Bloom's Modern Critical Views

Bloom's Modern Critical Views

Bloom's Modern Critical Views

F. SCOTT FITZGERALD

Edited and with an introduction by
Harold Bloom
Sterling Professor of the Humanities
Yale University

CHELSEA HOUSE
P U B L I S H E R S
An imprint of Infobase Publishing

Bloom's Modern Critical Views: F. Scott Fitzgerald, Updated Edition

Copyright © 2006 by Infobase Publishing
Introduction © 2006 by Harold Bloom

Chelsea House
An imprint of Infobase Publishing
132 West 31st Street
New York NY 10001

Library of Congress Cataloging-in-Publication Data
F. Scott Fitzgerald / Harold Bloom, editor.— Updated ed.
    p. cm. — (Bloom's modern critical views)
  Updated ed. of same title published 1985, in series: Modern critical views.
  Includes bibliographical references and index.
  ISBN 0-7910-8570-8
  I. Bloom, Harold. II. Series.
  PS3511.I9Z6137 2006
  813'.52—dc22   2006001775

Contributing Editor: Allison Stielau
Cover design by Takeshi Takahashi
Cover Photo: F. Scott Fitzgerald © CORBIS

Printed in the United States of America

Bang EJB 10 9 8 7 6 5 4 3 2 1

This book is printed on acid-free paper.

Contents

Editor's Note

My Introduction comments upon the two major influences that Fitzgerald sustained in his vocation as a writer: John Keats and Joseph Conrad. But I also note the rhetorical influence of T. S. Eliot, whose *The Waste Land* (1922) reverberates in *The Great Gatsby* (1925).

The 1920's critic Paul Rosenfeld shrewdly prophesies what Fitzgerald was about to do in *Gatsby*: which was to see his material simultaneously from the inside and the outside.

Glenway Wescott, an admirable novelist, laments the early death of Fitzgerald, in 1941, aged just forty-four, while the critic William Troy analyzes the sense of failure that the author of *Gatsby* and the greater short stories nevertheless felt in himself.

The richness and depth of *Gatsby* are emphasized by W.J. Harvey, after which John W. Aldridge grants Gatsby himself legendary status.

"Babylon Revisited," to me Fitzgerald's best story, is found by Seymour L. Gross to be a farewell to hope, while Leonard A. Podis meditates upon Fitzgerald's *The Beautiful and Damned*, and uncovers in it a prophetic lament for lost youth.

The *Crack-Up* articles are chronicled by Scott Donaldson as instances of self-alienation, after which Judith Fetterley interprets *Tender is the Night* as a manifestation of "sexual politics," in which both genders at last are victimized.

The Last Tycoon, unfinished at Fitzgerald's death, is judged by Robert Giddings as almost a great novel, while John F. Callahan explores the American Dream throughout the novelist's major works.

Nancy P. Van Arsdale rereads Fitzgerald's first book, *This Side of Paradise*, as a vision of Princeton University rather than of Fitzgerald, after which Meredith Goldsmith studies *Gatsby* as performance art, and Pearl James changes our perception of *This Side of Paradise* to the intersection of war and masculinity.

My Afterthought argues that Gatsby is the major literary character of twentieth century America.

HAROLD BLOOM

Introduction

It is difficult to imagine John Keats writing the fictions of Joseph Conrad, since there is nothing in common between the Great Odes and *The Secret Sharer* or *Heart of Darkness*. But such an imagining is not useless, since in some sense that was Scott Fitzgerald's accomplishment. *The Great Gatsby* does combine the lyrical sensibility of Keats and the fictive mode of Conrad, and makes of so odd a blending a uniquely American story, certainly a candidate for *the* American story of its time (1925). *Gatsby* has more in common with T. S. Eliot's "The Hollow Men," also published in 1925, than it does with such contemporary novels as the *Arrowsmith* of Sinclair Lewis or the *Manhattan Transfer* of John Dos Passos. Eliot's admiration for *The Great Gatsby* is understandable; the book, like the visionary lyric of Hart Crane, struggles against Eliot's conclusions while being compelled to appropriate Eliot's language and procedures. Fitzgerald, the American Keats, and Crane, even more the American Shelley, both sought to affirm a High Romanticism in the accents of a belated counter-tradition. The Keatsian belief in the holiness of the heart's affections is central to Fitzgerald, and *Tender Is the Night* owes more than its title to the naturalistic humanism of the Great Odes.

Fitzgerald's canonical status is founded more upon *Gatsby* and his best short stories, such as "Babylon Revisited," than it is upon the seriously flawed *Tender Is the Night*, let alone upon the unfinished *The Last Tycoon*. Oddly praised as "the best Hollywood novel" despite its manifest inferiority to Nathanael West's *The Day of the Locust*, *The Last Tycoon* is more an embryo than it is a torso. Edmund Wilson's affectionate overestimation of this fragment has been influential, but will fade away each time the book is actually read. *Tender Is the Night* demonstrates that Fitzgerald, unlike Conrad and Lawrence, cannot sustain too long a narrative. The book, though coming relatively late in his career, is Fitzgerald's *Endymion*, while *Gatsby* is, as it were, his *Fall of Hyperion*. Keats desired to write epic, but was more attuned to romance and to lyric. Fitzgerald desired to write novels on the scale of Thackeray and of Conrad, but his genius was more fitted to *Gatsby* as his mode of romance, and to "Babylon Revisited" as his version of the ode or of the reflective lyric.

The aesthetic of Scott Fitzgerald is quite specifically a personal revision of Keats's hope for Negative Capability, which Fitzgerald called "a romantic readiness" and attributed to his Gatsby. It is certainly part of the achievement of Fitzgerald's best novel that its hero possesses an authentic aesthetic dignity. By an effective troping of form, Fitzgerald made this a book in which nothing is aesthetically wasted, even as the narrative shows us everyone being humanly wasted. Edith Wharton rather nastily praised Fitzgerald for having created the "perfect Jew" in the gambler Meyer Wolfsheim. Had she peered closer, she might have seen the irony of her patrician prejudice reversed in the ancient Jewish wisdom that even Wolfsheim is made to express:

> "Let us learn to show our friendship for a man when he is alive and not after he is dead," he suggested. "After that, my own rule is to let everything alone."

Whether Nick Carraway is capable of apprehending this as wisdom is disputable but Fitzgerald evidently could, since Wolfsheim is not wholly devoid of the dignity of grief. Lionel Trilling commended *The Great Gatsby* for retaining its freshness. After eighty years, it has more than retained its moral balance and affective rightness. Those qualities seem augmented through the perspective of lapsed time. What has been augmented also is the Eliotic phantasmagoria of the *Waste Land* imagery that is so effectively vivid throughout Fitzgerald's vision. Carraway begins by speaking of "what preyed on Gatsby, what foul dust floated in the wake of his dreams." These are also "the spasms of bleak dust," above which you perceive the blue and gigantic eyes of Doctor T. J. Eckleburg, which brood on over the dumping ground of the gray land. "My heart is a handful of dust," the monologist of Tennyson's *Maud* had proclaimed in a great phrase stolen by Eliot for his *Waste Land*. Fitzgerald's dust is closer to Tennyson's heart than to Eliot's fear:

> to where Myrtle Wilson, her life violently extinguished, knelt in the road and mingled her thick dark blood with the dust.

Michaelis and this man reached her first, but when they had torn open her shirtwaist, still damp with perspiration, they saw that her left breast was swinging loose like a flap, and there was no need to listen for the heart beneath.

Fitzgerald's violence has that curious suddenness we associate with the same narrative quality in E. M. Forster. Something repressed in the phantasmagoria of the ordinary returns, all too often, reminding us that Fitzgerald shares also in Conrad's sense of reality and its treacheries, particularly as developed in *Nostromo*, a novel that we know Fitzgerald rightly admired. *Heart of Darkness*, which Fitzgerald also admired, is linked to "The Hollow Men" by that poem's epigraph, and many critics have seen Carraway as Fitzgerald's version of Marlow, somewhat sentimentalized but still an authentic secret sharer in Gatsby's fate. Like the Eliot of "The Hollow Men," Fitzgerald found in Conrad a seer of the contemporary abyss of:

Shape without form, shade without color,
Paralysed force, gesture without motion;

or, in the language of *Heart of Darkness*: "A vision of grayness without form."

Writing to his daughter about the "Ode on a Grecian Urn," Fitzgerald extravagantly observed: "For awhile after you quit Keats all other poetry seems to be only whistling or humming." Fitzgerald's deepest affinity to Keats is in the basic stance of his work, at once rhetorical, psychological, and even cosmological. In both Keats and Fitzgerald, the perpetual encounter is between the mortal poet or man-of-imagination (Gatsby, Diver) and an immortal or perpetually youthful goddess-woman. Fitzgerald's women—Daisy, Nicole, Rosemary—are not so much American dreams as they are Keatsian Lamias or perpetually virgin moon-maidens. "Virginity renews itself like the moon" is a Keatsian apothegm of Yeats's and the quester in Fitzgerald would have concurred. The murdered Gatsby is truly Daisy's victim; rather more grimly, Diver is emptied out by his relationship with Nicole, and to some degree, by his repetition of that pattern with Rosemary.

This has been read as misogyny in Fitzgerald but, as in Keats, it tends largely to be the reverse. Confronting his immortal women, the Keatsian quester seeks what at last Keats himself obtains from the harshly reluctant Muse, Moneta, in *The Fall of Hyperion*: recognition that he is *the* poet in and for his own time. "I sure should see / Other men here; but I am here alone." Fitzgerald was greatly ambitious, but his audacity did not extend quite that far. Yet his surrogates—Gatsby and Diver—are no more deceived than

Keats's poets are deceived. Daisy, Nicole, and Rosemary do not matter as personalities, not to us as readers and not much more to Gatsby or Diver. Gatsby, the more sublime quester, is allowed his famous touch of genius when he dismisses Daisy's love for her husband, the brutal Tom Buchanan: "In any case, it was just personal." Diver, less magnificently, also knows better, but is just as doom-eager as Gatsby. The inadequacies of the actual women do not matter, because the drive is not for satisfaction or for happiness. It is Freud's uncanny death-drive, which replaces the drive for self-preservation, and exists in a dialectical balance with the libido. Gatsby somehow chooses to die in his own fashion, while Diver chooses the death-in-life of erotic and professional defeat.

Tender Is the Night survives the weakness of its characterizations and the clumsiness of its narrative structure precisely because of Diver's own fated sense that there are no accidents. His character is his fate, and his relationship with Nicole is not so much a failed counter-transference as it is another pathetic version of the sublime Romantic vision of sexual entropy set forth overtly in Blake's "The Mental Traveller" and implicitly in James's *The Sacred Fount*: "And she grows young as he grows old." For the Blakean "young" we can substitute "whole," yet for the "old" we cannot quite substitute "weak" but something closer to Fitzgerald's "interior laughter," the quality in Diver that drives him down and out until he ends up practicing medicine in progressively smaller towns in the Finger Lakes Section of the Western Reserve of New York State. The pathos of that dying fall is anything but Keatsian, and may have been Fitzgerald's trope for his own self-destructiveness.

A curious self-appropriation, or perhaps indeliberate self-repetition, links the close of *Tender Is the Night* to the close of "Babylon Revisited," which seems to me Fitzgerald's most impressive single short story. On the day before he leaves the Riviera for America, after his rejection by Nicole, Diver spends all his time with his children: "He was not young any more with a lot of nice thoughts and dreams to have about himself, so he wanted to remember them well." The penultimate sentence of "Babylon Revisited" is "He wasn't young anymore, with a lot of nice thoughts and dreams to have about himself."

Whichever came first, the repetition is central to Fitzgerald. "Nice thoughts and dreams" are the essence, and Fitzgerald's regressive vision, like Gatsby's and Diver's and Charlie Wales's, is a Keatsian and Stevensian study of the nostalgias. Keats, staring at the face of the unveiled Moneta, prophesies the Stevens of *The Auroras of Autumn*, with his unabashed, Freudian celebration of the imago: "The mother's face, the purpose of the poem, fills the room." Charlie Wales, in "Babylon Revisited," longing for his daughter, remembers his dead wife as any man remembers his mother: "He was absolutely sure Helen wouldn't have wanted him to be so alone." As the last sentence of what may be Fitzgerald's most memorable story, it reverberates with a peculiar plangency in American Romantic tradition.

PAUL ROSENFELD

F. Scott Fitzgerald

The utmost that can be charged against F. Scott Fitzgerald is that too oftentimes his good material eludes him. Of the ultimate value of said material there is no dispute. Certain racehorses run for the pure joy of running, and the author of *The Beautiful and Damned* and *Tales of the Jazz Age* is such an animal. He is the born writer, amusing himself with tales and pictures; and eventually nothing is interesting except natural bent. Salty and insipid, exaggeratedly poetical and bitterly parodistic, his writing pours exuberantly out of him. Flat paragraphs are redeemed by brilliant, metaphors, and conventional descriptions by witty, penetrating turns. Ideas of diamond are somewhat indiscriminately mixed with ideas of rhinestone and ideas of window glass; yet purest rays serene are present in veritable abundance. They must come to this bannerman of the slickers and flappers in a sort of dream, unexpectedly out of some arcana where they have been concealing themselves, and surprise him by smiling up at him from underneath his pen. For so they startle the reader, unprepared to encounter in writing as carelessly undertaken, ideas so mature and poignant and worthy of fine settings.

Not a contemporary American senses as thoroughly in every fiber the tempo of privileged post-adolescent America. Of that life, in all its great hardness and equally curious softness, its external clatter, movement and

From *Men Seen: Twenty-Four Modern Authors*. © 1925 Lincoln Macveagh, The Dial Press.

boldness, he is a part; and what he writes reflects the environment not so much in its superficial aspects as in its pitch and beat. He knows how talk sounds, how the dances feel, how the crap-games look. Unimportant detail shows how perfect the unconscious attunement: the vignette of a boy drawing gasoline out of an automobile tank during a dance so that a girl can clean her satin shoe; the vignette of a young fellow sitting in his B.V.D.'s after a bath running his hand down his naked shin in indolent satisfaction; the vignette of two bucks from a pump-and-slipper dance throwing hash by the handful around Childs' at six A.M. Not another has gotten flashes from the psyches of the golden young intimate as those which amaze throughout *The Beautiful and Damned*. And not another has fixed as mercilessly the quality of brutishness, of dull indirection and degraded sensibility running through American life of the hour.

Taken as things, nevertheless, both the novels of Fitzgerald, and the majority of his tales as well, lie on a plane inferior to the one upon which his best material extends. He has the stuff for pathos, and this fact he fairly consistently ignores. Certain preconceptions seem to intrude between him and his material, spoiling his power to correctly appreciate it. Hence, instead of the veritable stories he has to tell, there appear smart social romanzas and unhappy happy endings. Of Fitzgerald's preconceptions, the chief sinner appears to be the illusion that the field of his vision is essentially the field of "youth." Now, it would be insanity to deny the author's almost constant preoccupation with exquisite creatures in chiffon and their slender snappy companions, or to deny the jolly subjects of his observations vivacity and frankness of spirit, and perfect elegance of texture. There is a place where an eternal dance proceeds, and this place for the while they occupy, filling it with their proper motions and gestures. And whatever the quality of these, who can for even an instant maintain that it is inferior to that of the dreadful motions and gestures which filled it a generation, or two or three generations ago? What one does affirm, however, and affirm with passion, is that the author of *This Side of Paradise* and of the jazzy stories does not sustainedly perceive his girls and men for what they are, and tends to invest them with precisely the glamour with which they in pathetic assurance rather childishly invest themselves. At the time of the appearance of Fitzgerald's first book, it was evident that to an extent he was indebted to Compton Mackenzie for the feeling with which he regarded the "dreaming spires" of Princeton; and since then it has become apparent that he tends a trifle overmuch to view everything which he sees in the light of Europe's past experiences. His protagonists he observes through the enchanted eyes of a perpetual Maytime, perceiving among the motors and crap-games a wave of cool spring flowers, a flutter of white and yellow ephemeridae. Even when he marks the cruel and shabby side, the decay and the ignobility of his objective, he tends to overplay the general attractiveness more than the detail warrants. The couple in *The Beautiful and Damned*, charming and comely enough and yet portrayed at length in the horrible effort to perpetuate a state of narcissistic irresponsibility, we are begged to perceive as iridescently wonderful bodies and souls.

And it is fresh, juicy and spontaneous that the American juveniles of the class described by Fitzgerald exactly are not. Superficially perhaps. But was not the forest green which Europe called by the name of youth somewhat more a thing of courage? And the number of us willing to face the world without the panoply of elaborate material protections is not overwhelming. It is claimed that in the American South virgins are carefully trained to inquire out the income and prospects of suitors, and nip in the bud any passion which threatens to direct itself upon an unworthy object. But it does not seem probable there is any truth in the report. For such maneuvers can scarcely be necessary. It is undoubtedly physically impossible for any really nice American girl South or North to respond to the desires of a male who does not make the spiritual gesture paralleling the Woolworth Building's. Through either external persuasion or inherent idealism, and which it is we know not, and undoubtedly it is both, the self-respecting damsels early acquire the conviction that splendidly complete orientation onto the business of material increase is the primary characteristic of maleness, and that any offer of love unaccompanied by the tautness for money is the profoundest of insults to the psyche seated in the tender depths of them. And the strapping, college-bred, Brooks-clad youths no less than they share this beautiful innate belief. They too seem unable to face life without having at the back of them the immense upholstery of wealth. Nothing which they might be or do, were they relieved of the necessity of being a worldly success, appears to them capable of making good to the lady the absence of the fur garment and the foreign roadster, and the presence of inevitable suffering. Thus the spirit of the business world is established well before the advent of puberty; and the spirit of business is compromise, which is not exactly it would seem the spirit of youth.

And even the lightest, least satirical of Fitzgerald's pages bear testimonial to the prevalence of the condition. A moralist could gather evidence for a most terrible condemnation of bourgeois America from the books of this protagonist of youth. And yet, *Lieb Vaterland, magst ruhig sein.* It is not a state of immorality in the general sense of the word that might be uncovered. If by morality we mean obedience to the *mores* of the tribe, then

Fitzgerald's diverting flappers and slickers are in no sense licentious. By means of necking parties and booze fights of the sort he describes the republic is maintained. Business rests on them. But immorality may be taken to signify a falling away from the ideal spirit of life, and in that sense America is proven the breeding ground of a kind of decay. In all unconsciousness Fitzgerald shows us types of poor golden young too shallow to feel, vainly attitudinizing in the effort to achieve sensation: girls who know they cannot live without riches and men perpetually sucking the bottle for solace. The people aren't young; they are merely narcissistic. Knowledge of life is gotten from books, and the naïveté is not quite lovely. That is all very well; one has no fault to find with it; it is quite sanitary and not at all messy as passion usually is; but why call it spring? And occasionally Fitzgerald drops the light guitar and with cool ferocity speaks the veritable name. *May Day*, perhaps the most mature of all his tales, brings the bitter brackish dry taste of decay fully to the mouth. With an air of almost glacial impersonality Fitzgerald gives a curious atmosphere of mixed luxury and rottenness of the heart. Through the entire story there seems to run the brutishness of the two soldiers hiding among pails and mops in the dust closet waiting for some stolen liquor to be handed in to them. And in the fantasia *The Diamond Big as the Ritz*, Fitzgerald strikes perhaps quite undeliberately further notes of satire: Mr. Braddock Washington, the richest and most profoundly unsympathetic man in the world looks dangerously like a jazz-age portrait of the father of the country.

But the world his subject-matter is still too much within Fitzgerald himself for him to see it sustainedly against the universe. Its values obtain too strongly over him, and for that reason he cannot set them against those of high civilizations, and calmly judge them so. Hence, wanting philosophy, and a little overeager like the rest of America to arrive without having really sweated, he falls victim to the favorite delusions of the society of which he is a part, tends to indulge it in its dreams of grandeur, and misses the fine flower of pathos. He seems to set out writing under the compulsion of vague feelings, and when his wonderfully revelatory passages appear, they come rather like volcanic islands thrown to the surface of a sea of fantasy. By every law *The Beautiful and Damned* should have been a tragedy, the victims damned indeed; yet at the conclusion Fitzgerald welched, and permitted his pitiful pair to have the alleviations of some thirty millions of dollars, and his hero tell the readers he had won out. To be sure, a steady growth has been going on within this interesting author. The amusing insolence of his earlier manner of writing has persistently given away before a bolder, sharper stroke less personal in reference. The descriptions in *May Day*: the sight of the avenue, the drinking scene in Delmonico's, the adventures of Mr. In and Mr.

Out, are done with quiet virtuosity. A very genuine gift of fantasy arrives in *Benjamin Button*. There are even Lawrence-like strong moments in *The Beautiful and Damned*. And still, in spite of *May Day*, Fitzgerald has not yet crossed the line that bounds the field of art.

He has seen his material from its own point of view, and he has seen it completely from without. But he has never done what the artist does: seen it simultaneously from within and without; and loved it and judged it too. For *May Day* lacks a focal point, and merely juxtaposes a number of small pieces. Should Fitzgerald finally break his mold, and free himself of the compulsions of the civilization in which he grew, it might go badly with his popularity. It will be a pathetic story he will have to tell, the legend of a moon which never rose; and that is precisely the story a certain America does not wish to hear. Nevertheless, we would like hugely to hear him tell it. And Fitzgerald might scarcely miss his following.

GLENWAY WESCOTT

The Moral of F. Scott Fitzgerald

F. Scott Fitzgerald is dead, aged forty-four. *Requiescat in pace; ora pro nobis.* In the twenties, his heyday, he was a kind of king of our American youth; and as the news of his end appeared in the papers there were strange coincidences along with it. A number of others—a younger writer who was somewhat of his school and, like him, had committed his talent unfortunately to Hollywood, and that writer's pretty, whimsical wife, and another young woman who was a famous horse-trainer, and the young leader of a popular jazz-band—also met sudden deaths that week. I was reminded of the holocausts by which primitive rulers were provided with an escort, servants and pretty women and boon companions, for eternity. The twenties were heaven, so to speak, often enough; might not heaven be like the twenties? If it were, in one or two particulars, Scott Fitzgerald would be sorry; sorry once more.

His health failed, and with a peculiar darkness and deadweight in mind and heart, some five years ago. Then in a wonderful essay entitled "The Crack-Up" he took stock of himself, looking twenty years back for what flaws were in him or in the day and age, what early damage had been done, and how. Thanks to that, one can speak of his weaknesses without benefit of gossip, without impertinence. And so I do, asking for charity toward him and clarity about him; and a little on my own mortal account; and for certain innocent immature American writers' benefit.

From *The New Republic* (February 17, 1941). © 1941 by The New Republic, LLC.

My theme is as usual personality rather than esthetics; but my sentiment on this occasion is not personal. Aside from our Midwestern birth and years of foreign residence, you could scarcely find two men of the same generation less alike than we two. Neither our virtues nor our vices appeared to overlap at all. I did not have the honor of his particular friendship. I have only one vivid memory of conversation with him, which was on a Mediterranean beach. Across the Bay of Angels and over the big good-for-nothing city of Nice, some of the Alps hung in the air as pearly as onions; and that air and that sea, which has only delicate tides, quivered with warm weather. It was before the publication of *The Sun Also Rises*, the summer of 1925 or 1926, and Hemingway was what he wanted to talk to me about. He came abruptly and drew me a little apart from our friends and relations, into the shade of a rock.

Hemingway had published some short stories in the dinky deluxe way in Paris; and I along with all the literary set had discovered him, which was fun; and when we returned to New York we preached the new style and peculiar feeling of his fiction as if it were evangel. Still, that was too slow a start of a great career to suit Fitzgerald. Obviously Ernest was the one true genius of our decade, he said; and yet he was neglected and misunderstood and, above all, insufficiently remunerated. He thought I would agree that *The Apple of the Eye* and *The Great Gatsby* were rather inflated market values just then. What could I do to help launch Hemingway? Why didn't I write a laudatory essay on him? With this questioning, Fitzgerald now and then impatiently grasped and shook my elbow.

There was something more than ordinary art-admiration about it, but on the other hand it was no mere matter of affection for Hemingway; it was so bold, unabashed, lacking in a sense of humor. I have a sharp tongue and my acquaintances often underestimate my good nature; so I was touched and flattered by Fitzgerald's taking so much for granted. It simply had not occurred to him that unfriendliness or pettiness on my part might inhibit my enthusiasm about the art of a new colleague and rival. As a matter of fact, my enthusiasm was not on a par with his; and looking back now, I am glad for my sake that it was not. He not only said but, I believe, honestly felt that Hemingway was inimitably, essentially superior. From the moment Hemingway began to appear in print, perhaps it did not matter what he himself produced or failed to produce. He felt free to write just for profit, and to live for fun, if possible. Hemingway could be entrusted with the graver responsibilities and higher rewards such as glory, immortality. This extreme of admiration—this excuse for a morbid belittlement and abandonment of himself—was bad for Fitzgerald, I imagine. At all events he soon began to waste his energy in various hack-writing.

I was told last year that another talented contemporary of ours had grown so modest in the wage-earning way, fallen so far from his youthful triumph, that he would sign a friend's stories and split the payment. Under the friend's name it would have been hundreds of dollars, and under his, a thousand or thousands. Perhaps this was not true gossip, but it is a good little exemplary tale, and of general application. It gives me goose-flesh. A signature which has been so humiliated is apt never to be the same again, in the signer's own estimation. As a rule the delicate literary brain, the aching creative heart, cannot stand that sort of thing. It is better for a writer even to fancy himself a Messiah, against the day when writing or life goes badly. And there is more to this than the matter of esthetic integrity. For if his opinion of himself is divided by disrespect—sheepish, shameful, cynical—he usually finds his earning capacity as well as his satisfaction falling off. The vast public, which appears to have no taste, somehow senses when it is being scornfully talked down to. The great hacks are innocent, and serenely class themselves with Tolstoy and Dickens. Their getting good enough to compare with P.G. Wodehouse or Zane Grey may depend upon that benign misapprehension.

Probably Fitzgerald never fell into any abuse of his reputation as unwise and unwholesome as the above-mentioned confrères. His standard of living did seem to the rest of us high. Publishers in the twenties made immense advances to novelists who had and could lend prestige; and when in the thirties Fitzgerald's popularity lapsed, movies had begun to be talkies, which opened up a new lucrative field of literary operation. Certainly he did write too much in recent years with his tongue in his cheek; his heart in his boots if not in his pocket. And it was his opinion in 1936 that the competition and popular appeal of the films—"a more glittering, a grosser power," as he put it—had made the God-given form of the novel archaic; a wrong thought indeed for a novelist.

This is not the ideal moment to reread and appraise his collectable works. With the mind at a loss, muffled like a drum—the ego a little inflamed as it always is by presentness of death—we may exaggerate their merit or their shortcomings. I remember thinking, when the early best sellers were published, that his style was a little too free and easy; but I was a fussy stylist in those days. His phrasing was almost always animated and charming; his diction excellent. He wrote very little in slang or what I call baby-talk: the pitfall of many who specialized in American contemporaneity after him. But for other reasons—obscurity of sentiment, facetiousness—a large part of his work may not endure, as readable reading matter for art's sake. It will be precious as documentary evidence, instructive example. That is not, in the way of immortality, what the writer hopes; but it is much more than most writers of fiction achieve.

This Side of Paradise haunted the decade like a song, popular but perfect. It hung over an entire youth-movement like a banner, somewhat discolored and wind-worn now; the wind has lapsed out of it. But a book which college boys really read is a rare thing, not to be dismissed idly or in a moment of severe sophistication. Then there were dozens of stories, some delicate and some slap-dash; one very odd, entitled "Head and Shoulders." I love *The Great Gatsby*. Its very timeliness, as of 1925, gave it a touch of the old-fashioned a few years later; but I have reread it this week and found it all right; pleasure and compassion on every page. A masterpiece often seems a period-piece for a while; then comes down out of the attic, to function anew and to last. There is a great deal to be said for and against his final novel, *Tender is the Night*. On the whole I am warmly for it. To be sane or insane is a noble issue, and very few novels take what might be called an intelligent interest in it; this does, and gives a fair picture of the entertaining expatriate habit of life besides.

In 1936, in three issues of *Esquire*, he published the autobiographical essay, ""The Crack-Up," as it were swan-song. I first read it at my barber's, which, I suppose, is according to the editorial devices of that magazine, a medium of advertising for men's ready-made clothing. There is very little in world literature like this piece: Max Jacob's *Defense de Tartuffe*; the confidential chapter of *The Seven Pillars of Wisdom*, perhaps; Sir Walter Raleigh's verse-epistle before his beheading, in a way. Fitzgerald's theme seems more dreadful, plain petty stroke by stroke; and of course his treatment lacks the good grace and firmness of the old and old-style authors. Indeed it is cheap here and there, but in embarrassment rather than in crudity or lack of courage. Or perhaps Fitzgerald as he wrote was too sensitive to what was to appear along with it in the magazine: the jokes, the Petty girls, the haberdashery. He always suffered from an extreme environmental sense. Still it is fine prose and naturally his timeliest piece today: self-autopsy and funeral sermon. It also, with an innocent air, gravely indicts our native idealism in some respects, our common code, our college education. And in general—for ailing civilization as well as one dead Fitzgerald—this is a day of wrath.

He had made a great recovery from a seemingly mortal physical illness; then found everything dead or deadish in his psyche, his thought all broken, and no appetite for anything on earth. It was not from alcohol, he said, evidently proud of the fact that he had not had any for six months, not even beer. We may be a little doubtful of this protestation; for protestation indeed is a kind of sub-habit of the alcoholic. Six months is no time at all, in terms of the things that kill us. Alcohol in fact never exclusively causes anything. Only, just as it will heighten a happy experience, it will deepen a rut or a pit, in the way of fatigue chiefly. Who cares, when a dear one is dying of a chest-cold or an embolism, whether he is a drunkard or a reformed ex-drunkard?— Yes, I know, the dying one himself cares! But when Fitzgerald wrote his essay he still had five years to live, quite a long time. It was not about ill health, and of course he was as sane as an angel. His trouble just then and his subject was only his lassitude of imagination; his nauseated spirit; that self-hypnotic state of not having any will-power; and nothing left of the intellect but inward observation and dislike. Why, he cried, why was I "identified with the objects of my horror and compassion"? He said it was the result of "too much anger and too many tears." That was his snap-judgment; blunt sentimentality of a boy or ex-boy. But since he was a storyteller above all, he did not stop at that; he proceeded to tell things about the past in which the mystery showed extraordinarily.

"The Crack-Up" has never been issued in book form; and perhaps because the pretty pictures in *Esquire* are so exciting to thumb-tack up on the wall, back numbers of it are not easy to come by. So I am tempted to try to summarize it all; but no, it must be published. Especially the first half is written without a fault: brief easy fiery phrases—the thinking that he compared to a "moving about of great secret trunks," and "the heady villainous feeling"—one quick and thorough paragraph after another, with so little shame and so little emphasis that I have wondered if he himself knew how much he was confessing.

He still regretted his bad luck in not getting abroad into the trenches as an army officer in 1918, and even his failure at football in 1913 or 1914. On certain of those unlucky days of youth he felt as badly as in 1936, and badly in the same way; he makes a point of the similarity. Perhaps the worst of the early crises came in his junior year, when he lost the presidency of one of the Princeton clubs. Immediately afterward, as an act of desperation and consolation, he made love for the first time; and also that year, not until then, he turned to literary art, as the best of a bad bargain. Ominous! Fantastic, too, that a man who is dying or at least done with living—one who has had practically all that the world affords, fame and prosperity, work and play, love and friendship, and lost practically all—should still think seriously of so much fiddledeedee of boyhood! Very noble convictions underlay Fitzgerald's entire life, and he explains them nobly. But when he comes to the disillusionment, that too is couched in alumnal imagery; it is along with "the shoulder-pads worn for one day on the Princeton freshman football field and the overseas cap never worn overseas" that his ideals are relegated to the junk-heap, he says. It is strange and baroque; like those large bunches of battle-trappings which appear decoratively in seventeenth-century architecture, empty helmets and empty cuirasses and firearms laid crossways, sculpurered up on the lintels of barracks and on the lids of tombs. Those condemned old European societies which have been too much militarized, too concerned with glory and glorious death, scarcely seem more bizarre than this: a kind of national consciousness revolving to the bitter end around college; and the latter also seems a precarious basis for a nation.

Aside from his literary talent—literary genius, self-taught—I think Fitzgerald must have been the worse educated man in the world. He never knew his own strength; therefore nothing inspired him very definitely to conserve or budget it. When he was a freshman, did the seniors teach him a manly technique of drinking, with the price and penalty of the several degrees of excess of it? If they had, it might never have excited him as a vague, fatal moral issue. The rest of us, his writing friends and rivals, thought that he had the best narrative gift of the century. Did the English department at Princeton try to develop his admiration of that fact about himself, and make him feel the burden and the pleasure of it? Apparently they taught him rather to appreciate this or that other writer, to his own disfavor. Did any wordly-wise critic ever remind him that beyond a certain point, writing for profit becomes unprofitable; bad business as well as bad art? Another thing: my impression is that only as he wrote, or just before writing, *Tender is the Night*, did he discover certain causes and gradations of mental illness which, nowadays, every boy ought to be taught as soon as he has mastered the other facts of life.

Even the army failed to inculcate upon Lieutenant Fitzgerald one principle that a good army man must accept: heroism is a secondary virtue in an army. Lieutenant Fitzgerald had no business pining for the front-line trenches in advance of his superior officers' decision that it was the place for him. The point of soldiering is to kill; not a mere willingness to be killed. This seems important today, as we prepare again for perhaps necessary war, and again too much is made of the spirit of self-sacrifice and embattlement of ideals; and not enough of the mere means of victory. And with reference to literature, too, as Fitzgerald drops out of our insufficient little regiment, we writers particularly blame him for that all-out idealism of his. No matter what he died for—if he died for anything—it was in too great a hurry; it was not worth it at his age.

In several of the obituary notices of Fitzgerald I detect one little line of mistaken moralizing, which I think is not uncommon; and his example and his fiction may have done something to propagate it. They seem to associate all rebellious morality somehow with a state of poor health. This is an unfair attack, and on the other hand a too easy alibi. Bad behavior is not always a feeble, pitiful, fateful thing. Malice of mind, strange style, offensive subject matter, do not always derive from morbid psyche or delicate physique. Wickedness is not necessarily weakness; and *vice versa*. For there is will-power in humanity. Its genuine manifestation is only in the long run; but, with knowledge, it can have the last word. Modern psychology does not deny it. Whether one is a moralist or an immoralist—a vengeful daily preacher like Mr. Westbrook Pegler, or an occasional devil's advocate like myself, or the quietest citizen—these little distinctions ought to be kept clear.

Fitzgerald was weak; we have the proof of it now in his demise. Fitzgerald, the outstanding aggressor in the little warfare which divided our middle classes in the twenties—warfare of moral emancipation against moral conceit, flaming youth against old guard—definitely has let his side down. The champion is as dead as a doornail. Self-congratulatory moral persons may crow over him if they wish.

There is bound to be a slight anger at his graveside; curse-words amid our written or spoken obsequies. The whole school of writers who went to France has been a bit maligned while the proletarian novelists and the politico-critics have enjoyed the general applause. Some of us are reckless talkers, and no doubt we have maligned each other and each himself as well. It was the beautiful, talented Miss Stein in her Paris salon who first called us "the lost generation." It was Hemingway who took up the theme and made it a popular refrain. The twenties were in fact a time of great prosperity and liberty, a spendthrift and footloose time; and especially in France you got your American money's worth of everything if you were clever. Still I doubt whether, in dissipation and unruly emotion, we strayed much farther out of the way than young Americans ordinarily do, at home as abroad. I think we were somewhat extraordinarily inclined to make youthful rebelliousness, imprudent pursuit of pleasure or ambition, a little easier for our young brothers. Heaven knows how it will be for our sons.

In any case, time is the real moralist; and a great many of the so-called lost are still at hand, active and indeed conspicuous: Bishop and Hemingway and Bromfield and Cummings and V. Thomson and Tate, Gordon and Porter and Flanner and others, the U.S.A.'s odd foreign legion. We were a band of toughs in fact, indestructible, which perhaps is the best thing to be said for us at this point. For the next step is to age well. Relatively speaking,

I think we are aging well; giving evidence of toughness in the favorable sense as well: tenacity and hardiness, and a kind of wordly wisdom that does not have to change its platform very often, and skepticism mixed in with our courage to temper it and make it last. Sometimes we are still spoken of as the young or youngish or "younger" writers, but there can be no sense in that, except by lack of competition; every last one of us is forty. That is the right age to give advice to the immature and potential literary generation. For their sake, lest they feel unable to take our word for things, it seems worthwhile to protest against the strange bad name we have had.

In any case we are the ones who know about Fitzgerald. He was our darling, our genius, our fool. Let the young people consider his untypical case with admiration but great caution; with qualms and a respect for fate, without fatalism. He was young to the bitter end. He lived and he wrote at last like a scapegoat, and now has departed like one. As you might say, he was Gatsby, a greater Gatsby. Why not? Flaubert said, "*Madame Bovary*, c'est moi! "On the day before Christmas, in a sensible bitter obituary, *The New York Times* quoted a paragraph from "The Crack-Up" in which the deceased likened himself to a plate. "Sometimes, though, the cracked plate has to be kept in service as a household necessity. It can never be warmed up on the stove nor shuffled with the other plates in the dishpan; it will not be brought out for company but it will do to hold crackers late at night or to go into the ice-box with the left-overs." A deadly little prose-poem! No doubt the ideals Fitzgerald acquired in college and in the army—and put to the test on Long Island and in the Alpes-Maritimes and in Hollywood—always were a bit second-hand, fissured, cracked, if you like. But how faithfully he reported both idealization and ordeal; and how his light smooth earthenware style dignifies it!

The style in which others have written of him is different. On the day after Christmas, in his popular column in *The New York World-Telegram*, Mr. Westbrook Pegler remarked that his death "recalls memories of a queer bunch of undisciplined and self-indulgent brats who were determined not to pull their weight in the boat and wanted the world to drop everything and sit down and bawl with them. A kick in the pants and a clout over the scalp were more like their needing...." With a kind of expert politeness throughout this *in memoriam*, Mr. Pegler avoids commenting upon the dead man himself exactly. His complaint is of anonymous persons: the company Fitzgerald kept, readers who let themselves be influenced by him, and his heroes and heroines: "Sensitive young things about whom he wrote and with whom he ran to fires not only because he could exploit them for profit in print but because he found them congenial...." I suppose Mr. Pegler's column is profitable too; and if I were doing it I should feel easier in my mind, surer of my aim, if I knew and liked my exploitees. Joking aside, certainly this opinion of his does not correspond in the least to my memory of the gay twenties. Certainly if sensitive young men and women of the thirties believe Pegler, they will not admire Fitzgerald or like the rest of us much.

Too bad; there should be peace between the generations now, at least among the literary. Popularity or no popularity, we have none too many helpful friends; and in a time of world war there may be panic and conservatism and absent-mindedness and neglect of literature in general, and those slight acts of obscure vengeance so easy to commit when fellow citizens have begun to fear and imagine and act as a mass. There should not be any quarrel between literature and journalism either. Modernly conceived and well done—literary men sticking to the truth and newspapermen using imagination—they relate to each other very closely, and may sustain and inspire each other back and forth. In a time of solemn subject matter it is more and more needful that they should.

In any case Mr. Pegler's decade is out as well as ours; the rude hard-working thirties as well as the wild twenties. The forties have come. Those of us who have been youthful too long—which, I suppose, is the real point of his criticism—now certainly realize our middle age; no more time to make ready or dawdle, nor energy to waste. That is one universal effect of war on the imagination: time, as a moral factor, instantly changes expression and changes pace. Everyman suddenly has a vision of sudden death.

What is the difference, from the universal angle? Everyone has to die once; no one has to die twice. But now that mortality has become the world's worst worry once more, there is less sophistication of it. Plain as day we see that the bull in the arena is no more fated than the steer in the slaughterhouse. The glamorous gangster's cadaver with bellyful of bullets is no deader than the commonplace little chap overcome by pernicious anemia. Napoleon III at the battle of Sedan, the other battle of Sedan, roughed his cheeks in order not to communicate his illness and fright to his desperate army. An unemployed young actor, a friend of a friend of mine, lately earned a living for a while by roughing cheeks of well-off corpses at a smart mortician's. All this equally—and infinitude of other things under the sun— is jurisdiction of death. The difference between a beautiful death and an ugly death is in the eye of the beholder, the heart of the mourner, the brain of the survivor.

The fact of Scott Fitzgerald's end is as bad and deplorable as could be; but the moral of it is good enough, and warlike. It is to enliven the rest of the regiment. Mere tightening the belt, stiffening the upper lip, is not all I mean;

nor the simple delight of being alive still, the dance on the grave, the dance between holocausts. As we have it—documented and prophesied by his best work, commented upon in the newspaper with other news of the day—it is a deep breath of knowledge, fresh air, and an incitement to particular literary virtues.

For the private life and the public life, literary life and real life, if you view them in this light of death—and now we have it also boding on all the horizon, like fire—are one and the same. Which brings up another point of literary criticism; then I have done. The great thing about Fitzgerald was his candor; verbal courage; simplicity. One little man with eyes really witnessing; objective in all he uttered, even about himself in a subjective slump; arrogant in just one connection, for one purpose only, to make his meaning clear. The thing, I think, that a number of recent critics have most disliked about him is his confessional way, the personal tone, the *tete-à-tete* or a man-to-man style, first person singular. He remarked it himself in "The Crack-Up." "There are always those to whom all self-revelation is contemptible."

I on the other hand feel a real approval and emulation of just that; and I recommend that all our writers give it serious consideration. It might be the next esthetic issue and new mode of American letters. It is American enough; our greatest fellows, such as Franklin and Audubon and Thoreau and Whitman, were self-expressers in so far as they knew themselves. This is a time of greater knowledge, otherwise worse; an era which has as many evil earmarks as, for example, the Renaissance: awful political genius running amok and clashing, migrations, races whipped together as it were by a titanic egg-beater, impatient sexuality and love of stimulants and cruelty, sacks, burnings and plagues. Fine things eventually may be achieved amid all this, as in that other century. I suggest revelation of man as he appears to himself in his mirror—not as he poses or wishes or idealizes—as one thing to try a revival of, this time. Naked truth about man's nature in unmistakable English.

In the Renaissance they had anatomy: Vesalius in Paris at midnight under the gallows-tree, bitten by the dogs as he disputed with them the hanged cadavers which they wanted to eat and he wanted to cut up. They had anatomy and we have psychology. The throws of dice in our world—at least the several dead-weights with which the dice appear to be loaded against us—are moral matters; and no one ever learns much about all that except in his own person, at any rate in private. In public, in the nation and the inter-nation and the anti-nation, one just suffers the weight of the morality of others like a dumb brute. This has been a dishonest century above all: literature lagging as far behind modern habits as behind modern history;

democratic statesmanship all vitiated by good form, understatement, optimism; and the nations which could not afford democracy, finally developing their supremacy all on a basis of the deliberate lie. And now is the end, or another beginning.

Writers in this country still can give their little examples of truth-telling; little exercises for their fellow citizens, to develop their ability to distinguish truth from untruth in other connections when it really is important. The importance arises as desperately in the public interest as in private life. Even light fiction can help a society get together and agree upon its vocabulary; little strokes of the tuning-fork, for harmony's sake. And for clarity's sake, let us often use, and sanction the use of, words of one syllable. The shortest and most potent is the personal pronoun: I. The sanctified priest knows that, he says *credo*; and the trustworthy physician only gives his opinion, not a panacea. The witness in the courtroom does not indulge in the editorial we; the judge and the lawyers will not allow it; and indeed, if the case is important, if there is life or liberty or even a large amount of money at stake, not even supposition or hearsay is admitted as evidence. Our worldwide case is important.

Not only is Anglo-Saxondom all at war with the rest of the world in defense of its accustomed power and prosperity, and of the luxuries of the spirit such as free speech, free publication, free faith—for the time being, the United States is the likeliest place for the preservation of the Mediterranean and French ideal of fine art and writing: which puts a new, peculiar obligation upon us ex-expatriates. The land of the free should become and is becoming a city of refuge; but there is cultural peril even in that. France has merely committed her tradition to our keeping, by default; whereas Germany has exiled to us her most important professors and brilliant writers. Perhaps the latter are bound to introduce into our current literature a little of that mystically philosophic, obscurely scientific mode which sometimes misled or betrayed them as a nation. Therefore we must keep up more strictly and energetically than ever, our native specific skeptical habit of mind; our plainer and therefore safer style.

In any consideration of the gravity of the work of art and letters—and upon any solemn occasion such as the death of a good writer like Scott Fitzgerald—I think of Faust, and that labor he dreamed of when he was blind and dying, keeping the devil waiting. It was the drainage of a stinking sea-marsh and the construction of a strong dyke. Fresh fields amid the eternally besieging sea: room for a million men to live, not in security—Goethe expressly ruled out that hope of which we moderns have been too fond—but free to do the best they could for themselves. Does it seem absurd to compare a deceased best seller with that mythic man: former wholesome Germany's demigod? There must always be some pretentiousness about literature, or else no one would take its pains or endure its disappointments. Throughout this article I have mixed bathos with pathos, joking with tenderness, in order to venture here and there a higher claim for literary art than is customary now. I am in dead earnest. Bad writing is in fact a rank feverish unnecessary slough. Good writing is a dyke, in which there is a leak for every one of our weary hands. And honestly I do see the very devil standing worldwide in the decade to come, bound to get some of us. I realize that I have given an exaggerated impression of Fitzgerald's tragedy in recent years: all the above is based on his confession of 1936, and he was not so nearly finished as he thought. But fear of death is one prophecy that never fails; and now his strength is only in print, and his weakness of no account, except for our instruction.

WILLIAM TROY

F. Scott Fitzgerald:
The Authority of Failure

Of course, in any absolute sense, Scott Fitzgerald was not a failure at all; he has left one short novel, passages in several others, and a handful of short stories, which stand as much chance of survival as anything of their kind produced in this country during the same period. If the tag is so often attached to his name, it has been largely his own fault. It is true that he was the victim, among a great number of other influences in American life, of that paralyzing high pressure by which the conscientious American writer is hastened to premature extinction as artist or as man. Upon the appearance of *The Crack-Up*, a selection by Edmund Wilson of Fitzgerald's letters, notebooks, and fugitive pieces, it was notable that all the emptiest and most venal elements in New York journalism united to crow amiably about his literary corpse to this same tune of insufficient production. Actually their reproaches betrayed more of their own failure to estimate what was good and enduring in his writing than his acknowledgeable limitations as an artist. If Fitzgerald had turned out as much as X or Y or Z, he would have been a different kind of writer—undoubtedly more admirable from the standpoint of the quasi-moral American ethos they were tarred with the same brush. But in *Gatsby* is achieved a dissociation, by which Fitzgerald was able to isolate one part of himself, the spectatorial or esthetic, and also the more intelligent and responsible, in the person of the ordinary but quite sensible narrator,

From *Selected Essays of William Troy*, pp. 140–146. © 1967 Rutgers University Press.

from another part of himself, the dream-ridden romantic adolescent from St. Paul and Princeton in the person of the legendary Jay Gatsby. It is this which makes the latter one of the few truly mythological creations in our recent literature—for what is mythology but this same process of projected wish fulfillment carried out on a larger scale and by the whole consciousness of a race? Indeed, before we are quite through with him, Gatsby becomes much more than a mere exorcizing of whatever false elements of the American dream Fitzgerald felt within himself: he becomes a symbol of America itself, dedicated to "the service of a vast, vulgar and meretricious beauty."

Not mythology, however, but a technical device which had been brought to high development by James and Conrad before him made this dissociation possible for Fitzgerald. The device of the intelligent but sympathetic observer situated at the center of the tale, as James never ceases to demonstrate in the Prefaces, makes for some of the most priceless values in fiction—economy, suspense, intensity. And these values *The Great Gatsby* possesses to a rare degree. But the same device imposes on the novelist the necessity of tracing through in the observer or narrator himself some sort of growth in general moral perception, which will constitute in effect his story. Here, for example, insofar as the book is Gatsby's story it is a story of failure—the prolongation of the adolescent incapacity to distinguish between dream and reality, between the terms demanded of life and the terms offered. But insofar as it is the narrator's story it is a successful transcendence of a particularly bitter and harrowing set of experiences, localized in the sinister, distorted, El Greco-like, Long Island atmosphere of the later twenties, into a world of restored sanity and calm, symbolized by the bracing winter nights of the Middle Western prairies. "Conduct may be founded on the hard rock or the wet marshes," he writes, "but after a certain point I don't care what it's founded on. When I came back from the East last autumn I felt that I wanted the world to be in uniform and at a sort of moral attention forever; I wanted no more riotous excursions with privileged glimpses into the human heart ever recurring." By reason of its enforced perspective the book takes on the pattern and the meaning of a Grail romance—or of the initiation ritual on which it is based. Perhaps this will seem a farfetched suggestion to make about a work so obviously modern in every respect; and it is unlikely that Fitzgerald had any such model in mind. But like *Billy Budd*, *The Red Badge of Courage*, or *A Lost Lady*—to mention only a few American stories of similar length with which it may be compared—it is a record of the strenuous passage from deluded youth to maturity.

Never again was Fitzgerald to repeat the performance. *Tender Is the Night* promises much in the way of scope but it soon turns out to be a backsliding into the old ambiguities. Love and money, fame and youth, youth and money—however one shuffles the antitheses they have a habit of melting into each other like the blue Mediterranean sky and sea of the opening background. To Dick Diver, with a mere change of pronoun, may be applied Flaubert's analysis of Emma Bovary: "Elle confondait, dans son désir, les sensualités du luxe avec les joies du coeur, l'élégance des habitudes et les délicatesses du sentiment." And it is this Bovaryism on the part of the hero, who as a psychiatrist should conceivably know more about himself, that in rendering his character so suspect prevents his meticulously graded deterioration from assuming any real significance. Moreover, there is an ambiguous treatment of the problem of guilt. We are never certain whether Diver's predicament is the result of his own weak judgment or of the behavior of his neurotic wife. At the end we are strangely unmoved by his downfall because it has been less a tragedy of will than of circumstance.

Of *The Last Tycoon* we have only the unrevised hundred and thirty-three pages supported by a loose collection of notes and synopses. In an unguarded admission Fitzgerald describes the book as "an escape into a lavish, romantic past that perhaps will not come again into our time." Its hero, suggested by a well-known Hollywood prodigy of a few years ago, is another one of those poor boys betrayed by "a heightened sensitivity to the promises of life." When we first meet him he is already a sick and disillusioned man, clutching for survival at what is advertised in the notes as "an immediate, dynamic, unusual, physical love affair." This is nothing less than "the meat of the book." But as much of it as is rendered includes some of the most unfortunate writing which Fitzgerald has left; he had never been at his best in the approach to the physical. Nor is it clear in what way the affair is related to the other last febrile gesture of Stahr—his championship of the Hollywood underdog in a struggle with the racketeers and big producers. Fortuitously the sense of social guilt of the mid-thirties creeps into the fugue, although in truth this had been a strong undertone in early short stories like "May Day" and "The Rich Boy." It is evident that Stahr is supposed to be some kind of symbol—but of what it would be hard to determine. From the synopses he is more like a receptacle for all the more familiar contradictions of his author's own sensibility—his arrogance and generosity, his fondness for money and his need for integrity, his attraction toward the fabulous in American life and his repulsion by its waste and terror. "Stahr is miserable and embittered toward the end," Fitzgerald writes, in one of his own last notes for the book. "Before death, thoughts from *Crack-Up*." Apparently it was all to end in a flare-up of sensational and not too meaningful irony: Stahr, on his way to New York to call off a murder which he had ordered for the best of motives, is himself killed in an airplane crash, and his possessions are rifled by a group of schoolchildren on a mountain. If there is anything symbolic in this situation, could it be the image of the modern Icarus soaring to disaster in that "universe of ineffable gaudiness" which was Fitzgerald's vision of the America of his time?

Inquiry into what was the real basis of Fitzgerald's long preoccupation with failure will not be helped too much by the autobiographical sketches in *The Crack-Up*. The reasons there offered are at once too simple and too complicated. No psychologist is likely to take very seriously the two early frustrations described—inability to make a Princeton football team and to go overseas in the last war. In the etiology of the Fitzgerald case, as the psychologists would say, the roots run much deeper, and nobody cares to disturb them at this early date. His unconscionable good looks were indeed a public phenomenon, and their effect on his total personality was something which he himself would not decline to admit. The *imago* of the physical self had a way of eclipsing at times the more important *imago* of the artist. But even this is a delicate enough matter. Besides, there were at work elements of a quite different order—racial and religious. For some reason he could never accept the large and positive influence of his Celtic inheritance, especially in his feeling for language, and his harking back to the South has a little too nostalgic a ring to be convincing. Closely related to this was the never resolved attitude toward money and social position in relation to individual worth. But least explored of all by his critics were the permanent effects of his early exposure to Catholicism, which are no less potent because rarely on the surface of his work. (The great exception is "Absolution," perhaps the finest of the short stories.) Indeed, it may have been the old habit of the confession which drove him, pathetically, at the end, to the public *examen de conscience* in the garish pages of *Esquire* magazine.

To add to his sense of failure there was also his awareness of distinct intellectual limitations, which he shared with the majority of American novelists of his time. "I had done very little thinking," he admits, "save within the problems of my craft." Whatever he received at Princeton was scarcely to be called an education; in later years he read little, shrank from abstract ideas, and was hardly conscious of the historical events that were shaping up around him. Perhaps it is not well for the novelist to encumber himself with too much knowledge, although one cannot help recalling the vast cultural apparatus of a Tolstoy or a Joyce, or the dialectical intrepidity of a Dostoievski or a Mann. And recalling these Europeans, none of whom foundered on the way, one wonders whether a certain coyness toward the things of the mind is not one reason for the lack of development in most

American writers. Art is not intellect alone; but without intellect art is not likely to emerge beyond the plane of perpetual immaturity.

Lastly, there was Fitzgerald's exasperation with the multiplicity of modern human existence—especially in his own country. "It's under you, over you, and all around you," he protested, in the hearing of the present writer, to a young woman who had connived at the slow progress of his work. "And the problem is to get hold of it somehow." It was exasperating because for the writer, whose business is to extract the unique quality of his time, what Baudelaire calls the quality of *modernité*, there was too much to be sensed, to be discarded, to be reconciled into some kind of order. Yet for the writer this was the first of obligations; without it he was nothing—"Our passion is our task, and our task is our passion." What was the common problem of the American novelist was intensified for him by his unusually high sense of vocation.

In the last analysis, if Fitzgerald failed, it was because the only standard which he could recognize, like the Platonic conception of himself forged by young Jay Gatsby in the shabby bedroom in North Dakota, was too much for him to realize. His failure was the defect of his virtues. And this is perhaps the greatest meaning of his career to the younger generation of writers.

"I talk with the authority of failure," he writes in the notebooks, "Ernest with the authority of success. We could never sit across the same table again." It is a great phrase. And the statement as a whole is one neither of abject self-abasement nor of false humility. What Fitzgerald implies is that the stakes for which he played were of a kind more difficult and more unattainable than "Ernest" or any of his contemporaries could even have imagined. And his only strength is in the consciousness of this fact.

W.J. HARVEY

Theme and Texture in
The Great Gatsby

Criticism of *The Great Gatsby*, when it has not been sidetracked into biography or reminiscence of the Jazz Age, has tended to concentrate on two issues. The first of these has been concerned with the moral seriousness of the book, with what answer, if any, can be given to the hostile critic of whom John Farelly, writing in *Scrutiny*, is a good example:

> I want to suggest that there is an emptiness in his work that makes 'convincing analysis' honestly difficult, but leaves a hollow space where critics can create their own substitute Fitzgerald. And I should probe for that hollow space in what we call the *centre* of a writer's work—that around which and with reference to which he organizes his experiences; in short, his values.[1]

Closely related to this is the problem of what status we should allow Gatsby himself; in particular, we may note the attempt to see him as a mythic character and the novel as the expression of some deep-rooted and recurrent 'American Dream'.[2]

The first of these questions has been exhaustively debated and if neither side has much shaken the other's conviction, the issues are at least clearly defined; while anyone who is not an American will feel a natural

From *English Studies*, Vol 38, No. 1. Pp. 12–20. (c) 1957 Taylor & Francis Ltd., http://www.tandf.co.uk/journals.

diffidence about expressing any opinion on the second topic. In fact, what immediately impresses itself upon most readers—especially if they have come to *The Great Gatsby* after reading Fitzgerald's earlier novels—is not moral theme or national archetype but something much simpler, something so obvious, perhaps, that it has received remarkably little close critical skill. I mean the astonishing accession of technical power and critical attention. Less pretentious than his earlier work, *The Great Gatsby* achieves much more; in it Fitzgerald discovers not only his true subject but a completely adequate form. To say this, no doubt, is to say also that he has attained a maturity that transcends the merely aesthetic, that reveals itself also in the moral implications of the fable.

Nearly every critic of *The Great Gatsby* has stressed the tremendous structural importance of the narrator, Nick Carraway, the character through whom Fitzgerald is able to achieve that aesthetic distance from his own experience necessary for firmness of control and clarity of perception, through whom he can express that delicately poised ambiguity of moral vision, the sense of being 'within and without, simultaneously enchanted and repelled by the inexhaustible variety of life' out of which insight into the truth of things must grow. William Troy has summed it up neatly and concisely:

> In the earlier books author and hero tended to melt into one another because there was no internal principle of differentiation by which they might be separated; they respired in the same climate, emotional and moral; they were tarred with the same brush. But in *Gatsby* is achieved a dissociation, by which Fitzgerald was able to isolate one part of himself, the spectatorial or esthetic, and also the more intelligent and responsible, in the person of the ordinary but quite sensible narrator, from another part of himself, the dream-ridden romantic adolescent from St. Paul and Princeton, in the person of the legendary Jay Gatsby.[3]

Again, most critics of the novel have amply demonstrated its economy, the clarity of its narrative outline and the forceful, unbroken drive of it forward from the first page to the last, an impetus which incorporates, and even gains momentum from, the cunningly interpolated flashbacks. Many critics have expanded and expounded the significance of the major symbolic structures of the book; indeed, to insist upon its legendary nature is to insist upon these. What more, then, can be said about the mastery of Fitzgerald's technique; what aspect of it has received less than its fair share of attention?

I should like, quite simply, to discuss the language of the book. Here we find, co-existing with economy, clarity and force, an extreme density of texture. It is this which ultimately gives richness and depth to the novel, this without which the larger symbols would lose their power of reverberating in the reader's mind and the major themes of the book would seem intellectual or emotional gestures, without the pressure of felt and imaginatively experienced life behind them.

We may best begin with a fairly detailed analysis of one passage; my aim here will be to show that textural detail is not merely local in its point and effect but relates to the central themes and dominant moral attitudes expressed in the book. Analysis of prose is always liable to be cumbrous and clumsy but this very clumsiness is an oblique tribute to the dexterity and economy with which Fitzgerald achieves his effects. I take as my example a passage dealing with the end of the first of Gatsby's parties to be described in the book. The glamour and enchantment of the party, so brilliantly evoked by Fitzgerald, has here dissolved; the intoxication of night and music, champagne and youth, has vanished and the scene is closed by a dismal return to the world of sober reality, or more precisely, to the disenchanted world of the hangover. The party is over; it is time to go home. Here is the passage:

> I looked around. *Most of the remaining women were now having fights with men said to be their husbands.* (1) Even Jordan's party, the quartet from East Egg, were rent asunder by dissension. *One of the men was talking with curious intensity to a young actress,* (2) and his wife, after attempting to laugh at the situation in a dignified and indifferent way, broke down entirely and resorted to flank attacks—at intervals she appeared suddenly at his side like an angry diamond, and hissed 'You promised!' into his ear.
>
> The reluctance to go home was not confined to wayward men. *The hall was at present occupied by two deplorably sober men and their highly indignant wives.* (3) The wives were sympathizing with each other in slightly raised voices.
>
> 'Whenever he sees I'm having a good time he wants to go home.'
>
> 'Never heard anything so selfish in my life.'
>
> 'We're always the first ones to leave.'
>
> 'So are we.'

'Well, we're almost the last tonight,' said one of the men sheepishly. 'The orchestra left half an hour ago.'

In spite of the wives' agreement that such malevolence was beyond credibility, the dispute ended in a short struggle, and both wives were lifted, kicking, into the night. (4)

At first we might seem to be concerned with a piece of merely slick, glossy writing; the simile, *like an angry diamond*, is perhaps a little too smart, a little too consciously clever and contrived; it trembles on the verge of preciosity. But leaving this aside, we may see how most of the main themes are touched on tangentially in what appear to be superficial and cynical comments. I wish to concentrate on the four short passages I have, for convenient reference, italicized and numbered.

(1) This sentence, apart from the obvious implication about the sexual morality of such a society, relates as well to the rootlessness and transience of these people, the lack of any stable relationship—a point I shall discuss later. It is also one strand in the complex network of gossip, rumour and innuendo which fills the whole book.

(2) Here, the intensity is in one sense anything but curious; the relationship implied is obvious; but in another sense the intensity is curious in that this is a society which is flippant and cynical, gay and hedonistic, but definitely not intense in its feeling for anyone or anything; as such, it contrasts with the real intensity of the outsider who is its host, with the passion of Gatsby's dream of Daisy.

(3) Here Fitzgerald is employing a common satirical device; he is enforcing his morality by pretending to accept its opposite as the norm—sobriety becomes deplorable. Further, however, the syntactical balance of the sentence leads us to infer a causal relationship between the balanced parts—the wives are indignant because the men are sober and want, therefore, to go home. We may link this with another device Fitzgerald often uses, namely, his method of making his point by simple juxtaposition without any comment. It is a method akin to Pope's in, for example, the often-quoted line:

Puffs, powders, patches, Bibles, billets-doux

In a catalogue like this each object assumes an equal status, and the fact that a bible may be seen as sharing the importance or triviality of its context is comment enough on the society in which such an equivalence can be contemplated. So in Fitzgerald. For example, we are told that Tom and Daisy drifted around 'wherever people played polo and were rich together'. There, the juxtaposition of playing a game and being wealthy indicates the superficiality and frivolity of the rich. One finds a rather different effect achieved when Fitzgerald describes Gatsby's party: 'In his blue gardens men and girls came and went like moths among the whisperings and the champagne *and the stars*', where the phrase I have italicized illuminates by contrast the transience and evanescence of the whisperings, champagne and the moth-like men and girls.

(4) Here Fitzgerald achieves yet another effect, this time by a contrast of diction. The first half of the sentence, with its polysyllabic abstraction, approaches the inflation of mock-heroic; it is promptly deflated by the abrupt, racy description of action in the second half of the sentence.

Such analysis may seem to be breaking a butterfly upon a wheel, but the fact that it is so laboured is merely the result of trying to bring to a conscious formulation something that we respond to immediately and unconsciously in our casual reading of the novel. But it will have served its purpose if it helps to show that beneath the gaiety and wit of his prose Fitzgerald is maintaining a light but insistent moral pressure and is guiding and preparing our attitudes and responses so that we shall make a correct evaluation when the need arises. All this is done through his manipulation of the point of view afforded us by the narrator, Nick Carraway, who acts as the moral seismograph of the novel's uneasiness, premonitory quakings and final eruption into catastrophe.

We may extend this analysis by noticing how keyphrases are repeated subtly but insistently and how the work is so admirably organized, so intact as well as compact, that any one of these phrases inevitably leads to another and then to another, so that wherever the reader enters the book—whatever aspect of it he chooses to emphasize—his attention is engaged in a series of ever-widening perspectives until the whole of the novel is encompassed. Let us take, quite arbitrarily, the word restless; if we follow up this tiny and apparently insignificant verbal clue we shall find that it leads us swiftly and decisively to the heart of the book. Any one of a dozen other starting-points would do the same. Consider these examples:

(a)   Of Nick: 'A little later I participated in that delayed Teutonic migration known as the Great War. I enjoyed the counter-raid so thoroughly that I came back restless.'

(b)   Of Tom, surveying his Long Island estate: ' "I've got a nice place here", he said, his eyes flashing about restlessly.' Later he is seen 'hovering restlessly about the room.'

(c)   Of Jordan Baker: 'Her body asserted itself with a restless
       movement of her knee, and she stood up.'

These instances of our chosen key-word, all occurring within the first
twenty pages of the novel, are complicated and supplemented by other
phrases suggesting sudden movement, either jerky and impulsive, as of
Tom:

> Wedging his tense arm imperatively under mine, Tom Buchanan
> compelled me from the room as though he were moving a
> checker to another square.

or, by contrast, of Jordan:

> She yawned and with a series of rapid, deft movements stood up
> into the room.

We may notice again how Fitzgerald often obtains his local effects; how
in the second example the unusual preposition *into* gives a peculiar force to
the sentence, how, in the description of Tom, the word *imperatively* interacts
with the word *compelled* so that the latter also contains the sense of *impels* and
how the simile of checkers gives one the sense of manipulation, a sense which
expands into the whole complex of human relationships, plots, intrigues and
dreams that fills the novel.

In this context, repose is seen as a strained effort, the result of which is
precarious; thus Jordan

> was extended full length at her end of the divan, completely
> motionless, and with her chin raised a little, as if she were
> balancing something on it which was likely to fall.

Even the house seems unable to stay still:

> A breeze blew through the room, blew curtains in at one end and
> out the other like pale flags, twisting them up toward the frosted
> wedding-cake of the ceiling, and then *rippled over the wine-coloured
> rug, making a shadow on it as a wind does on the sea.*

> The only completely stationary object in the room was an
> enormous couch on which two young women *were buoyed up*, as

though upon an *anchored* balloon. They were both in white, and their dresses were *rippling* and fluttering as though they had just been blown back in after a short flight around the house. I must have stood for a few minutes listening to the whip and snap of the curtains and the *groan of a picture on the wall.*

In this passage one verbal trail intersects another and it is by this continual criss-cross of phrases and images that Fitzgerald achieves the effect I have already mentioned of a widening perspective. The image here, submerged beneath the surface elaboration of the prose and coming out in the phrases I have italicized is not, as one might expect, of flight but rather one of ships and the sea; a complicated image, a double exposure, so to speak, in which the whole house is seen as a ship groaning in the wind, with its flags flying, and at the same time in which the divan is a kind of ship within ship, upon the wine-coloured sea of the rug. The connecting link between the two aspects of the image is, of course, the activity and effect of the wind; both curtains and dresses ripple. There is a great deal that could be said about this kind of submerged activity in the novel to which we respond unconsciously in a casual non-analytical reading of it; for the moment, however, I am concerned only to note how the idea of restlessness is linked with the idea of the sea. We will return to this connection shortly: we may first notice how this restlessness expands and fills the opening of the book, especially the scene of the first dinner party at the Buchanans.

The dinner begins quietly enough 'with a bantering inconsequence that was never quite chatter' but the inconsequence is soon out of control; people are continually interrupting each other, changing the subject, Tom becomes vehement. Daisy is possessed by 'turbulent emotions', the air is full of whispers, implications, innuendos, people are always shifting around, 'the shrill metallic urgency' of the telephone is never absent for long. The following passage is a good example of the general atmosphere:

Miss Baker and I exchanged a short glance consciously devoid of meaning. I was about to speak when she sat up alertly and said 'Sh!' in a warning voice. A subdued impassioned murmur was audible in the room beyond, and Miss Baker leaned forward unashamed, trying to hear. The murmur trembled on the verge of coherence, sank down, mounted excitedly and then ceased altogether.

This atmosphere is most completely expressed in Nick's feeling about Daisy:

> as though the whole evening had been a trick of some sort to exact a contributory emotion from me. I waited, and sure enough, in a moment she looked at me with a smirk on her lovely face, as if she had asserted her membership in a rather distinguished secret society to which she and Tom belonged.

Just as this passage anticipates the moments after the catastrophe when Daisy and Tom look as though they are conspiring together, so the whole scene prepares us for the picture of Tom's affair with Mrs. Wilson which by its squalor, its triviality, its commonplaceness is a preparatory contrast with the naïve grandeur of Gatsby's schemes to meet Daisy once again. The atmosphere of the dinner, as I have tried to describe it, is thus established as part of the emotional and moral climate of the whole book. But it is much more than mere scene-setting; let us follow out a little further some of the implications of the restlessness motif. Ultimately this derives from the rootlessness of those people; they are strangers not only to their own country but also to their past. They live in houses that may be palaces but are certainly not homes; their intellectual ideas are shoddy and their moral attitudes to life are at best the detritus of a collapsed social framework, second-hand and conventionally assumed, so that Nick is tempted to laugh at Tom's abrupt 'transition from libertine to prig' while the most he can find to admire is the 'hardy scepticism' of Jordan Baker.

All the implications of this rootlessness radiate from another key-word, *drifting*, and we may notice how Fitzgerald, early in the book, links this idea with the idea of restlessness, when he writes of Daisy and Tom:

> Why they came back East I don't know. They had spent a year in France for no particular reason, and then drifted here and there unrestfully wherever people played polo and were rich together.

Each example of this kind of thing, when taken in isolation, may seem neutral, empty of metaphorical richness, but the interaction of these two ideas is so insistent that each tiny accretion of phrase and image builds up a powerful cumulative charge. We have already seen the image of the sea at work beneath a passage of descriptive prose, but it extends with a deceptive casualness throughout the whole book; at Gatsby's parties Nick notes 'the sea-change of faces and voices and colour' and is 'rather ill at ease among swirls and eddies of people'; at these parties Tom says one meets 'all kinds of crazy fish' and later protests that people will 'throw everything overboard'. Examples could be multiplied but we need only notice the recurrence of the metaphors of sea, drifting and voyaging in two crucial passages. The first is towards the end of Nick's prefatory comments:

> No—Gatsby turned out all right at the end; it is what preyed on Gatsby, what foul dust floated in the wake of his dreams that temporarily closed out my interest in the aborted sorrows and short-winded hopes of men.

and in the very last words of the book: 'So we beat on, boats against the current, borne back ceaselessly into the past.'

I would like to suggest that far below the surface of *The Great Gatsby*—below the particular interest of the narrative, below Fitzgerald's analysis of society, below even the allegedly 'mythic' qualities of the book—is a potent cliché, a commonplace of universal human experience to which we all respond. To say one of the bases of the novel is a cliché is not to dispraise Fitzgerald—most great art is built upon similar platitudes and it is probably why the novel is alive for another age than Fitzgerald's and for non-Americans—what we should admire is the way in which he has refreshed the cliché, given it a new accession of life in his story. The cliché I refer to is easily summed up; in the words of a popular hymn it is this:

> *Time, like an ever-rolling stream,*
> *Bears all its sons away;*
> *They fly forgotten, as a dream*
> *Dies at the opening day.*

The simple truth of this fact of life is everywhere implicit in the texture of the novel, and sometimes it is more than implicit. The appropriateness of the way in which Nick records the names of all those people who went to Gatsby's house that summer has often been remarked:

> Once I wrote down on the empty spaces of a time-table the names of those who came to Gatsby's house that Summer. It is an old time-table now, disintegrating at its folds, and headed 'This schedule in effect July 5th, 1922.'

There could be no more decorous memorial to those 'men and girls' who 'came and went like moths among the whisperings and the champagne and the stars.'

It is essential to Gatsby's tragic illusion, his belief in 'the unreality of reality; a promise that the rock of the world was founded securely on a fairy's wing,' that he should deny this fact of life and try to make the ever-rolling stream flow back up-hill.

> 'I wouldn't ask too much of her,' I ventured. 'You can't repeat the past.' 'Can't repeat the past?' he cried incredulously. 'Why of course you can!'

It is not insignificant that Nick should be so acutely aware of the passing of time, while in this context Gatsby's apology, 'I'm sorry about the clock' acquires a new level of unconscious ironic meaning. This has been stressed often enough before; the point I wish to make is that the theme, basic to *The Great Gatsby*, is not merely adumbrated, is not merely translated into terms of narrative and character, but is also expressed in the very texture of the prose, in the phrases and images, for example, which centre on words like *restless* and *drifting*. Thus the moral attitude of Nick is conveyed in precisely these terms. We may note in passing that Nick is not the fixed, static point of view some critics have supposed him; he is not the detached observer but is deeply implicated in the story he is telling and his attitude evolves and changes as the story progresses; in a sense what *The Great Gatsby* is about is what happens to Nick. At the outset he 'began to like New York, the racy adventurous feel of it at night, and the satisfaction that the constant flicker of men and women and machines gives to the restless eye'. The attractiveness and glamour of Gatsby's parties needs no stressing but Nick begins to feel oppressed and uneasy at the 'many-coloured, many-keyed commotion'. And his reaction after the catastrophe is naturally expressed in an antithesis to the terms already established.

> When I came back from the East last autumn I felt that I wanted the world to be in uniform and at a sort of moral attention forever.

Similarly, the ambiguity of Gatsby himself comes over to us in these terms. He is not the simple antithesis of Tom and Daisy; he is implicated in their kind of corruption too, and his dream is proved hollow not only by the inadequacy of the actual correlative—that is, Daisy—to the hunger of his aspiring imagination, but also by the means he uses to build up the gaudy fabric of his vision. He, too, shares in the restlessness of the actual world which will defeat his ideal, Platonic conceptions:

> This quality was continually breaking through his punctilious manner in the shape of restlessness. He was never quite still; there was always a tapping foot somewhere or the impatient opening and closing of a hand.

and a little later he tells Nick:

> 'You see, I usually find myself among strangers because I drift here and there trying to forget the sad thing that happened to me.'

This note of drifting is frequently reiterated in connection with Gatsby but it does not, as in the case of Daisy and Tom, remain unqualified; Gatsby comes out all right at the end. What we remember about him is not the restlessness or the drifting but 'an unbroken series of successful gestures', Gatsby standing in the moonlight outside the Buchanans' house, rapt in 'the sacredness of the vigil'; Gatsby in his own temple-cum-roadhouse between 'the great doors, endowing with complete isolation the figure of the host, who stood on the porch, his hand up in a formal gesture of farewell', or above all, Gatsby stretching out his arms towards the green light that is the vain promise of his future. We remember these formal poses as something theatrical or religious, but they *are* poses, moments of suspended time, something static and as such are the stylistic equivalents of Gatsby's attempt to impose his dream upon reality, his effort to make the ever-rolling stream stand still. We remember Gatsby not as drifting but as voyaging to some end and it is this sense, hinted at all the way through the book, which gives impetus to that imaginative leap whereby we encompass the ironic contrast between Gatsby and Columbus or those Dutch sailors in that moment when:

> man must have held his breath in the presence of this continent, compelled into an aesthetic contemplation he neither understood nor desired, face to face for the last time in history with something commensurate to his capacity for wonder.

Thus, starting with the idea of restlessness and going by way of its enlargement into the idea of drifting we are brought to face the largest issues that the novel propounds. This is, of course, not the only—or even the most important—strand in the textural pattern of the whole; any one of a dozen other starting points might have been taken—the contrast between East and West, for example, the subtle choreography of the terms *reality* and *unreality*, the functional role of the machine which enlarges to provide metaphors for the emotional and moral life, the religious overtones that some critics have noted, or the ideas of money and value. All of these combine and interact to give *The Great Gatsby* its satisfying depth and richness of suggestion without which the themes so often abstracted for discussion would lack both definition and reverberant power and the novel would fail to achieve that quality which Mark Schorer has described as 'language as used to create a certain texture and tone which in themselves state and define themes and meanings; or language, the counters of our ordinary speech, as forced, through conscious manipulation, into all those larger meanings which our ordinary speech almost never intends'.[4]

NOTES

1. John Farelly: Scott Fitzgerald: Another View (*Scrutiny*, Vol. XVIII, No. 4, June 1952).

2. For example, Edwin S. Fussell: Fitzgerald's Brave New World (*English Literary History* Vol. 19, No. 4, December 1952).

3. William Troy: Scott Fitzgerald: The Authority of Failure (*Accent*, 1945).

4. Mark Schorer: Technique as Discovery (*Hudson Review*, Spring, 1948).

JOHN W. ALDRIDGE

The Life of Gatsby

It is probably about time we stopped writing essays on *The Great Gatsby*, just at the moment, this is to say, when a really proper criticism seems threatening to begin. Certainly, it has been a saving paradox of criticism up to now that it has taken very little precise note of *Gatsby* while appearing to take vast general note of it. If we are not going to disturb that happy state of affairs, we had perhaps better call a halt before we yield up the book altogether to the dignifying but always transforming fire of criticism, and risk finding, after we have done so, that we are left not with the cleansed bones of the novel itself but with the ashes of one or more of its several meanings. I ask simply that we hold onto the living object in hand: the well-wrought urn on the mantelpiece can remain empty a while longer. Posterity, if it is to get at *Gatsby* at all, will most assuredly have to breathe back into it the life we take out, and we should take care to see that posterity does not waste its breath on a corpse. For *Gatsby* is above all a novel to be directly experienced and responded to; it is a fragile novel, to be sure, in some ways imperfect, in some ways deeply unsatisfactory, but it is clearly alive because produced by a directly experiencing, living imagination, one that habitually and with great innocence so perfectly confused its own longings, fears, defeats, and chimeras with those of a certain portion of American society, that a certain portion of American society ever since has confused its own image with it

From *Twelve Original Essays on Great American Novels*, Charles Shapiro, ed. pp. 210–237. © 1977 by Charles Shapiro.

and made its plans for itself on the vision of an accessible future which, as a skeptical imagination, it took pains to condemn. *Gatsby*, therefore, is a work of art particularly prone to being confused with its meanings, just as its meanings, if we are not careful, can be made to substitute for its life as a work of art.

Such a cautionary approach to *Gatsby* should count for something with us, although it probably counts for less than it would have at one time. We are accustomed now to having our experience of life abstracted for us by fiction, and our experience of fiction abstracted for us by criticism, both life and literature projected into a construct twice removed from the original and signed, sealed, and delivered over to our captive imaginations. We no longer want to do the imaginative job ourselves: we cannot quite afford the time; the code governing the division of imaginative labor would not permit it, nor do we really believe it can or need be done. Undoubtedly one of the reasons *Gatsby* continues to seem alive to us is that it represents one of the last attempts made by an American writer to come directly at the reality of the modern American experience while its outlines were still visible and before the social sciences convinced us that they could do the job and do it better. I assume that those outlines have not since been so visible and that we no longer have the sense of a distinctive American experience or even much of a certainty that there is one. After Fitzgerald, one feels, the door onto the native scene banged shut for American writers; the process of creation ceased to be a matter of opening the eyes and letting the sensibility take moral readings; the forms of social conduct, the traditional modes of action in which the drama of the will in crisis had formerly been displayed, no longer seemed directly accessible to the novel; suddenly no one appeared to know how anyone else behaved. Among the newer writers, certainly, who aspire to something more than journalism, there has been a sort of retreat of consciousness from the nearly insupportable task of dealing creatively with the fluid social situation and with the immense complication of status values and drives that the sociologists have discovered to be typical of the present age, and in comparison with which Fitzgerald's reality seems almost banally primitive. But Fitzgerald came to the novel at a time when the patterns of our present society were just being laid down; he had the inestimable advantage of the primal view, and so we return to him, particularly in *Gatsby*, with the feeling that we are seeing ourselves as we were in the light of an intensity that we are unable to direct upon ourselves as we are. If *Gatsby* is one of the very few books left from the twenties that we are still able to read with any kind of enduring pleasure and without always having to suffer a reminder of emotions we no longer care to feel, I suspect it is so because it dramatizes for us those basic assumptions and modes of assumption about the nature of American experience that belong to the antique furniture of our minds but that our experience of the present age and its literature has not been able to renew or replace. In this sense, *Gatsby* constitutes not only a primal view but, at least to date, a final view; it crystallizes an image of life beyond which neither our books nor our own perceptions seem able to take us; for two generations in fact, in that turgid area of consciousness where life and literature seem interchangeable, it has pretty largely done our perceiving for us. It therefore has about it some of that particular poignancy that we reserve for the lost moments of the past when we felt the emotions we would like still to feel, if we were able to and had again those exactly right opportunities. In this sense too *Gatsby* is mythopoeic: it has created our legend of the twenties, which at the present time is our common legend, and like *Moby-Dick* and *Huckleberry Finn*, it has helped to create, by endowing with significant form, a national unconscious; its materials are those of the collective American mind at its closest approach to the primary source of native frontier symbols. As a result, we must all feel on reading it a little as Nick Carraway felt on hearing Gatsby's words—"reminded of something—an elusive rhythm, a fragment of lost words, that I had heard somewhere a long time ago." I do not mean that I much hold to the more obvious and popular mythological view of *Gatsby*: carried too far, as it usually is, it threatens always to smother the novel within the strictures of meaning. But I can understand its attraction and its relevance: Fitzgerald's technique of pictorial generalization, along with what Lionel Trilling has called his "ideographic" method of character portrayal, insists on far more than the novel primarily signifies. Yet at this late stage in Fitzgerald criticism one can hope to escape cliché only by refusing to rest content with meaning and by inducing some contemplation of *Gatsby*'s life as fiction.

A prime feature of that life is of course the marvelous style that shows it forth, and while it is now commonplace to say that in *Gatsby* Fitzgerald found, certainly for the first time and probably for the last, his proper form, it is less so to say that he could not have found the form had he not experienced an immense deepening as well as a marked shift of his relation both to himself and to language. The essentially expressive form of the earlier novels had indulged Fitzgerald in all his younger, easier, and more sentimental mannerisms; it encouraged him to describe emotion rather than to embody it, and whenever he could not find emotion, to fake it; it put up no resistance whatever to his habit of seeking, and then descending to, the lowest level of feeling his characters could sustain, or of making use, whenever he thought he could get away with it, of the cheapest rhetorical devices cribbed from Compton Mackenzie and the gothic novel. It is also evident, particularly now, that the subjects of his first novels were not suitable vehicles for his real emotions, and if they were bad, it is partly because they never allowed him to discover what his real emotions were. Fitzgerald never believed with anything like his full heart in the life he was describing; his deeper sensibilities were not only not engaged but offended, and the necessity to appear to believe, to try to pass off childish infatuation as adult devotion, only served to make him seem frivolous and girlishly Beardsleyan. In this sense, of course, Fitzgerald's first subjects kept him young: they arrested him for the time at a level of emotional development precisely adequate to their capacity for receiving emotion, and they asked nothing more of him than that he disguise the deficiency behind effusion and rhetoric.

It is not clear from his biography exactly what happened in the time between *The Beautiful and Damned* and *Gatsby* to mature Fitzgerald, nor is it very likely that his biography knows. Obviously he found a way of untangling his moral imagination from the gothic bric-a-brac of ghosts, mysterious medieval gentlemen, and wispy lurking presences, among which it had searched for an object through the earlier novels, and under the sponsorship of that imagination he was able to achieve a sufficient penetration of his subject to engage for the first time his real emotions and his best talents. In *This Side of Paradise* "the problem of evil had solidified" for Amory Blaine "into the problem of sex," and one felt that this had behind it some affront to Fitzgerald's romanticism stemming from the discovery that a physical act could be imagined for nice girls beyond the kiss. By the time he wrote *The Beautiful and Damned* the problem appeared to have risen on the anatomical scale and lodged somewhere near the heart, although one could never be certain whether it really belonged there or in Wall Street. But with *Gatsby* there was no longer any doubt: the problem of evil had by then solidified into a problem of responsibility and spiritual condition in those rich enough to be able to choose their morals; Fitzgerald's opposing selves, the giddy, bibulous boy and the morose, hung-over tallier of emotional chits, had struck a bargain and a balance.

This deepened understanding of his subject inevitably brought Fitzgerald to an awareness of the need for a narrative form far stricter and at the same time far subtler than that demanded by his earlier novels. It is doubtful if up to *Gatsby* he had given any serious thought at all to matters of form, and considering the limited conception he had of his subject at the time, he probably felt little necessity to. By Jamesean standards *This Side of Paradise* was abominably constructed, and *The Beautiful and Damned* was only slightly less so. But the loosely episodic, rather spongy form of the juvenile *bildungsroman* borrowed from Mackenzie and Wells was not hopelessly unsuited to the situation of the young man only faintly disenchanted with the life of glamour, particularly so long as in Fitzgerald's mind the difference between the rich and you and me could still be equated with the possession of more money, better looks, looser morals, and greater daring. All that was required was an involved, naïve consciousness capable of moving more or less horizontally through a series of episodes, the function of which was slow instruction in a kind of eager irony, and for this the one-dimensional mock-heroes, Amory Blaine and Anthony Patch, were perfectly competent pupils. But with *Gatsby* Fitzgerald's talent took a dramatic turn; his sense of his subject and his involvement with it became too complex and ambivalent to be portrayed through the limited single consciousness; he needed a narrative form at once firm enough to correct his tendency toward emotional bloat and supple enough to allow full range for the development of a set of individual characters who would display his theme and at the same time serve as suitable dramatic equivalents for his contradictory feelings toward it. He had suddenly and without quite knowing it arrived at a point where he was ready to put to use his mature understanding of his material within the framework of his advanced knowledge of the formal art of fiction.

The pictorial method of Conrad, James, and Wharton, combining the "single window" technique of the engaged narrator with that of the scenic tableau, made it possible for Fitzgerald to overcome in *Gatsby* the severe limitations of the merely expressive form and to achieve the kind of distance between himself and his subject that must be achieved before the job of true fictional creation can properly begin. In Nick Carraway he found the protagonist of his own most central ambivalence, a median consciousness and conscience vacillating between admiration and judgment, a "first-rate intelligence" able "to hold two opposed ideas in the mind at the same time, and still retain the ability to function." The foil-figures of Gatsby and Tom Buchanan serve him as devices for breaking down into contrasting parts and recombining in even more ambiguous relation his twin senses of the physical glamour of the rich and their spiritual corruption, their force of character and their moral weakness, the ideal nature of romantic vision and the baseness of the methods employed in its service, the essential shabbiness of romantic vision in a society that can measure vision only in money. Daisy Buchanan and Jordan Baker function on a somewhat simpler level to complete the symbolism of identity and contrast—Daisy standing initially as an embodiment of the purity of the vision, finally of the corruption and the baseness of method; Jordan holding up to the world a mask of sophisticated, though precarious, self-composure, but concealing behind it, like Nicole Diver, an awful secret of interior derangement. George and Myrtle Wilson alone remain almost untouched by the process of imaginative revision through which Fitzgerald transformed, by immensely complicating; his typical thematic effects in the novel: Wilson carries forward and for the first time fully characterizes Fitzgerald's earlier horror of poverty and illness, while Myrtle dramatizes his formerly incoherent, at moments hysterical, aversion to direct sexuality when unaccompanied by beauty and wealth.

Lionel Trilling is undoubtedly right in calling this method of characterization "ideographic" and in applying the term as well to the method of the novel as a whole. Nothing and no one in the course of the narrative is really developed; everything is seen in tableau, in a state of permanent pictorial rest. The characters are little more than a collection of struck attitudes, frieze figures carved on the entablature of a moral abstraction, a greatly generalized intuitive view of the nature of American experience. Their individual identities are subordinated to the central idea they are meant to signify, perfectly embodying the "platonic conception" behind the remark made by Gatsby when he admits the possibility that Daisy may perhaps have once loved her husband: "In any case it was just personal." The secret of the entire technique of the novel may in a sense be said to lie hidden in this remark, for its effect is to divert attention from the personal and particular to the abstract conception, the allegorized whole.

In achieving this effect Fitzgerald carried the pictorial method considerably beyond James; in fact, the closest parallel to its use in *Gatsby* is the Joycean "signature" or "epiphany" technique where character is broken down into its separate parts, and one or two of the parts are made to stand for the whole. The result for Joyce, in both *A Portrait of the Artist* and *Ulysses*, was the establishment of a virtual iconography of character, a system of extravagantly distilled symbolic essences, usually suggested by a gesture or an article of clothing, through which the soul of being was shown forth. The result for Fitzgerald is not nearly so elaborate, but it is very similar in kind. Nick Carraway is revealed to us through his signature of honesty; Gatsby is identified by his pink suits, Tom Buchanan by his rippling pack of muscle, Daisy by her voice, Jordan by her balancing act, Myrtle by her fleshy vitality, Wilson by his hollow-eyed stare, Wolfsheim by his hairy nostrils, the butler by his nose. In the case of each of the major characters these attributes take on metaphorical significance in the thematic design of the novel. Nick's honesty is called into ironic question by Jordan in an effort to shift the blame for her own dishonesty; Gatsby's pink suits suggest the meretriciousness of his role, Tom's muscle the brutal strength of his; Jordan's balancing act is indicative of her precarious control over herself and her need for stabilizing moral convention, while Daisy's voice serves as the gauge of her "basic insincerity," which it is the principal business of the novel to penetrate. Initially full of warm excitement and promise, it is finally shown to be "full of money," and in the long interval between the two observations the pathetic futility of Gatsby's dream is gradually made clear.

To create an effect of involvement and movement while retaining the advantage of the pictorial method, Fitzgerald made constant use of ironic parallelisms of both character and event, still very much in the manner of Joyce. Both Gatsby and Daisy are "insincere," Gatsby about his past, Daisy about her present feelings; Tom's unfaithfulness to Daisy is balanced by Gatsby's faithfulness to her; yet Tom and Daisy belong to a "secret society" of ultimately deeper faithfulness. Nick keeps faith with Gatsby to the end, but not with Jordan. Jordan's dishonesty is revealed in time with the Buchanans' and Gatsby's; Jordan like Daisy is a "careless driver," and the episode in which this fact is first made clear to Nick prefigures the moment when Daisy's carelessness results in Myrtle's death; both, furthermore, are anticipated by the comic accident scene in Gatsby's driveway and are finally commented upon during Nick's last meeting with Jordan when, to conceal her own dishonesty, she insists that she met in Nick another bad driver. Just before the showdown scene with Gatsby in the Plaza Hotel Tom feels that he has lost in one afternoon both his wife and his mistress; during the scene he wins back his wife, and Gatsby loses his mistress and is symbolically murdered by Tom—all to the accompaniment of Mendelssohn's Wedding March being played in the ballroom below. As Gatsby the dreamer dies, Nick remembers that it is his own thirtieth birthday, the time of life when, in his and Fitzgerald's romantically limited chronology, all dreams must end. On the way back to East Egg Daisy kills Tom's mistress, Wilson loses a wife, and a while later Tom arranges through Wilson to murder Gatsby in fact, Wilson believing that Gatsby has been Myrtle's lover as well as her murderer. All the principal male characters lose the women they love, and in each case through some act of faithlessness on the part of one or more of the women.

This system of carefully plotted interior parallels and cross-references serves greatly to enhance the thematic "size" of the novel and to give back to it some of the quality of dramatic specification that the method of static character portrayal takes away. The same can be said for the reflexive relationship of the parts in the narrative design as a whole. Each of the nine chapters is composed of one, or very occasionally more than one, dramatic scene presented pictorially and surrounded by skillfully foreshortened panoramic material, and each achieves significance not through the standard depth-wise plumbing of character, but through its contribution of fresh facts to the linearly developing sequence of facts that gradually illuminate Gatsby's central dilemma and mystery. Each functions, furthermore, in reciprocal relation to every other, at times ironically, at times by simple contrast, so that an effect of counterpointed motifs comes ultimately to stand, very much as it does in *The Waste Land*, in place of the more conventional and predictable effect of events arranged chronologically and naturalistically.

The opening and closing pages of the novel frame Gatsby's story within the parentheses of an elegiacally retrospective vision of time, history, and moral conduct. The first two pages state the terms of the ambivalent attitude that Nick is to take toward the subsequent action and which it is to be the task of that action to resolve. Presented initially as a young man taught by his father to "reserve all judgments" in the knowledge that "all the people in this world haven't had the advantages that you've had," Nick describes himself immediately afterward as one who has since been taught better by first-hand contact with some of the people who have had even more of the advantages than he, and who have left him with the feeling of wanting "the world to be in uniform and at a sort of moral attention forever." He then goes on to substitute a new and much more complex ambivalence for the one that, on looking back over his experience, he feels has now been resolved: he has been educated in the power of condemnatory judgment, but he is still unable to condemn Gatsby—"Only Gatsby ... was exempt from my reaction—Gatsby who represented everything for which I have an unaffected scorn." It is to be Nick's fate in the course of the novel, as unquestionably it was Fitzgerald's, that while he is to learn intolerance and finally moral indignation, he is never to come to terms with his contradictory feelings toward Gatsby: his moral indignation remains to the end the slave of his moral idealism. After Gatsby's death it is simple enough for Nick to recognize the Buchanans as "careless people," for he has accumulated more than sufficient evidence of their irresponsibility to cancel out his earlier admiration of them. But of Gatsby the poseur, racketeer, and liar he can only speak in the name of Gatsby the dreamer, and eulogize him only in the name of the founding of America itself, for Gatsby is one who escapes the monitory conscience of the "spoiled priest" by being himself priestlike, with a priest's passionate and self-sacrificing dedication to an ideal, a religion, of romantic transcendence. Nick's point of view, which we see in the process of gradually becoming reeducated with regard to the Buchanans, is incapable of reeducation with regard to Gatsby, for Gatsby is both a suitable object for the fascination that Nick earlier felt for the Buchanans and an embodiment of the ideal against which he measures and condemns them. It is an inadequate ideal, and Nick—

or at least Fitzgerald—is entirely aware of the fact, but within the limits of his given experience it is the only one he has to set against the world of Buchanan values, the only one he has, therefore, to exalt into triumph over those values at the end.

But the image of Nick that dominates the opening chapters is of another, as yet uneducated idealism, the kind indigenous to his Middle West, a rural frontier fascination with the appearance of culture and worldly manners. In fact, the first chapter centered in the scene depicting the dinner party at the Buchanan estate is clearly intended to dramatize Nick in his primal condition of reserved judgment juxtaposed with the gradually emerging facts of spiritual corruption and deceit that finally cause him to arrive at condemnatory judgment and become morally initiated. Firmly established amid the grandeur of his physical setting, Tom Buchanan first appears to Nick as an heroic figure, but almost at once Nick is struck by the change in him since their New Haven years.

> Now he was a sturdy straw-haired man of thirty with a rather hard mouth and a supercilious manner. Two shining arrogant eyes had established dominance over his face and gave him the appearance of always leaning aggressively forward. Not even the effeminate swank of his riding clothes could hide the enormous power of that body.... It was a body capable of enormous leverage—a cruel body. His speaking voice, a gruff husky tenor, added to the impression of fractiousness he conveyed. There was a touch of paternal contempt in it, even toward people he liked— and there were men at New Haven who had hated his guts.

This swift appraisal of Tom establishes him in the role he is later to play and constitutes the first element in the developing contrast between appearance and reality on which the chapter turns.

A moment later Nick is taken in to see Daisy and Jordan, and the picture of glamorous buoyancy and charm that they present temporarily restores his powers of admiration. In fact, the quality of physical inflation, suggested entirely in tableau, that pervades the scene stands as an exact equivalent for the emotion the sight of the women arouses in him.

> The only completed stationary object in the room was an enormous couch on which two young women were buoyed up as though upon an anchored balloon. They were both in white, and their dresses were rippling and fluttering as if they has just been

blown back in after a short flight around the house.... Then there
was a boom as Tom Buchanan shut the rear windows and the
caught wind died out about the room, and the curtains and the
rugs and the two young women ballooned slowly to the floor.

But the effect is only temporarily. As the scene deflates itself, so subsequent
events deflate Nick's illusion and impel him toward condemnatory judgment.
At the dinner table he learns that "Tom's got some woman in New York."
Gatsby's name is brought into the conversation and hastily dropped. Nick
dimly remembers, having seen Jordan, or a picture of her, somewhere before.
Sitting on the porch with Daisy after dinner and listening to her tell about
the birth of her child and her feelings about life in general, he is suddenly
struck by "the basic insincerity of what she had to say" and begins to feel "the
whole evening had been a trick of some sort to extract a contributory
emotion" from him. A moment later Daisy smirks "as if she had asserted her
membership in a rather distinguished secret society to which she and Tom
belonged." Nick leaves East Egg that night sufficiently disturbed to want
Daisy to "rush out of the house, child in arms," and upon returning home he
catches sight of Gatsby standing in the darkness of his lawn and looking
across the water to the green light at the end of the Buchanans' dock: Thus,
by the end of the first chapter the basic dramatic situation has been
established; all the principal characters have been introduced or alluded to;
and the destructive element in the Buchanans has been brought into fatal
juxtaposition with both Nick's naïve admiration and Gatsby's naïve
aspiration. The contest now will be between the force of the secret society,
epitomized by Daisy's insincerity and Tom's cruel selfishness, and the
persuasive power of Gatsby's illusion. But we already know the outcome: it
has been ordained by the quality and content of the action itself.

    The second chapter develops the destructive statement of the first in
two ways: through the contextual symbolism of the "valley of ashes" image
dominated by the gigantic eyes of the oculist Dr. T. J. Eckleburg, and
through the pictorial scene of the drunken party at Tom's New York
apartment. The valley of ashes establishes the situation of evil that is
conventionally, and in Fitzgerald habitually, associated with hopeless poverty,
and it projects that evil into literal contrast with the kind that wealth and
privilege induce in the Buchanans. Theirs is at once a more serious and
reprehensible kind because it involves the possibility of moral choice and an
identical kind because it has behind it an equivalent impoverishment of soul.
The eyes of Dr. Eckleburg can be variously and, if one is not careful to
preserve a sense of humor, fatuously interpreted. They are reminiscent of

some of Fitzgerald's earlier gothic figures of evil—The ghostly apparitions and "somber palls" of *This Side of Paradise* and *The Beautiful and Damned*— but they have the virtue of thematic relevance that these lacked, as well as the dramatic advantage of association with a developed physical milieu. They are, of course, suggestive of Nick's monitory conscience and are related to the image of "the casual watcher in the darkening streets" that is evoked during the party scene by his sense of being "within and without, simultaneously enchanted and repelled by the inexhaustible variety of life." They are also specifically associated by George Wilson in the eighth chapter with the eyes of God and, since Gatsby is represented as a son of God, we are probably justified in associating them in turn with the holiness of his romantic aspiration. More generally, they operate as an open symbol of transcendence and judgment set down in an opposing environment of defeat and subhuman amorality, or, to put it differently, they serve as a terminal point for the two principal thematic lines of the novel: the evil of the human condition overseen and modified by conscience.

The party episode pictorializes in scenic form the evil implicit in the valley of ashes, and since it stands in ironic contrast with the earlier scene at the Buchanans', it shows up that evil to be merely the nether side of theirs: the moral debasement of the party is the Buchanans' moral hypocrisy with its clothes off, the ugly truth beneath the veneer of social elegance that first charmed Nick, the corruption behind Daisy's enchanting voice and Jordan's delicate balancing act—in effect, the vulgar barroom scene in *The Waste Land* in comparison with the sterile "game of chess" episode.

The third through the sixth chapters perform for Gatsby the same service that the first two chapters performed for the Buchanans: they present him in the alternating conditions of illusion and reality, mystery and fact, successively as genial host, shady character, and romantic visionary. In the third chapter he is dramatized in his public role of host, but like Conrad's Heyst he is seen by various observers in the roles created for him by his legend, and this has the effect of endowing him with the mythic generality and largeness that his thematic role requires. It also gives concrete endorsement to the premise that he is the product of his "Platonic conception of himself." Nick is himself momentarily taken in by the "Oggsford man" role, but quickly recognizes its absurdity, especially after the luncheon with Wolfsheim when he becomes acquainted with the underworld role. He shortly discovers, however, that the truth about Gatsby, as it is gradually revealed to him, first by Jordan, then by Gatsby himself, is far more remarkable than any of the stories circulated about him, and ultimately far more compelling. By the end of the sixth chapter he has become convinced of the high quality of Gatsby's aspiration, but he has also gathered fresh evidence in the form of the Buchanans' high-handed behavior at one of the parties that that aspiration will eventually be defeated. Daisy has initially been hypnotized by Gatsby's display of wealth and ardor and for the moment is attracted by the prospect of an affair, but during the party she reveals her snobbish inability to participate wholly in any form of life outside herself.

> She was appalled by West Egg, this unprecedented 'place' that Broadway had begotten upon a Long Island fishing village— appalled by its raw vigor that chafed under the old euphemisms and by the too obtrusive fate that herded its inhabitants along a short-cut from nothing to nothing. She saw something awful in the very simplicity she failed to understand.

Like Daisy's first show of "basic insincerity," this reaction is proof that she will never finally join Gatsby in his efforts to "repeat the past."

It is interesting to see how these chapters devoted to Gatsby exactly reverse the revelatory processes of those devoted to the Buchanans. The illusion of sophisticated elegance was penetrated in their case to reveal a basic sickness and poverty of spirit. Gatsby, on the other hand, is seen initially against a veneer of fraudulent finery, is then revealed as actually fraudulent as well as lawless, and finally as morally innocent in the midst of the lawless. Superficially, he is as bad as the Buchanans, but only superficially. Theirs is a fundamental lawlessness of the heart: they are "careless people" in the worst and deepest sense. His is the lawlessness of the merely illegal and is excusable on the ground of the service it renders in enforcing the highest laws of the heart.

The seventh and climactic chapter brings into dramatic conflict the opposing elements of destruction and aspiration, the morally lawless and the morally innocent within the illegal, which have been separately developed in the chapters alternately devoted to the Buchanans and Gatsby. The occasion is a gathering at the Buchanan estate, precisely like that of the first chapter, but the tonal differences between the two are obviously intended to unite them in ironic contrast. Again Daisy and Jordan are seen in tableau, but where formerly they had about them a quality of inflation and buoyancy suggestive of the emotion they first aroused in Nick, they now appear in a state of fatigued deflation, as if the intervening events had drained away their vitality along with their charm. "The room, shadowed well with awnings, was dark and cool. Daisy and Jordan lay upon an enormous couch, like silver idols weighing down their own white dresses against the singing breeze of the fans." The whole situation, furthermore, seems to Nick to be touched with nightmare. He imagines he overhears the butler replying to a telephone request for "the master's body." Daisy impulsively kisses Gatsby the moment Tom leaves the room. Daisy's child is led in by a nurse and introduced to Gatsby who, Nick is certain, had never "really believed in its existence before." Finally, as the party prepares to leave for New York, Gatsby has his first insight into the quality of Daisy's that is to prevent him from winning her.

> "Her voice is full of money," he said suddenly.... That was it. I'd never understood before. It was full of money—that was the inexhaustible charm that rose and fell on it, the jingle of it, the cymbal's song of it.... High in a white palace the king's daughter, the golden girl....

This is the quality that indemnifies Daisy's commitment to Tom's world, but it finally involves much more than just money: it is a whole philosophy and tradition of life belonging to those who have always had money and marking them as a separate breed superior to those who have not. And in the chapter's closing scene, following on Gatsby's defeat and Myrtle's death, the difference is epiphanized:

> Daisy and Tom were sitting opposite each other at the kitchen table, with a plate of cold fried chicken between them, and two bottles of ale.... They weren't happy, and neither of them had touched the chicken or the ale—and yet they weren't unhappy either. There was an unmistakable air of natural intimacy about the picture, and anybody would have said that they were conspiring together.

The "secret society" has at last won out over romantic illusion, and Gatsby, standing outside in the dark just as he was at the end of Chapter I, is now "watching over nothing."

The movement of the novel, then, is from illusion to reality, innocence to knowledge, aspiration to defeat, and of course suffusing them all, tolerance to judgment. It is Gatsby who pays the price for the learning, who functions by turns as the hapless Mme. de Vionnet and the finally unteachable Chad, but it is Nick who does his learning for him and through whose experience—as through Strether's in the case of Chad—it is made dramatically concrete. Gatsby's dream is dramatically unspecific because it is unspecific to him. That is, symbolically, its limitation and meaning: it is based not on things as they are, but on things as they might become. It is real only to the extent that one can imagine for it some successful embodiment in action, and this the logic of the novel never permits. Nick's sensibility, therefore, serves as a surrogate for Gatsby's, making external all that the dream, because it lacks concrete basis in fact and action, cannot make external by itself. In doing this, Nick's sensibility fleshes Gatsby out to very nearly epic size, endowing him with the character of heroism seen against a broadly generalized conception of national life and history.

This is accomplished in the novel in two ways: through Nick's direct participation in the life of the Buchanans, which educates him in the folly of innocence, and through the larger symbolism of place against which Nick measures the meaning of both his own and Gatsby's experience. In practice, however, the two function as one: Nick records the experience as well as the meaning lost entirely in terms of place. Place affords him his basis of vision and evaluation, and the change that occurs in his vision and valuation results in a change in his evaluation of place.

At the beginning of the novel the East appears to Nick—as by implication it does to Gatsby—as a land of wealth and future glittering with the promise of "shining secrets." But as the action proceeds, the "shining secrets" tarnish, and it becomes clear that the wealth and quality of purposeful movement into the future are illusory virtues imposed upon the East by the innocence of the beholder. Like Gatsby's isolated dream, the wealth feeds on itself; the Easterners are imprisoned by it to the point of spiritual stagnation; the "flow of life" moves in a purposeless circle. "The rich grow richer" because they have no other way to grow; "the poor get—children" as well as poorer and end ultimately in a "valley of ashes." But the Middle West too is stagnant. There "dwellings are still called through decades by a family's name"; one is oppressed by the "interminable inquisitions" and by a moral code that demands that life survive as a tradition rather than flow dynamically into the future. It follows, therefore, that West Egg, the Eastern analogue of the Middle West, should also end in a "valley of ashes," and that *both* East and West Egg should be imperfect ovals "crushed flat at the contact end," equally defective in their reception to life.

Fundamentally Gatsby is, as Nick says, "a story of the West, after all." It begins in the Middle West, makes a "riotous excursion" into the heart of Eastern promise, and returns to the Middle West in what at first appears to be disillusionment. Actually, of course, it is an affirmation of the true values following on disillusionment: the initial image of Middle

Western stolidity resolves itself into a closing image of Middle Western solidity. Upon Nick's return from war the Middle West, "instead of being the warm centre of the world ... seemed like the ragged edge of the universe." Coming East to learn the bond business he settles down in West Egg in a "small eyesore" of a house to enjoy "the consoling proximity of millionaires" and to plumb if he can "the shining secrets that only Midas and Morgan and Maecenas knew." Having just left the restrictive environment of the Middle West, he is at first especially aware of the free flow of life in the East, although he is also aware that it is intimately associated with the free flow of wealth. He speaks of Tom and Daisy as drifting "here and there ... wherever people were rich together." But they "drift unrestfully," and he sees that Tom "would drift on forever seeking, a little wistfully, for the dramatic turbulence of some irrecoverable football game." Like Gatsby's dream, the Buchanans' drifting is an effort to recover in the present some of the lost sensations of the past as well as the sensibilities of youth that, in Americans, alone seem capable of deep response.

But Nick's first impression of the East is one of exciting, restless movement, and throughout the scene of his visit with the Buchanans his enchantment with their kinetic radiance alternates with moments of insight into their superficiality. Their lawn "started at the beach and ran toward the front door for a quarter of a mile, jumping over sundials and brick walls and burning gardens—finally when it reached the house drifting up the side in bright vines as though from the momentum of its run." Tom appears to be "leaning aggressively forward," filling his "glistening boots until he strained the top lacing, and you could see a great pack of muscle shifting when his shoulder moved under his thin coat." Inside the house as well everything seems to be flowing, but only because of a momentary breeze. "A breeze blew through the room, blew curtains in at one end and out the other like pale flags, twisting them up toward the frosted wedding-cake of the ceiling, and then rippled over the wine-colored rug, making a shadow on it as wind does on the sea." On the "only completely stationary object in the room" Daisy and Jordan appear to be "buoyed up as though upon an anchored balloon." But as soon as Tom shuts the window, the wind dies, and the floating effect proves to have been only an appearance. Nick is charmed and enchanted by the appearances, but soon begins to recognize them for they are. Tom and Daisy make only a "polite, pleasant effort to entertain and be entertained. They knew that presently dinner would be over and casually put away." There is little meaning or sincerity in what is going on. Daisy suddenly declares that Nick is an "absolute rose," but he realizes that she is only "extemporizing." Daisy and Jordan converse in language that "was as cool as their white dresses and their impersonal eyes in the absence of all desire." Inevitably Nick compares the scene with similar occasions in the West "where an evening was hurried from phase to phase toward its close, in a continually disappointed anticipation, or else in sheer nervous dread of the moment itself." But here in the East among expatriated Middle Westerners even anticipation has been lost; all desire is dead; the Buchanans are the spent shadows of action. "You make me feel uncivilized, Daisy," Nick says. "Can't you talk about crops or something," and the "or something substantial" is implied.

In the second chapter culminating in the party at Tom's New York apartment the contrast of place motifs is reinforced by an implicit symbolism relating place to dream and ultimately to Gatsby. The natives of West Egg are depicted as a race of the living dead, "ash grey men ... who move dimly and already crumbling through the powdery air." Only Myrtle Wilson is alive: "There was an immediately perceptible vitality about her as if the nerves of her body were continually smouldering." She alone is free of the "white ashen dust" that veiled her husband's "dark suit and pale hair as it veiled everything in the vicinity," and we learn later that she has remained alive and uncontaminated because she is nourished by her dream of an eventually legal life with Tom in the West.

During the party a change occurs in Myrtle that pictorializes a crucial fact about the nature of her own dream and, by implication, Gatsby's. Although the dream has kept her alive, now that she is surrounded by circumstances approaching those of its fulfillment she undergoes an ugly transformation: "The intense vitality that had been so remarkable in the garage was converted into impressive hauteur." She now presents a pathetic, ridiculous figure dressed in expensive clothes that contrast sharply with her commonness and her "violent and obscene language." Apparently the dream, by the very fact of its existence, can be lifegiving, but as it approaches realization it invests life with inconsistency and vulgarity: it is doomed to remain a "Platonic conception," an ideal incapable of embodiment in fact, particularly when the fact can only be material. But Myrtle's dream is a long way from realization. It is confined, as it turns out permanently, to illegality and the East.

For Nick the party represents a vulgarization of what he previously experienced at the Buchanans. The "flow" of the East has become confusion. "People disappeared, reappeared, made plans to go somewhere and then lost each other, searched for each other, found each other a few feet away." There is a photograph on the wall apparently of "a hen sitting on a blurred rock. Looked at from a distance, however, the hen resolved itself into a bonnet, and the countenance of a stout old lady beamed down into the room." It seems to him that there is a "blurred air" to the faces in the room, and in a fatuous effort to restore order he wipes from McKee's cheek "the spot of dried lather that had worried [him] all afternoon." But he is still "simultaneously within and without, simultaneously enchanted and repelled by the inexhaustible variety of life." Tom has told Myrtle that he cannot get a divorce because his wife is a Catholic, and although Nick "is a little shocked at the elaborateness of the lie," he has not yet learned to relate the lie, in all is elaborateness, to the false promise of the East or to the larger lie on which his whole experience rests.

But we cannot help but see the relation, just as we cannot help but see Nick, Myrtle, and the Buchanans as actors in a dumb show caricaturing Gatsby's tragedy. Like Nick, Gatsby is enchanted by the "shining secrets" of the East and mistakes the purposeless movement for the free flow of life into the future; like Myrtle he is given vitality by a dream that is far larger than any possibility of fulfillment; and like the Buchanans he is thwarted in his efforts to "repeat the past." He shares with them all the deficiency that makes them "subtly unadaptable to Eastern life," but he also shares their fate of inhabiting a culture in which dreams along with most demands of the spirit have no place. He aspires to the good life as though it were a thing of the spirit, while the culture can afford him the means only for a life of material achievement—a material woman or a woman corrupted by materialism. In his aloofness from his own material possessions he dramatizes his uncompromising faith that life can and will yield more, if only he can manipulate circumstances properly. And it is no more than the justice of irony that he should finally be thwarted by an utterly faithless but infinitely more powerful materialism than his own. For the Buchanans, wealth is not a means to the fulfillment of any dream: it is the hard fact of life against which the hard fact of Gatsby's manipulations can have no effect. It is also ironic that the illusions of Gatsby's party guests are seen in conjunction with his cold and aloof factualness, and that this factualness is the product of an illusion far more romantic than theirs. The guests come to his parties in pursuit of some final ecstasy, some ultimate good time that the American Dream has always promised them. Gatsby is the self-appointed agent of that dream, but they can never get close to him or discover his true identity, just as neither he nor they can hope to discover an identity for the dream.

It is dramatically just, therefore, that at the close of the novel Nick should relate Gatsby's aspiration to the feelings aroused in the early Dutch voyagers to America by their first glimpse of the "fresh, green breast of the new world."

> For a transitory enchanted moment man must have held his breath in the presence of this continent, compelled into an aesthetic contemplation he neither understood nor desired, face to face for the last time in history with something commensurate to his capacity for wonder.... And as I sat there brooding on the old, unknown world, I thought of Gatsby's wonder when he first picked out the green light at the end of Daisy's dock. He had come a long way to this blue lawn, and his dream must have seemed so close that he could hardly fail to grasp it. He did not know that it was already behind him, somewhere back in that vast obscurity beyond the city, where the dark fields of the republic rolled on under the night.

But it is also logically just that he should go on to say that those voyagers were face to face "for the last time in history with something commensurate to" their capacity for wonder. For it may well be that the moment when America was first settled was the last moment when America was able to embody the dream that the settlers brought to its shores, and that ever since the wonder and the dream have lacked a suitable object, or have had to languish and die in pursuit of an unworthy object—mere money or mere surface display—just as Gatsby's dream had to die in part because Daisy was, and could not help but be, unworthy of it.

It is perhaps too much to say, as at least one critic has, that Gatsby is a symbol of America itself. But he is a major figure in the legend created by the complex fate of being American, and he is the hero of the tragic limitations of that fate in a world that, as the eclipsing myth of the twenties recedes, seems more contemporary than we knew.

SEYMOUR L. GROSS

Fitzgerald's "Babylon Revisited"

Thus, though we cannot make our sun
Stand still, yet we *will* make him run.
                              —*Marvell*

In the little hours of the night every
    move from place to place was an enormous human
    jump, an increase of paying for the privilege
of slower and slower motion.
                              —"Babylon Revisited"

I

The two epigraphs which introduce this essay define, in one sense, the polar limits of Fitzgerald's life. His frenetic, attempts, almost heroic in their intensity and pathetic in their ultimate ineffectiveness, to stay ahead of "Time's winged chariot" (though he was afraid the race was lost at thirty) are too well known, have been too fully documented, to need much elaboration here. "I wanted to enjoy, to be prodigal and open-hearted, to miss nothing." What Fitzgerald wanted, finally, was to fill each moment of life so full of living that time would stand still for him. This was the way to "beat" time— to run a dead heat with the galloping stallions of mortality. It is one of

From *College English* 25 (November 1963), 128–135. © 1963 by the National Council of Teachers of English.

Fitzgerald's accomplishments that he can still make us respond to the purity of this desire even as we recognize, as we are so often meant to, the spurious materials and self-defeating methods by which his characters strive to make life go glimmering. Those of us for whom the Twenties as Fitzgerald's metaphor of what life may offer by way of glamour has not yet become a whipping boy of middle-age can still acknowledge, as he wrote in his notebook, how "any given moment has its value; it can be questioned in the light of after-events, but the moment remains. The young prince in velvet gathered in lovely domesticity around the queen amid the hush of rich draperies may presently grow up to be Pedro the Cruel or Charles the Mad, but the moment of beauty was there."

But at the polar opposite of Fitzgerald's presentations of "the romantic enlargement of the possibilities of life" (to use Professor Bewley's phrase) emerge the results of the toughened vision of the "spoiled priest"—as Fitzgerald once called himself—who watches with horror as the "filled moment" collapses of its own weight. In this region of Fitzgerald's moral geography—whose supreme history and topography have been written into "Babylon Revisited" (1931)—there is nothing of the confusion of attitude to be found in such essays as "Echoes of the Jazz Age" (1931) or "My Lost City" (1932), in which the seemingly firm-eyed recapitulation of catastrophe and self-delusion finally counts for less than the nostalgic yearnings with which they end.[1] Nor is there anything here of that troubled ambivalence which characterizes our response to that fantastic ambiguity, Jay Gatsby, whose exquisite dream moves us even as we acknowledge the cloud of foul dust which trails in its wake. In the world of "Babylon Revisited" winter dreams do not drift sweetly into sad memories, but erupt into nightmares of irrevocable loss, leaving only the waste and horror of the twisted shapes that lie on the decimated plains of the Babylonian Captivity.

II

The action of "Babylon Revisited" begins and ends in the Ritz bar. This structural maneuver is absolutely right, for the bar is one of the story's chief symbols of the relentless impingement of the past on the present, though it is not until the end of the story after Charlie's defeat, that it clearly takes on this signification. Indeed, ironically enough, Charlie's initial appearance at the Ritz seems to imply precisely the opposite: the apparent separation of the past from the concerns, needs, and desires of the present. The very fact that Charlie can return to the hub of a life which had cost him his wife and his child does not at all indicate, as the story's most recent commentator has it, that the old way of life "still appeals to him,"[2] but rather demonstrates the extent and depth of his self-mastery and the confidence he feels in his belief that his wildly squandered yesterdays are over and done with, that there is no tab left for him to have to pick up.

The opening scene's primary function is to show how divorced Charlie feels from the blurred life of several years ago. His questions to the bartender about cronies from the past are mechanically curious but fundamentally uninterested. The news that "Mr. Campbell [is] a pretty sick man" and that Claude Fessenden cheated the bar of thirty thousand francs and is now "all bloated up" evokes no comment. The pricks to memory of "familiar names from the long list of a year and a half ago" strike no responsive chord. Charlie feels out of place and "polite" in the bar that, in the time of wine and roses, he had felt he had "owned." "It had gone back into France," he thinks. When he goes through the remembered ritual of placing his foot firmly on the bar rail and turning to survey the room, only a single pair of indifferent eyes "fluttered up from a newspaper in the corner." Charlie's dissociation from his past is capped by the brief bit of dialogue with which the scene ends:

"Here for long, Mr. Wales?"
"I'm here for four or five days to see my little girl."
"Oh-h! You have a little girl?"

In the Babylon who "saith in her heart [I] shall see no sorrow," there can be neither children nor the risk of their loss. The figures there float rootlessly free of human ties and responsibilities, having sprung full-born from their skyrocketing blue chips and capacity for dissipation. The adults are the only children. "We *did* have such good times that crazy spring [Lorraine wistfully recalls in the letter to Charlie], like the night you and I stole the butcher's tricycle, and the time we tried to call on the president and you had the old derby rim and the wire cane." But Charlie Wales's return to Paris is an attempted return to fatherhood, an attempt to lay the ghost of his past childishness through the recovery of his lost child, Honoria. "Oh-h! You have a little girl?" is a bitterly reasonable question for one whose life had been nothing more than a "catering to vice and waste ... on an utterly childish scale." After all, children have no children.

The tragedy is that Charlie no longer deserves such a question. There is in us a desire to find the present Charlie somehow deserving of his wretched fate—which is what perhaps accounts for Professor Harrison's reading—for it is easier to live with a belief in reasonable justice. But Fitzgerald does not allow us this luxury. Throughout the story he ironically stresses the splendid achievement of Charlie's reform. His sensitivity, poised intelligence, and quiet power over himself *should* be enough to get his daughter back. That moral renovation may not be enough is the injustice that lies at the center of the story.

Charlie's recovery of "character"—"the eternally valuable element"— which was implied in the opening scene in his being unafraid to confront the old life, is made explicit as he leaves the bar. Walking the street, he feels, all at once, "the sudden provincial quality of the left bank." But Charlie is not a prig: his self-mastery is too final to need the subtly corrupt support of the moral outrage of a libertine turned puritan. He can still be moved by the "pink majesty" of the Place de la Concord and "the blue hour spread over the magnificent façade" of the Avenue de l'Opera; he can even afford to indulge in the fantasy of imagining that "the cab horns, playing endlessly the first few bars of *Le Plus que Lent*, were the trumpets of the Second Empire." Paris is not, after all, Babylon. Only the Left Bank, which in the "crazy years" had seemed the epitome of romantic possibility, strikes him with "its sudden provincialism." Brentano's, cheap restaurants (in which he had never eaten), such as Duval's, with its "trim little bourgeois hedge," had never been "spoiled," because they had never been touched, by the crowd of three years ago who had made "months into days." Babylon, Charlie thinks sadly, had been an American creation.

The following scene with Marion and Lincoln Peters, Charlie's sister-in-law and her husband, who had been given custody of Honoria when Charlie's wife, Helen, was dying and he himself was broke and in a sanitarium for alcoholism, is the symbolic obverse of the opening scene at the Ritz bar, which had depicted the repudiated past. Here the "warm and comfortably American room," the intimate movements of children, "the cheer of six o'clock" as dinner is being prepared, and Honoria (in Charlie's mind) at the center of the bustle, represent the future which Charlie anticipates with excruciating need. The contrasts between the two scenes are extensive. The mechanical exchange in the bar has become the sincerely interested conversation between Charlie and Lincoln Peters; the "single bored voice in the once-clamorous women's room" has changed into "the eager smacks of the fire and sounds of French activity in the kitchen"; the shrill group of homosexuals ("strident queens") has been replaced by a family. Honoria's ecstatic shriek of welcome—"oh, daddy, daddy, daddy, daddy, dads, dads, dads!"—is the answer to the barman's surprised question.

Yet for all the obvious contrasts between the two scenes, there is also present an ominous similarity—a similarity which functions as the first of many symbolic foreshowings of Charlie's failure to redeem his daughter (and thus himself) from the carnival years. In both scenes Charlie is fundamentally isolated from the radical quality of the life going on around him: in the bar because of his maturity, in the home because of his position as a suppliant. Despite Honoria's presence (with its infinite promise), it is Marion Peters' hostility which dominates the scene, making Charlie's heart sit "up rigidly in his body." Although it is not until Part III that we come fully to understand why Marion has set herself against Charlie's future, her animosity, interposing itself as it does between father and daughter, so serves to consign Charlie's presence to the periphery of the room that the final effect of the scene is the disturbing implication that Charlie's proximity to the symbols of the life he hopes for is as deceptive as was his proximity in the opening scene to the symbols of the life he left behind him. It is significant that Honoria never speaks again in the scene after her cry of joy and that the last bit of dialogue is Marion's frigid reply to Charlie's statement that he takes but one drink a day—"I hope you keep to it."

The parallelism between the two scenes is reinforced by the similarity of Charlie's response to both the bar and the Peters' home: relief at being able to get away and a desire to roam the streets alone to see Paris "with clearer and more judicious eyes than those of other days." His second view is more severely contemptuous, the result, no doubt, of his recent contact with Honoria. Montmartre, "where he had parted with so many hours and so much money," stripped of its alcoholic haze, reveals itself as cheap, meretriciously exuberant, and corrupt. As he watches the prowling prostitutes, devouring cafes, and "bleak and sinister cheap hotels," he "suddenly realized the meaning of the word 'dissipate'—to dissipate into thin air; to make nothing out of something." Then follows what is perhaps Fitzgerald's most profound insight into the nature of Babylon, Jazz Age style: "In the little hours of the night every move from place to place was an enormous human jump, an increase of paying for the privilege of slower and slower motion."

On the literal level, the sentence describes early morning bar-hopping: greater and greater expenditures of cash for the "privilege" of more and more uncertain physical movement. But the passage reaches out to larger significances. The impulse towards the enlargement of experience which lies behind the spree manifests itself in the *little* hours of the night (which Fitzgerald elsewhere described as "the dark night of the soul")—"little" not only in the sense of early, but also in the ironic sense of compressed and constricted. The "enormous human jump" required of the drunk in moving from place to place, for whom physical space is constantly hostile, enlarges to an understanding of the expense of spirit which the movement entails.

Not only is money being spent ("an increase of paying"), but the human quality is being spent, used up, too. The desire to make the sun run by filling each moment so full of gaiety and abandon that time will seem to stand still succeeds only in so weighting down the figures that they can manage only the contrived movements of an artificially slowed-down motion picture. Life, not time, has stopped.

Part II opens deceptively. The "fine fall day," Charlie's euphoria, and lunch with Honoria at the only restaurant Charlie can think of "not reminiscent of ... long luncheons that began at two and ended in a blurred and vague twilight," seem to promise, structurally, that the happier of the alternatives symbolically offered in Part I will occur. This scene—the only extended contact between father and daughter—is particularly poignant because in dramatizing a glimpse of the future Charlie yearns for, Fitzgerald makes us *feel* (and not merely abstractly acknowledge) the absolute rightness of Charlie's desire to be reunited with his daughter. Though Charlie knows that he needs his daughter back in order to give shape and direction to his renascence, to redeem his lost honor, and, in a sense, to recover something of his wife "escaped to a grave in Vermont," he is aware of the danger in the very intensity of his need. He knows how perilously easy it would be to make Honoria into a smothered surrogate for all that he has irremediably lost. For example, when Honoria "tranquilly" agrees that she won't always love her daddy best, but will someday "grow up and meet somebody her own age and go marry him and forget [she] ever had a daddy," Charlie is not upset. The conversation between father and daughter is tender and loving and wholly free of sinister psychiatric pressures, dramatic proof of Charlie's ability to act in terms of his understanding as it is articulated in Part IV:

> The present was the thing—work to do and someone to love. But not to love too much, for he knew the injury that a father can do to a daughter ... by attaching [her] too closely: afterward, out in the world, the child would seek in the marriage partner the same blind tenderness and, failing probably to find it, turn against love and life.

Hawthorne once observed that every crime we commit destroys more Edens than our own. In focusing on Charlie's need it is easy to miss Honoria's. Though Fitzgerald does not cheapen the scene by sentimentalizing the unsatisfactoriness of Honoria's present life, it is clear that Honoria likes neither Marion nor Marion's daughter, though she is too well-bred and sensitive to engage in spiteful recriminations that could only serve to deepen her father's unhappiness. Her sudden "Daddy, I want to come and live with you," though unaccompanied by Dickensian emotional fanfare, is an eloquent plea that broadens the base of the tragedy, much as does the silent presence of the children at the end of the *Oedipus*. This encounter will painfully remind us, when Charlie's undeserved defeat is at the center of our response, of Honoria's loss as well.

The past and future, which were structurally separated in Part I (though the past was made to impinge symbolically upon the future) are narratively intersected in Part II. Duncan Schaeffer and Lorraine Quarles— "Sudden ghosts out of the past"—intrude themselves upon the promise of tomorrow. They are ghosts not only because they will eventually haunt Charlie to defeat, but also because they are disembodied, dislocated spirits inhabiting a world which exists only in their self-conscious strivings. Lorraine's "This your little girl?" (which echoes the bartender's question) announces her exclusion from reality; similarly, when Charlie tries to stop the banal bantering about his being sober by indicating Honoria with his head, both Lorraine and Duncan can only laugh. The innocent pleasure of father and daughter attending the vaudeville at the Empire becomes, in Lorraine's "There! That's what I want to do.... I want to see some clowns and acrobats and jugglers," an obscene activity, a Babylonian revel of ruinous irresponsibility and desperate hilarity. But they are ghosts in yet another sense, for Lorraine and Duncan are the anonymous figures in slow motion in the passage already quoted. Doomed as they are to being out of time, where gestures pass through all the essential realities, they can only drift, "trite, blurred, worn away," in search of some vampiristic contact with those who inhabit the real world. "They liked him," Charlie thinks, "because he was serious ... because he was stronger than they were, because they wanted to draw a certain sustenance from his strength." He has located their essential weakness; but he has miscalculated their power to destroy. Human blood cannot make vampires normally human; but vampires destroy what is human in achieving temporary sustenance.

The intrusion of the ghosts from Charlie's past accounts, symbolically, for the tableau with which Part II ends. Charlie does not accompany his daughter into the Peters's house. He waits, instead, "in the dark street until she appeared all warm and glowing, in the window above, and kissed her fingers out into the night." The distance between the shadowed father and radiant daughter, which the kiss can only symbolically but not actually traverse, is the measure of their inevitable separation. Honoria, framed in the window, has become, the passage seems to imply, a portrait—something that was once livingly available but is now only accessible as a memory in a gallery of remembrances of things past. The tableau, moreover, looks back to the terminal passage of Part I, in which Charlie eludes the "encouraging stare" of a streetwalker, though he buys her supper and gives her a twenty-franc note (as he is later to buy Honoria lunch and give her a doll), and forward to the terminal passage of Part III, when Charlie in a half-dream tries to talk to his dead wife, who "was in a swing in a white dress, and swinging faster and faster all the time, so that at the end he could not hear clearly all that she said." These structural juxtapositions indicate that although Charlie has wilfully removed himself from the sterility of his past, as represented by the prostitute, he is nevertheless actually closer to her than he is to the distanced Honoria or receding Helen. He is offered the physical presence of a non-wife, non-mother, but only the "portrait" of his child and the "ghost" of his wife.

In Part III Marion becomes a significant actor in the drama. Having dressed herself in a black dress "that just faintly suggested mourning," as if already prepared to preside over the death of Charlie's hopes, Marion sets herself squarely against her brother-in-law's dream of the future. Although she has obviously convinced herself that she is motivated solely by a concern for Honoria's welfare and duty to her dead sister, it soon becomes apparent that her hard stance is not morally unequivocal. In Marion we see a subtly corrupt desire for self-justification masking itself in the virtues of duty and responsibility. Marion, because she had never really loved her sister,[3] jealously resented her sister's materially superior marriage. Lincoln, though a wholly decent person, has never been capable of making much money; even in the boom time he "never got ahead enough to carry anything but [his] insurance." Indeed, although Charlie has had recently to start over again from scratch, he is already making twice as much money as Lincoln. Marion's response to this "injustice" has been to take psychological refuge in the cliché that the rich are never happy; she has submerged her envy in "a curious disbelief in her sister's happiness." Marion's hostility did not originate, as Lincoln believes, in the Babylonian days—"Marion felt there was some kind of injustice in ... you not even working toward the end, and getting richer and richer"—but long before that. The party years merely aggravated—and seemed to give justification for—an already existing mean condition of mind. Marion's vindication came in "the shock of one terrible night" when Helen was locked out in a snowstorm and barely escaped pneumonia. Convinced, because she wanted to be, that this was "one of many scenes from her sister's martyrdom," Marion's repressed envy was able to flower forth as self-righteous "hatred" for Charlie. The death of Helen (which Marion falsely insists on blaming Charlie for) and Charlie's own crack-up affirmed once and for all the superiority of her own married life. Her "investment" has paid off in the legal guardianship of Honoria; and the power to beat Charlie with this moral triumph is what she has instead of a materially lavish life.

Marion, however, is not merely an interesting piece of psychological portraiture, for she complicates what might otherwise have been an unqualified commitment to the life of the "solid citizen." Though "Babylon Revisited" is centrally an exploration of the waste inherent in the quest for the gorgeous life, it is not thereby a paean to Main Street. It is clear that Charlie's "plans, vistas, futures for Honoria and himself" are organized around what we have come to call middle-class values and virtues—home, responsible job, hard work, the respect of the community. But it is also clear—as Marion's presence in the story indicates—that the achievement of worth is not to be found in the middle class automatically. Every mode of life is shadowed by its own kind of treachery and means of self-aggrandizement. Marion, no less than Lorraine and Duncan, "needs" Charlie, in her case as a "tangible villain." It is therefore both ironic and apt that although Marion is revolted by people like Lorraine and Duncan—they "make her really physically sick"—she will, in Part IV, unwittingly ally herself with them to destroy Charlie. She too has set herself against Charlie's attempt to extricate himself from his past: "from the night you did that terrible thing [Charlie's accidental locking out of his wife in the snow] you haven't really existed for me." Indeed, without Marion, Lorraine and Duncan are without effect. How fully she has committed herself to keeping Charlie from escaping into the future is revealed when, after being forced to acknowledge that Charlie "had somehow arrived at control over the situation" and that Lincoln will not help her keep Honoria from her father, she responds with hysterical viciousness, "I think if she were my child I'd rather see her—" and retreats to her bed with a neurasthenic headache.

In Part IV, which ironically opens with Charlie's ecstatic feeling that the "door of the world was open again," Charlie is to feel the full weight of his history. As if duplicating the ultimate movement of the entire section, Charlie's happiness fades suddenly into the sad memory of all the plans he and Helen had made that would never materialize. Though he turns away from the past— "The present was the thing"—the arrival of a letter from Lorraine, nostalgically recalling the "good times that crazy spring," reinforces the mounting sense of an unreasonably vengeful past. It will turn out to be of no avail that Charlie can dismiss the thought of a "trite, blurred, worn away" Lorraine to "think of Sundays spent with [Honoria] ... and knowing she was there in his house at night, drawing her breath in the darkness."

For at the very threshold of Charlie's new life, the "ghosts from the past" drift up the corridors of time. Fitzgerald's paragraph describing their emergence is appropriately eerie. First, like an annunciation of doom, the long peal of the bell; then the voices in the corridor coming closer, "which developed under the light into Duncan Schaeffer and Lorraine Quarles." Drunk, incoherent, irresponsible, the world of Babylon has shattered the world of "people together by a fire." In a brilliant symbolic gesture, Charlie, horrified, moves closer to them, "as if to force them backward down the corridor." That it is Charlie's own past that he is trying to force backward into time is amply demonstrated by the fact that Lorraine and Duncan are specifically identified with the figures in the "little hours of the night" passage: "Still in slow motion, with blurred, angry faces, with uncertain feet, they retired along the corridor."

But Charlie's power is finally useless: the door of the world opens to both the past and the future. Charlie is now more isolated than he had ever been before. Marion stands rigidly with an arm encircling each of her children and Lincoln is "swinging Honoria back and forth like a pendulum from side to side." The implications of this tableau are totally devastating. The past has set the pendulum of the future in motion; time will serve only to take Honoria further away from him; "the tangible, visible child" will swing away into dimmer and dimmer memory, like Helen in the dream in Part III, who was "swinging faster and faster all the time, so that in the end he could not hear clearly all that she said." All that is left for Charlie to do is to return alone down the corridor, turning to say a final goodbye—"Good night, sweetheart.... Good night, dear children."

The story ends in the Ritz bar, where Charlie furiously goes to find Lorraine and Duncan. But he soon realizes that "there was nothing he could do." The return to the bar, as well as the first appearance of Paul, the head barman, "who in the latter days of the bull market had come to work in his custom-built car," symbolizes Charlie's bondage to a world which he mistakenly supposed could be cast off completely. Charlie does not change in the course of "Babylon Revisited"; his undeserved defeat does not become an occasion for either self-pity or self-indulgence; in the bar he neither talks of his loss nor takes more than the one drink a day he has allowed himself.

But his substantial endowments have not been enough. Though he thinks that he will "come back someday; they couldn't make him pay forever," the whole movement of the story makes it bitterly clear that they can. When he asks the waiter "What do I owe you?" the answer the story supplies is "your hopes and dreams."

A part of Charlie's life had stopped in the little hours of some night when if you didn't want something to be real, "you just paid some money." Looking back, Charlie now realizes how utterly he "lost everything [he] wanted in the boom"; and Fitzgerald, in the final sentence of the story, crushes any lingering hopes by indicating that there is nothing left for Charlie to do but turn for comfort to the dead, for whom time has also stopped. "He was absolutely sure Helen wouldn't have wanted him to be so alone."

NOTES

1. "... and it all seems rosy and romantic to us who were young then, because we will never feel quite so intensely about our surroundings any more" ("Echoes of the Jazz Age"). "For the moment I can only cry out that I have lost my splendid mirage. Come back, come back, O glittering and white!" ("My Lost City").

2. James M. Harrison, "Fitzgerald's 'Babylon Revisited,'" *Explicator*, 16 (Jan. 1958), item 20.

3. When Marion intimates a tremendous love for her sister, Charlie thinks that "he had never been certain how fond of each other the sisters were in life." The contrast between the two sisters is symbolically emphasized by Marion's black dress, which opens the section, and Helen's white one, with which the section closes.

LEONARD A. PODIS

The Beautiful and Damned:
Fitzgerald's Test of Youth

During the early years of the republic, America's youth had little choice but to find a living as soon as they reached physical maturity. As the country prospered with the maturation of industrialism, allowing the middle class to encroach upon the leisure-ground traditionally reserved for the elite, youth gained education and freedom of movement as well. That women's emancipation was coming into its own in the early 1900's is common knowledge. What is not so often realized is that youth—both young men and women—were also gaining new freedom. People had begun to enjoy themselves before seeking the sober responsibilities of family life.[1]

F. Scott Fitzgerald was perhaps the first, certainly the best-known, writer to monitor this trend in American culture, and capitalize on it in his fiction. It was, in fact, largely Fitzgerald's glamorous conception and treatment of the "new" American girl that popularized the notion of the "flapper," and brought him early success. So completely was Fitzgerald tied to the public's awareness of wild youth and "the jazz age," that many readers (including a few critics) could never accept him as the writer of serious literature he was during most of his career.[2]

Taken together, *This Side of Paradise* and Fitzgerald's early short stories demonstrate his penchant for dealing with people I prefer to think of as

From *Fitzgerald/Hemingway Annual* 1973, pp. 141–147. ©1973 Leonard A. Podis.

"moral orphans." Stories like "The Ice Palace," "The Off-Shore Pirate," "The Jelly Bean," and "The Camel's Back," to name but a few, are filled with supremely youthful characters who drink and dance through an amusement-park world uninformed by parents, or any sense of parental morality. The fact that they seem to have no parents is somehow less important than the feeling one gets from their antics that they never had any to begin with. By totally separating youth from parents and elders, Fitzgerald created the atmosphere which enabled him to write the shocking, unprecedented, "now" tales of the post–World War period.

Yet while it is true that Fitzgerald peopled his early works with youthful heroes and heroines, it is equally true that much of his writing, most noticeably beginning with *The Beautiful and Damned*, expressed a tragic vision of the consequences of unfettered, misspent youth, failing to condone, while hesitating to glamorize the idea of young life divorced from parental stability. As he later noted in retrospect:

> All the stories that came into my head had a touch of disaster in them—the lovely young creatures in my novels went to ruin, the diamond mountains of my, short stories blew up, my millionaires were as beautiful and damned as Thomas Hardy's peasants. In life these things hadn't happened yet, but I was pretty sure living wasn't the reckless, careless business these people thought—this generation just younger than me.[3]

In *The Beautiful and Damned* we can see Fitzgerald's first major attempt ("May Day" was his most notable minor attempt) to reconcile his romantic faith in the magic of youth with his morally ingrained suspicions that life wasn't "the reckless business" for which he and his young creatures had been taking it.

As Fitzgerald wrote his publisher, Charles Scribner, the novel would show the ruin of a young marriage "on the shoals of dissipation."[4] That it succeeded in this end critics agree. Most, however, feel that Fitzgerald failed to supply the groundwork necessary to explain the couple's decline. Thus the book delineates very well the pathetic landscape of mental and physical deterioration, but sheds no light on underlying causes.[5]

Fitzgerald originally intended to call his second novel "The Flight of the Rocket."[6] To me, this provisional title seems more appropriate than the more poetic one he finally chose. For the characters are not really beautiful, and they are certainly not damned—morally irresponsible, to be sure, but not damned in that lofty, tragic sense the phrase might suggest.

"The Flight of the Rocket" is a more adequate description of the temporarily brilliant exhaustion of youth which occurs in the novel. Anthony Patch and his wife, Gloria, launch their lives with all the majesty and fury of a moon rocket. But, losing sight of moral wisdom and truths in the thrust of their consuming onward motion, they slip into total hedonism. They lack responsibility in any traditional sense of the word. Living without work or apparent purpose, thinking only of each moment as it comes in terms of their own enjoyment, Anthony and Gloria exploit their ephemeral youth imprudently, and, inevitably, fizzle out like spent rockets, disintegrating as they plummet earthward with the recognition that youth alone has not been enough.

Fitzgerald's abundant use of moral orphans notwithstanding, Anthony Patch is one of his few literal orphans. He lives with his parents as a very small boy, but his mother, an opera singer, dies when he is not more than six or seven. His memories of her are faint and "nebulous."[7] Anthony's father is often drunk, and generally negligent in the care of his son. "He was continually promising Anthony hunting trips and fishing trips and excursions to Atlantic City, 'oh, some time soon now'; but none of them ever materialized" (6). On the one trip they do take, Anthony's father dies amid "much sweating and grunting and crying aloud for air," leaving the child an orphan at eleven.

Anthony soon finds himself under the guidance of the fatuous Adam Patch, his paternal grandfather, who, had Fitzgerald so desired, might have been as moral a force as the image of Nick Carraway's father would later be in *The Great Gatsby*. But in *The Beautiful and Damned*, it appears that Fitzgerald felt he must portray youth unhindered by any ubiquitous sense of morality. Just as Henry James wrote about people who did not work so he could examine their everyday lives in a purer context, so Fitzgerald used moral orphans to enable him to study youth in an isolated setting. Thus, far from providing Anthony with a moral heritage, "Cross" Patch, a fanatical social reformer of the day, is a simpering prig who:

> levelled a varied assortment of uppercuts and body-blows at liquor, literature, vice, art, patent medicines, and Sunday theatres. His mind, under the influence of ... insidious mildew ... gave itself up furiously to every indignation of the age. From an armchair in the office of his Tarrytown estate he directed against the enormous hypothetical enemy, unrighteousness, a campaign which went on through fifteen years, during which he displayed

himself a rabid monomaniac, an unqualified nuisance, and an intolerable bore (4).

Fortunately for Anthony, his grandfather does not want much to do with him. Anthony goes abroad to study, and only occasionally pays a visit to his doddering benefactor—the closest thing to a father he has known since the age of eleven. During one conversation with Anthony, Cross Patch demonstrates his lack of cordiality and understanding. His mind appears to be as mired in its own narrow conception of life as his body is confined in his gloomy Tarrytown estate, surrounded by a "veritable maze of walls and wire fences" (13). When Anthony states that he feels himself most qualified to be a writer, the old man winces, "visualizing a family poet with long hair and three mistresses" (15). Anthony wants to write a history of the Middle Ages, however, not poetry. To this, his grandfather characteristically replies, "'Middle Ages? Why not your own country? Something you know about? ... Why you should write about the Middle Ages, I don't know. Dark Ages, we used to call 'em. Nobody knows what happened, and nobody cares, except that they're over now'" (15).

Thus, although Adam Patch might easily have been a solid moral influence on Anthony, he emerges as a burlesque of the values and wisdom associated with the traditional image of fatherhood. His laughable sententiousness, and overzealous chauvinism tend to encourage Anthony's *carpe diem* life style, not temper it. Quite understandably, Anthony chooses to disregard totally his grandfather's presence, and live a youth of moral orphancy.

The Beautiful and Damned is unique among Fitzgerald's completed novels in that it has a heroine as well as a hero. Gloria Gilbert is the girl who matches Anthony in charm, vanity, and hedonistic tendencies, and is therefore the logical girl for him to marry. Although Anthony is probably the book's central character, much of the third-person narration is centered in Gloria's point of view.

Gloria has parents who fade out of the picture shortly after we meet them, but it is quite apparent that they have been powerless to control her for a long while. Fitzgerald shows them just long enough to establish their negative qualities as parents and as human beings in general. The mother, Mrs. Gilbert, is like an old figurine, capable of little more than sitting about decorously. Her manner is extremely affected, as we see on her first meeting Anthony. "'How do you do?' She spoke in the conventional American lady-lady language. 'Well, I'm awfully glad to see you—.... This is really lovely—lovely'" (38).

Mr. Gilbert is bland and ineffectual in his own right. "His ideas were the popular delusions of twenty years before; his mind steered a wabbly and anaemic course in the wake of the daily newspaper editorials" (40).

Thus Gloria, like Anthony, has lived a youth unguided by stable, sensible parental values. Just as Anthony has responded to false morality by completely rejecting Adam Patch, so Gloria rejects the parents she has been unable to obey, and joins with one of her own kind. The marriage of Anthony and Gloria consecrates the understanding they have made with themselves, and which they now make together—the terms of which are later outlined by Gloria—"'to use every minute of these years, when I'm young, in having the best time I possibly can'" (304).

Youth is central to Fitzgerald's depiction of Anthony and Gloria. When we first see Gloria, she is twenty two—certainly young enough—yet she looks "so young, scarcely eighteen" (62). She seems the personification of youth. When one of Anthony's friends tells of his accidental meeting with her, he says, "'She seemed—well, somehow the youngest person there'" (48). Symbolically as well as literally, she is constantly devouring gum-drops, no matter what the company around her. Anthony, too, is a "young soul." His friend Dick Caramel, the successful writer, calls him "young Anthony" (50), and notes that he is "very romantic and young" (51).

But soon after these auspicious beginnings, life for the Patches turns into wearying confusion. Wild party succeeds wild party, followed by petty, but enervating arguments, and more wild parties. Each day becomes "a jelly-like creature, a shapeless, spineless thing" (53). Borne along by a vague anticipation of more dissipation, and the excitement of the knowledge that they will someday inherit Adam Patch's seventy-five millions, Anthony and Gloria seem grossly immature. They have no work whatsoever, manual or intellectual. Anthony makes several abortive attempts at writing his "book on the Middle Ages," but as he never gets a word of it on paper, it becomes a mocking, standing joke. Parenthood might have rescued the couple from their morass of self-destructive indifference, but although Gloria becomes pregnant, no child is born, and it must be assumed that she has had an abortion.

Each dispute between Anthony and Gloria takes "relentlessly its modicum of youth" (195). As they begin to run out of money and their youthful beauty fades, both begin to sense the waste of their lives. Anthony feels "first of all, the sense of waste, always dormant in his heart" (284). Gloria wonders "whether after all she had not wasted her faintly tired beauty" (391). At the novel's end, despite the inheritance of thirty million dollars from Adam Patch, both Anthony and Gloria are aged and broken. Anthony, having reached his breaking point, is "a little crazy" (448), and sits swaddled in blankets on a deck chair, and Gloria is now ironically "—sort of dyed and *unclean*" (448)—both seem the diametric opposite of what they were scarcely ten years before.

In reality, neither character is "old" (Anthony is only a year or two past thirty, and Gloria is three years younger), yet Fitzgerald has ironically divested them of their precious youth. They are now condemned to an "old-age-in-youth," somewhat reminiscent of the Ancient Mariner's cursed "life-in-death." Gone is "... the fruit of youth or of the grape, the transitory magic of the brief passage from darkness to darkness—the old illusion that truth and beauty were in some way entwined" (417).

In *The Great Gatsby*, written almost four years after *The Beautiful and Damned*, one finds another significant attempt by Fitzgerald to reconcile his faith in youth's promise with his inbred sense of conventional morality. In that novel he introduces a tangible parental morality in the image of the narrator's father. Nick Carraway is fit to pass judgment on "the whole damn bunch put together," and to escape Jay Gatsby's (the moral orphan's) fate, primarily due to the strength he has drawn from his father: "In my younger and more vulnerable years my father gave me some advice that I've been turning over in my mind ever since."

Yet this evidence will not allow us to conclude that Fitzgerald had come to terms with moral orphancy and parental morality, for although Nick's parental heritage allows him to avoid what "preyed" on Gatsby, the novel does not finally condemn Gatsby's life style: "No—Gatsby turned out all right at the end."

Thus, whether or not Fitzgerald had adequately reconciled his romantic beliefs with his staid instincts by 1925 is doubtful. As the responsibilities of parenthood and family life pressed ever more heavily upon him, however, and his own youth receded before him, the author's sympathies turned increasingly toward more traditional moral values. In his later short stories and *Tender is the Night*, he was to forsake unguided youth almost entirely.

But of *The Beautiful and Damned*, we can be certain that Fitzgerald displayed his first significant literary doubt as to the "magical glory" of youth he had previously celebrated. While one may find other reasons—factors and deficiencies in character which contributed to the Patches' fall, such as vanity, lust for money and pleasure, idleness and lethargy—it is clear that all these are the accoutrements of moral orphancy, the obstacles and temptations to be overcome by the morally stable. In *The Beautiful and Damned*, youth has its first serious moral test. Uninformed by parental values, it fails. But it was only by isolating youth from a mature, conventional morality that Fitzgerald could administer the test.

NOTES

1. Henry Dan Piper, in *F. Scott Fitzgerald: A Critical Portrait* (New York: Holt, Rinehart, and Winston, 1965, pp. 59–60) draws on Alexis de Tocqueville and Van Wyck Brooks to support his somewhat fuller discussion of youth's emancipation.

2. Piper, pp. 58–61, 72–6.

3. F. Scott Fitzgerald, *The Crack-Up*, ed. Edmund Wilson (New York: New Directions, 1945), p. 87.

4. *The Letters of F. Scott Fitzgerald*, ed. Andrew Turnbull (New York: Scribners, 1963), p. 145.

5. For examples, see Arthur Mizener, *The Far Side of Paradise* (Boston: Houghton Mifflin, 1951), p. 142; William Troy, "Scott Fitzgerald—The Authority of Failure," and Edmund Wilson, "Fitzgerald before *The Great Gatsby*," both in *F. Scott Fitzgerald: The Man and His Work*, ed. Alfred Kazin (New York: World, 1951); and Kenneth Eble, *F. Scott Fitzgerald* (New York: Twayne, 1963), pp. 71–4.

6. *Letters*, p. 145.

7. F. Scott Fitzgerald, *The Beautiful and Damned* (New York: Scribners, 1922), p. 6. Hereafter, page numbers are given in parentheses following the quote.

SCOTT DONALDSON

The Crisis of Fitzgerald's Crack-Up

I. THE REACTION

F. Scott Fitzgerald's three "Crack-Up" articles that ran in *Esquire* for February, March, and April 1936 precipitated an extraordinary response from the magazine's readers. "I get letters from all over," Fitzgerald wrote editor Arnold Gingrich on March 20. These letters came from old friends who wanted to cheer him up, from total strangers who recognized something of their own plight in Fitzgerald's account of emotional exhaustion, and most of all from other writers, among them James Boyd, John Dos Passos, Ernest Hemingway, Nancy Hoyt, John O'Hara, Marjorie Kinnan Rawlings, G. B. Stern, Julian Street, and Alexander Woollcott.[1] As O'Hara put it in an April letter, "I suppose you get comparatively little mail these days that does not dwell at greater or less length on your Esquire pieces, and I guess few of the writers resist, as I am resisting, the temptation to go into their own troubles for purposes of contrast." (O'Hara then revealed that he had recently been jilted by his girl and had picked up a dose of clap on the rebound.)[2]

The very nature of Fitzgerald's articles called for some response. Here a well-known writer was admitting in print that he had cracked like a plate and lost much of the vitality that made him successful. Furthermore, at the end of the second article, Fitzgerald openly appealed for reader reaction. His story might not be of general interest, yet if anyone wanted more, he

From *Twentieth Century Literature* Vol. 26 (Summer 1980), pp. 171–188. © 1980 Hofstra University.

announced, there was plenty left. But perhaps his readers had already had enough. If so, he hoped they'd let him know.[3]

The correspondence that found its way back to Fitzgerald varied enormously in tone. Much of it sympathetically proposed solutions to his dilemma. Some letter-writers suggested God, some Alcoholics Anonymous, some a rendezvous. Others recounted their own troubles, delivered pep talks, tried to jolly him up. More than a few thought he should never have begun the series of autobiographical pieces at all. (Five more articles followed the three about the "Crack-Up" in *Esquire*, but the later pieces were not so painfully defeatist as the earlier ones.) "People have received this Esquire article ("An Author's Mother") with mingled feeling," he wrote Beatrice Dance in September 1936, "—not a few of them think it was a terrific mistake to have written any of them from *Crack-Up*. On the other hand, I get innumerable 'fan letters' and requests to republish them in the *Reader's Digest*, and several anthologist's requests, which I prudently refused."[4] As he'd acknowledged at the beginning of "Pasting It Together" (the second "Crack-Up" article)[5], there were "always those to whom all self-revelation is contemptible, unless it ends with a noble thanks to the gods for the Unconquerable Soul."[6] There were also those who could not resist the opportunity to preach at Fitzgerald. "Please write me," he asked Max Perkins in February 1937, "you are about the only friend who does not see fit to incorporate a moral lesson, especially since the *Crack Up* stuff. Actually I hear from people in Sing Sing & Joliet all comforting & advising me."[7]

Certainly "The Crack-Up" essays conveyed a strong impression of personal depression. *The New Yorker's* "Talk of the Town" dismissed them with its usual snide superiority. "F. Scott Fitzgerald has been telling, in *Esquire*, how sad he feels in middle life," the item began, and went on to refer to his "picturesque despondency."[8] *The San Francisco Chronicle* observed in similar vein that the "gentleman in question is being a little too sorry for himself," but acknowledged that one could "hardly help being interested in what he has to say," the more so since he seemed to strike a common chord, and his essays went far "to explain the spiritual troubles of many another member of the almost-lost generation."[9]

Such friends as Margaret Turnbull and Marie Hamm agreed. "Your story is a mental snapshot of a rather universal experience," Mrs. Turnbull wrote after reading his first article. All of us end up "more or less defeated," but since so many shared this experience, Fitzgerald would discover "a chain of people, stretching around the world, to catch hold of [his] hands."[10] One hand that reached out was that of Scott's first girl in St. Paul, Marie Hersey Hamm. "Cheer up, darling, life begins at forty!" she wrote early in October, responding both to the *Esquire* articles and to the account, in *Time*, of his disastrous 40th birthday interview with Michel Mok for the *New York Post*. Mrs. Hamm granted that Fitzgerald had probably gone "on a more prolonged binge than the rest of us," and that therefore his "hang-over, awakening, or what have you" was that much more oppressive. But life, she insisted, was pretty swell, especially when you considered the alternative. Among their mutual friends, for instance, Joe Ordway was in a sanitarium and Theodore Schultze had died the week before. "When you're dead, you're dead, my pet, so why not enjoy it while you're here."[11] Bob and Raye Sylvester on *The New York News* extended their hands from out of the blue, first itemizing reasons why Fitzgerald couldn't quit now (he was too old to go into a tailspin, he was the only writer in the world who understood kids, he'd deprive Bob Sylvester of his saloon argument that Fitzgerald's novels would outlive Caesar's *Gallic Wars*). They concluded by praising *Tender Is the Night* and wishing that the man who wrote it would get well and happy and back to work soon.[12]

Mostly, Fitzgerald refused to be cheered up by such correspondence. It was nice of Marie Hamm to try. "However, child," he told her, "life is more complicated than that." To the Sylvesters he sent a more discouraged reply:

> The thing is this: that you go along thinking, this is the way things are, and that is all right; you go along at the same time saying that this is the way things should be, but you are not sure; and you keep your tongue in your cheek about how things will be, but the safest prophecy is the most dismal.
>
> Now, second: You go along thinking that you will get by no matter what; you think that the methods you have used are all right. Then you come up, because the first two don't fit together, and you never thought you had character, anyhow.[13]

Some people thought he had demonstrated his lack of character by publishing the pieces in the first place. To Sara Murphy, for example, Fitzgerald seemed so wrapped up in himself as to be unable to sympathize with others. Did Scott really, honestly think that "life was something you dominated if you were any good?" That kind of arrogance brought an incident to mind:

> I remember once your saying to me—in Montana at Harry's Bar, you & Dotty (Parker) were talking about your disappointments, & you turned to me and said: I don't suppose

you have ever known despair? I remember it so well as I was
furious, & thought my god the man thinks no one knows despair
who isn't a writer & can describe it. This is my feeling about your
articles.[14]

John Dos Passos also proposed that Fitzgerald stop regarding his own
navel. "Christ, man, how do you find time in the middle of the general
conflagration to worry about all that stuff? ... We're living in one of the
damnedest tragic moments in history—if you want to go to pieces I think
it's absolutely O.K. but I think you ought to write a first-rate novel about
it (and you probably will) instead of spilling it in little pieces for Arnold
Gingrich—."[15]

The important thing, to Dos Passos and other writer-friends, was that
Fitzgerald should continue to do his work. "Katy & I ... wish like hell you
could find some happy way of getting that magnificent working apparatus of
yours to work darkening paper; which is its business," as Dos put it in
another letter.[16] Even if he remained unhappy, Fitzgerald ought to turn that
sorrow to literary account. "I suppose you know that nothing is wasted,"
Marjorie Kinnan Rawlings asserted. "The hell you've been through isn't
wasted. All you have to do, ever, is to forget everything and turn that terrible,
clear white light you possess, on the minds and emotions of the people it stirs
you to write about."[17] Ernest Hemingway had offered much the same advice
after reading *Tender Is the Night* and detecting traces of self-pity in the
portrayal of Dick Diver. Forget your personal tragedy, he told Fitzgerald.
"But when you get the damned hurt use it—don't cheat with it." Neither of
them were tragic characters. They were only writers, and what they should
do was write.[18]

Hemingway did not mean, however, that Fitzgerald should bleed all
over the page. "The Crack-Up" articles struck him as a despicable whining
in public. His old friend Scott had become the "Maxie Baer" of writers, he
wrote Max Perkins, sunk to the canvas in the "shamelessness of defeat."[19] In
"The Snows of Kilimanjaro," which appeared in the August 1936 *Esquire*,
Hemingway dismissed Fitzgerald openly. "Poor Scott Fitzgerald" had been
"wrecked," Ernest wrote, by his worship of the rich. When Fitzgerald
objected, Hemingway explained that since Scott had written himself off in
"The Crack-Up" he figured it was open season on him.[20] It must have been
something of the same savage distaste for public confession that inspired
syndicated columnist Westbrook Pegler's ill-spirited obituary of Fitzgerald,
whose death recalled to Pegler "memories of a queer band of undisciplined
and self-indulgent brats who were determined not to pull their weight in the

boat and wanted the world to drop everything and sit down and bawl with them."[21]

Though he did not share the vehemence of Hemingway or Pegler, the gentlemanly Perkins was also embarrassed by "The Crack-Up" articles. Parading one's troubles in public simply wasn't done. The essays constituted the author's "indecent invasion of his own privacy."[22] As an editor, therefore, Perkins faced a problem when Fitzgerald proposed on March 25, 1936 that his autobiographical magazine writing might be stitched together into a good and saleable book. Perkins had earlier discouraged this idea, but since "the interest in this *Esquire* series has been so big," Fitzgerald pointed out, "I thought you might reconsider the subject...."[23] Perkins replied tactfully that he'd much prefer "a reminiscent book—not autobiographical but reminiscent.... I do not think the Esquire pieces ought to be published alone. But as for an autobiographical book which would comprehend what is in them, I would be very much for it." It would need integration, however, and should not be a mere collection of articles.[24] Three months later Gilbert Seldes echoed the point in a letter to Fitzgerald. Collections of scattered articles rarely made sense or money, Seldes observed, and then went on to make an argument for the book of reminiscence Perkins had favored:

> ... more important, Scott, is that you seem more and more to me an essential figure in America and sooner or later you will have to say your complete say, not only in fiction, but in the facts about yourself and the part you played at the beginning and what you think of it now.[25]

By the fall of 1936, Fitzgerald had abandoned any idea of collecting "The Crack-Up" articles. Both Perkins and agent Harold Ober had by then indicated that the articles were doing real damage to his reputation as a writer. "My Hollywood deal ...," he wrote Beatrice Dance in September, "was seriously compromised by their general tone. It seems to have implied to some people that I was a complete moral and artistic bankrupt."[26] The Mok interview might never have come about, he felt, if he hadn't composed "those indiscreet *Esquire* articles."[27] As a consequence he began disavowing them. They were not to be taken too seriously, he told Hamilton Basso.[28] Later he withheld the articles from Sheilah Graham for some time before showing her the tearsheets with the admonition, "I shouldn't have written these."[29]

When Edmund Wilson began assembling the volume of Fitzgerald's nonfiction and others' critical acclaim which emerged in 1945 as *The Crack-*

Up, he encountered some opposition from both Perkins and Ober. As early as February 1941 Wilson had suggested to Perkins that "The Crack-Up" should be brought out in book form. "I hated it when it came out, just as you did," Wilson remarked, "but I have found several intelligent people that think highly of it. There was more truth and sincerity in it, I suppose, than we realized at the time. He wanted it published in a book himself, and after all I dare say it is a part of the real Fitzgerald record."[30] These were excellent reasons for Scribner's to publish such a book, but Perkins remained adamant. Eventually Wilson took his project to New Directions, but not before he'd lobbied on its behalf with Fitzgerald's financial executor, John Biggs. He intended to call his book *The Crack-Up*, editor Wilson explained, not because he was enamored of the title, but because

> Glenway Wescott's appreciation is largely based on *The Crack-Up*, and ... if you read *The Crack-Up* through, you realize that it is not a discreditable confession but an account of a kind of crisis that many men of Scott's generation have gone through, and that in the end he sees a way to live by application to his work.

"I hope," Wilson added, "that you can counteract with your influence any influence that Ober and Max Perkins may have had on Scottie, and that you can allay her misgivings."[31]

II. THE CIRCUMSTANCES

How did Fitzgerald come to write his three "gloom articles," as he referred to them in his Ledger? He finished "The Crack-Up" itself in October 1935, "Pasting It Together" and "Handle with Care" in December. At that time he was suffering through an extremely low period in his life, during which he attempted to drive off with liquor and sex the awareness that Zelda would never be wholly well, the realization that his earning power had drastically diminished while the bills mounted ever higher, and the sense that he'd let his life and his talent waste away. In 1935–1936, he observed, "all my products were dirges & elegies."[32]

When Arnold Gingrich came calling in Baltimore one day in the spring of 1935, he found Fitzgerald in a "ratty old bathrobe" moaning about having to write a story of young love for the *Saturday Evening Post*. He couldn't do such stories with enthusiasm anymore, and the idea of producing one brought up his "cold gorge." "Well, why not write about that?" Gingrich suggested, then thought no more of the matter until, in the fall, the first of the three "Crack-Up" pieces arrived on his desk.[33]

Fitzgerald had spent the intervening summer in Asheville, North Carolina, carrying on a reckless affair with a married woman and drinking vast quantities of alcohol. Laura Guthrie (later Laura Hearne), who was his "secretary" (that is, his always-to-be-available companion, good listener, potential conquest, and occasional typist) that summer, began by admiring and feeling sorry for her employer and ended in near-disgust. In the exhaustive diary she kept of those days, Mrs. Guthrie set down her initial impression of Fitzgerald:

> He is completely alone because no persons are near to him, and he has no religion to comfort him. He makes me think of a lost soul, wandering in purgatory—sometimes hell. He tries so hard to drown it out with drinking and sex. Sometimes in the heights of these moments he forgets for a brief time—then it all comes back in overwhelming force. "Life is not happy," as he says. It isn't for him. He said it was a good thing he was not a rich man or he would have been dead before now (killing himself with indulgences!) but that the necessity of doing work had kept him going. Now he hopes that life will continue to be just endurable, which will only be if he keeps enough health to work.[34]

One can detect here the humble secretary parroting the thoughts of the great man, but by the end of the summer—after she had been exposed to every sort of indignity, including lying to cover up Fitzgerald's affair with Beatrice Dance and witnessing his daily attempt to achieve oblivion through drink—Mrs. Guthrie was only hoping to get rid of him. She finally managed to do so on Friday the 13th of September, when Scott, who had switched from beer and ale to gin a week earlier, broke down physically and allowed himself to be placed in the local hospital. When she arrived at his hotel room that morning, Mrs. Guthrie found empty glasses everywhere and Fitzgerald himself in terrible condition, with bloodshot eyes, drawn lips, skin raw from eczema, twitching leg muscles, and a distorted look about the face that made her realize he couldn't last much longer. "My nerves are going," he told her. "I'm about to break." He could not work at all. He wept, as he often had that summer. He pretended he was having a heart attack. Then, though it didn't seem fair that she should have to get him to the hospital, Mrs. Guthrie helped her invalid pack up his filthy clothes and get dressed so that he could march through the lobby and check out as if he were on his way to the train.

Upon depositing him at the hospital she "felt like a kid out of school," her responsibility over. "Nothing could ever happen to get me to put my head in this noose again," she noted in her diary. "At first I had thought that I could save him and help him to write steadily and really be his good angel, but I have decided that no one can be this...."[35]

The collapse in Asheville was Fitzgerald's fourth breakdown from liquor in the space of about two years, he told Mrs. Guthrie.[36] Within a month he had dried out enough to write "The Crack-Up," but another year and more would elapse before his long spell of despondency and drunkenness came to an end. By mid-1937, he was able to confide most of the truth to his notebooks:

> What got me in the two years mess that reached its lowest point in the fall of 1936 [when he was again in Asheville under constant care by nurses, and attempted suicide twice] was the usual combination of circumstances. A prejudiced enemy might say it was all drink, a fond Mama might say it was a run of ill-luck, a banker might say it was not providing for the future in better days, a psychologist might say it was a nervous collapse—it was perhaps partly all these things—the effect was to prevent me from doing my work at the very age when presumably one is at the height of one's powers. My life looked like a hopeless mess there for a while and the point was I didn't *want* it to be better. I had completely ceased to give a good god-damn.[37]

III. THE ART

When *The Crack-Up* emerged as a book in 1945, several critics celebrated its honesty. Lionel Trilling hailed Fitzgerald's "heroic self-awareness."[38] Glenway Wescott praised his candor.[39] Andrews Wanning detected "a desperate effort at self-disclosure."[40] In some ways, the essays *were* unusually candid. "The Crack-Up" accurately reflected Fitzgerald's tendency toward sadness, for example. "Please don't be depressed," Zelda had written him in 1931, "Nothing is sad about you except your sadness and the frayed places in your pink kimono and that you care so much about everything ... O my love, I love you so—and I want you to be happy."[41] But her husband was temperamentally unsuited to happiness. Hemingway's "instinct [was] toward megalomania," he later commented, "and mine toward melancholy."[42]

Yet Fitzgerald was far from totally forthcoming in the articles for *Esquire*. One feels on reading them, as Alfred Kazin saw, "that something is being persistently withheld, that the author is somehow offering us certain facts in exchange for the right to keep others to himself."[43] In fact "The Crack-Up" is surprisingly short of that kind of concrete evidence which lends conviction to the greatest confessional writing.[44] The thing most conspicuously left out was, naturally, Fitzgerald's alcoholism—"naturally" because as both Wescott and Malcolm Cowley have observed, denying that one has a drinking problem constitutes one of the symptoms of the disease.[45] Still, it was disingenuous of Fitzgerald to dismiss the issue in the first of his "Crack-Up" articles. There he referred to William Seabrook's book about alcoholism which "tells, with some pride and a movie ending, of how he became a public charge." Seabrook's nervous system had collapsed, and so, admitted Fitzgerald, had his own, but not because of drink: "the present writer was not so entangled," he lied, "—having at the time not tasted so much as a glass of beer for six months."[46]

Such denials did not convince everyone. John V. A. Weaver, another writer associated with the Jazz Age, found the first two *Esquire* articles disturbing, since they described so exactly what had happened to him. And what was that? "I can't drink a *drop*," he wrote Fitzgerald. "I can only sit impotent, day by day, and see a strange world careen by—a world in which I have no place."[47] Weaver mailed his letter in February 1936, while George Martin (who did not know Fitzgerald) waited until after the publication of "An Alcoholic Case" in February 1937 to offer his assurance that he'd been in the same boat. "From the stuff you write in *Esquire* you seem to be having one hell of a time," Martin began. "If it's true … please know that I've lived all through it—will to die, dts, friends gone, money gone, job gone, self respect gone, guts gone … everything." He then suggested that Fitzgerald get hold of Peabody's *Common Sense of Drinking*.[48]

This letter obviously struck a nerve, for Fitzgerald answered by proposing external reasons for his malady. Martin gently chided him in reply: "Certainly, as you say, the cause precedes the curse; but it is also true that the old ego breeds rationalizations like guinea pigs."[49] Indeed, much of "The Crack-Up" reads like a rationalization of Fitzgerald's breakdown, and the three articles represent more an apologia than a confession. The blame for his crack-up, Fitzgerald implies, lies not within himself but elsewhere: the deficient genes he was bequeathed, the contemporary climate of materialism and insincerity, even the growth of motion pictures which threatened to put fiction writers out of business.

By the middle of 1937, when he was drafting his autobiographical essay on "Early Success," Scott had matured enough to recognize this self-deception. There, in a passage he later cut out of the essay, Fitzgerald compared himself unfavorably with his own father, a man who had failed without seeking scapegoats. This passage was intended to accompany the discussion of the relative importance of will and fate in determining success which appears in the published essay as "The man who arrives young believes that he exercises his will because his star is shining. The man who only asserts himself at thirty has a balanced idea of what will power and fate have each contributed...."[50] Then, in part of the typescript he later deleted, came the following, with Fitzgerald's lined-through corrections indicated in italics:

> *It is* This [difference] comes out when the various storms *of professional life* strike your craft *that this comes out. My own father was a failure, once, in his own business, and once as a "high-salaried man"*—What success my father *success he had* had come fairly late in life and was brief in duration and never did I hear him blame his failure on anything but his own incompetence. *He* Yet he might have since he was caught once in *the* panic of 93 and once in the first rush to weed *passion for weeding out* older men out of business. *When* On the contrary when I went through several years of private misfortune and impeded production, I felt no loss of *confidence and* morale until one day a comparatively small blow matter gave me that idea my star had miraculously gone out. *and I mean gone out, not gone into eclipse.* For two years I sulked in bitter discouragement *and indifference before I could struggle out. I was so sure of it* so sure about it that I told everyone about it and even wrote about it with as little reticence as if I'd lost a leg in a railroad accident.[51]

It is easy enough from half a century's perspective to gloss Fitzgerald's reference to "several years of private misfortune"—these were the years of Zelda's final relapse into schizophrenia and his own immersion in drink. But what was the "comparatively small blow" that toppled him into the slough of despond? The dramatic logic of "The Crack-Up" demanded that some immediate cause be located, and so in the first of his essays he indicated that it was a piece of unexpected good news from his doctor—a reprieve from an earlier death sentence—that led him to crack like an old plate. Such an event may have happened, but no biographer has documented it. Probably, Fitzgerald was exaggerating his own situation in order to contrast the dread loss of vitality (a bankruptcy that resulted, he wrote, from mortgaging himself "physically and spiritually up to the hilt") with the comparatively unimportant "small gift of life given back...." In the remaining "Crack-Up" essays, significantly, he dropped all reference to this medical reprieve. In "Pasting It Together," he cited three specific blows that led up to his breakdown: dropping out of Princeton because of ill health (he does not mention his academic difficulties), temporarily losing Zelda because of lack of money, and suffering an unspecified, more violent third blow that "cut off the sun last spring."[52]

Obviously and quite understandably, Fitzgerald was telling less than the whole truth about himself and his family. A similar reticence led him to eliminate almost all names from his articles, though he does acknowledge Edmund Wilson as his "intellectual conscience." In "The Crack-Up" Fitzgerald was working in a genre new to him. "Although presented as autobiography," Kenneth Eble has commented, the articles "have the air of highly wrought and intensely felt fiction." But that is not the case exactly, for how often in Fitzgerald's short stories would one find references to the Bible, to William Ernest Henley, to Wordsworth and Keats, to Lenin and Dickens and Tolstoy, to Spinoza, to Descartes, to the Euganean Hills? And how often would Fitzgerald as a writer of fiction allow metaphor to substitute for concrete action, as it does so often in "The Crack-Up" essays? Instead of providing specific detail, Fitzgerald compares himself to a cracked plate, a beggar carrying the "tin cup of self-pity," a bankrupt who had overdrawn his account, a lecturer about to lose his audience, an empty shell, a conjurer fresh out of tricks, a Negro lady cutting out a rival, a Negro retainer pretending to jollity, and a dog who will remain subservient if thrown a bone from time to time.[53] Saying what one is *like* provides an alternative to saying outright what one actually is. Like the wealth of learned references, it was a form of evasion.

The tone of the articles varied from the tough wise-guyism of "All rather inhuman and undernourished, isn't it? Well, that, children, is the true sign of cracking up" in the first essay to the ornate confusion of "The dullest platitude monger or the most unscrupulous Rasputin who can influence the destinies of many people must have some individuality so the question became one of finding why and where I had changed, where was the leak through which, unknown to myself, my enthusiasm and my vitality had been steadily and prematurely trickling away" in the third. Fitzgerald was searching for a form, but he had not quite found it. Re-reading "The Crack-Up" today, one is inclined to share the ambivalent reaction of the woman who wrote Fitzgerald that she found it hard to believe his articles really touched the depths of tragedy, yet they were "so convincing as to leave little room for doubt that the author had at some time *lived* those bitternesses and depressions."[54] The source of this ambivalence, according to William

Barrett, lay in the excessive artfulness of the essays. "The Crack-Up," he wrote,

> is a frightening thing to read: rapid, brilliant, but also jerky and almost metallically tense in tone, as if still vibrating with the receding hysteria of the breakdown. No doubt Fitzgerald, writing for *Esquire* magazine, felt he had to jazz up his material, but, even with allowance made for this, these pieces leave the impression that the author is still seeing life much too much in literary and dramatic terms. A man writing of his own human defeat and failure ought to have passed beyond "literature" altogether, even to the point of risking a matter-of-factness that might appear prosy and plodding....[55]

It is a dangerous business, this prescribing the correct technique for authors, but a more matter-of-fact approach would, it seems to me also, have given Fitzgerald's essays that authority and verisimilitude they now lack. In fact, apology masquerading as confession may well represent, in Alfred Kazin's words, "the best possible device for not revealing" the truth.[56]

As it stands, "The Crack-Up" tells its truths only between the lines. It is not about nervous exhaustion, emotional bankruptcy, or even an alcoholic breakdown. The subject of "The Crack-Up" is Fitzgerald's misanthropy, and the self-hatred behind it. All these essays, but especially the first and last, deal with the author's attempted escape from people—more particularly his escape from that large group of people to whom he has felt obliged to give something of himself. He has given too much in the past. He will, he says, give no more.

When the writing touches on this subject, it achieves a vividness missing elsewhere. Upon hearing the "grave sentence" of his doctor, Fitzgerald writes in the first article, he "wanted to be absolutely alone" and so cut himself off "from ordinary cares." Instead he sat around making lists. "It was not," he reveals, "an unhappy time." Then came the crack-up and with it the realization that "for a long time I had not liked people and things, but only followed the rickety old pretense of liking." In his casual relations—"with an editor, a tobacco seller, the child of a friend"—he had merely done what was expected. Even with love, he had been going through the motions. He had, in short, been guilty of emotional insincerity for some time, yet he does not publicly blame himself. Instead, he transfers his self-disgust into distaste for most other human beings.

He still admires the looks of Middle Western Scandinavian blondes. He likes "doctors and girl children up to the age of about thirteen and well-brought-up boy children from about eight years old on." He likes old men and Katherine Hepburn's face on the screen, and Miriam Hopkins' face, and old friends if he only has to see them once a year. But there is a larger category of people he has come to detest:

> I couldn't stand the sight of Celts, English, Politicians, Strangers, Virginians, Negroes (light or dark), Hunting People, all retail clerks, and middlemen in general, all writers (I avoided writers very carefully because they can perpetuate trouble as no one else can)—and all the classes as classes and most of them as members of their class....[57]

Under the pressure of his crack-up Fitzgerald withdrew from contact with the real world into a period of "vacuous quiet" during which he was forced to think for himself. He then discovered, according to the second article, that he had never done this before. All his ideas had been borrowed from Edmund Wilson and from four other unnamed men, one of whom, his "artistic conscience," was surely Ernest Hemingway. Not only had he given too freely of himself to people he didn't care about, but he had submerged his mental development by passively adopting the ideas of others. There was no "I" any more, Fitzgerald concluded, no basis on which he could organize his self-respect.[58]

The third article, "Handle with Care," picks up this theme. Unlike Descartes, Fitzgerald's motto had been, "I felt—therefore I was." He had, in fact, felt too much, and so he decides that if he wishes to survive he must cease "any attempts to be a person—to be kind, just or generous." Instead, he rather cynically resolves to develop a false smile to win the favor of those who might be of use to him, and otherwise to cultivate the habit of saying no in a voice that will make "people feel that far from being welcome they are not even tolerated...."[59]

In the last paragraph of this last "Crack-Up" article, Fitzgerald located the source of his malady in two telling comparisons. For too long he had concentrated on pleasing others, and in the process neglected his own development:

> ... And just as the laughing stoicism which has enabled the American negro to endure the intolerable conditions of his existence has cost him his sense of the truth—so in my case there is a price to pay.

Now that he has determined to change, life will no longer be as pleasant as it once was. He is a different sort of dog now, one who no longer likes "the postman, nor the grocer, nor the editor, nor the cousin's husband ... and the sign *Cave Canem* is hung permanently just above my door." He will only lick your hand now, Fitzgerald says, if you throw him a bone.[60] This cynicism, like much cynicism, is directed against the self. In repudiating a past in which he has too often played the fawning servant or the lovable lap dog, Fitzgerald was implicitly condemning himself and preparing the way for a fresh start.

Despite these protestations, Fitzgerald never became really antisocial. But he did reorder his priorities so that doing his work and fulfilling his obligations came ahead of his drive to charm other people. During the Hollywood years he seems finally to have achieved a sense of self-respect, a term which Joan Didion has defined in a passage that uncannily echoes the theme of "The Crack-Up":

> To have that sense of one's intrinsic worth which constitutes self-respect is potentially to have everything: the ability to discriminate, to love and to remain indifferent. To lack it is to be locked within oneself, paradoxically incapable of either love or indifference. If we do not respect ourselves, we are on the one hand forced to despise those who have so few resources as to consort with us, so little perception as to remain blind to our fatal weaknesses. On the other, we are peculiarly in thrall to everyone we see, curiously determined to live out—since our self-image is untenable—their false notions of us. We flatter ourselves by thinking this compulsion to please others an attractive trait: a gist (gift?) for imaginative empathy, evidence of our willingness to give. Of course I will play Francesca to your Paolo, Helen Keller to anyone's Annie Sullivan: no expectation is too misplaced, no role too ludicrous. At the mercy of those we cannot but hold in contempt, we play roles doomed to failure before they are begun, each defeat generating fresh despair at the urgency of divining and meeting the next demand made upon us.
>
> It is the phenomenon sometimes called "alienation from self." In its advanced stages, we no longer answer the telephone, because someone might want something; that we could say no without drowning in self-reproach is an idea alien to this game. Every encounter demands too much, tears the nerves, drains the will....[61]

This "alienation from self" lies behind Fitzgerald's breakdown, and behind his announced misanthropy. The very process of putting words down on paper helped free him from that alienation. The insightful Perkins, who maintained that no one "would write those articles if they were really true," came to the conclusion "that in some deep way, when he wrote those articles, Scott must have been thinking that things would be different with him." Other readers agreed that the articles must surely have a purgative effect. He'd be willing to bet, Burton Rascoe observed after seeing the first two essays, that Fitzgerald was "already feeling immensely better ... self-confident and creative again." "You've been finding out a lot of things that have hurt like hell," Julian Street told Fitzgerald, "and at the end of it you'll be grown up ... a bigger and better man and a bigger and better writer for it." In replying to Street on February 24, 1936, Fitzgerald acknowledged that since the intensity of despair had moderated somewhat, he could see that writing the articles "was a form of catharsis but at the time of writing them what I said seemed absolutely real." He could also see, he added defensively, that "an unfriendly critic might damn the series as the whining of a spoilt baby," but wasn't that true of most poetry?[62]

It is true of Fitzgerald not only that his characters are modeled on himself but that he sometimes becomes his characters after the fact. Thus his retreat to Asheville, Tryon, Hendersonville in North Carolina during the two years of his personal depression virtually repeated Dick Diver's drifting among the small towns of upstate New York. Like Diver too, Fitzgerald had to abandon his goal of becoming an "an entire man ... with an opulent American touch, a sort of combination of J. P. Morgan, Topham Beauclerk and St. Francis of Assisi."[63] He will now be "a writer only," he announces in the last of the "Crack-Up" articles, just as Dick Diver finally became only a doctor, no longer a scientist or entertainer or *bon vivant*. The difference is that Diver faded away, while Fitzgerald emerged from his fallen estate to live a useful and productive four years.

Fitzgerald referred to the "Crack-Up" articles in his ledger as "biography," not "autobiography." This apparent slip of the pen, as Robert Sklar has observed, revealed the "essential truth" that the Scott Fitzgerald described in the essays was not the same as the man who wrote about him.[64] "I don't know whether those articles of mine in *Esquire*—the 'Crack-Up' series—represented a real nervous breakdown," Fitzgerald remarked in July 1939. "In retrospect it seems more of a spiritual 'change of life'—and a most unwilling one...."[65] "Transformation" might be an even better term than "change of life," for in "The Crack-Up" Fitzgerald sloughed off the skin of the old Irish charmer and determined to let work instead of play dominate the time left to him. The articles hardly achieve what Trilling called a "heroic awareness."[66] It took courage to say as much as he did, but Fitzgerald left too much only hinted at and blamed too many external forces for his predicament to be adjudged a hero of self-revelation. Despite the false leads and evasions, however, Fitzgerald did uncover more of himself between the lines of these articles, and particularly of the last article, than anywhere else in his works. And, though the benefits did not surface immediately, the process did him good. "The Crack-Up" does not measure up to the best confessional writing, but it had something of the same therapeutic effect on the man who set it down on paper.

NOTES

1. F. Scott Fitzgerald to Arnold Gingrich, 20 March 1936, *The Letters of F. Scott Fitzgerald*, ed. Andrew Turnbull (New York: Scribner's, 1963), pp. 533–34.

2. John O'Hara to F. Scott Fitzgerald, April 1936, *Selected Letters of John O'Hara*, ed. Matthew J. Bruccoli (New York: Random House, 1978), p. 115.

3. F. Scott Fitzgerald, *The Crack-Up*, ed. Edmund Wilson (New York: New Directions, 1945), p. 79.

4. F. Scott Fitzgerald to Beatrice Dance, 15 September 1936, *Letters*, pp. 541–42. The only request for reprint I know of came from Kathryn Coe Cordell and William H. Cordell, who wanted to include "The Crack-Up" in their 1936 edition of the annual *American Points of View*: Cordells to F. Scott Fitzgerald, 8 September 1936, Fitzgerald Papers, Princeton University Library.

5. The titles of the second and third articles were transposed during the movement from *Esquire* to *The Crack-Up*. The original, and—one presumes—the correct order is this: the second article should be entitled "Pasting It Together" and the third "Handle with Care."

6. Fitzgerald, *Crack-Up*, p. 75.

7. F. Scott Fitzgerald to Maxwell Perkins, late February 1937, *Dear Scott/Dear Max: The Fitzgerald–Perkins Correspondence*, ed. John Kuehl and Jackson Bryer (New York: Scribner's, 1971), p. 235.

8. "Notes and Comment (The Talk of the Town)," *The New Yorker*, 12 (14 March 1936), 11.

9. "Between the Lines," *San Francisco Chronicle* (20 March 1936).

10. Mrs. Bayard Turnbull to F. Scott Fitzgerald, 12 February 1936, Fitzgerald Papers, Princeton University Library.

11. Mrs. William Hamm to F. Scott Fitzgerald, 5 October 1936, Fitzgerald Papers, Princeton University Library.

12. Bob and Raye Sylvester to F. Scott Fitzgerald, 26 September 1936, Fitzgerald Papers, Princeton University Library.

13. F. Scott Fitzgerald to Mrs. William Hamm, 28 October 1936, *Letters*, p. 545; F. Scott Fitzgerald to Bob and Raye Sylvester, 12 November 1936, Fitzgerald Papers, Princeton University Library.

14. Sara Murphy to F. Scott Fitzgerald, 3 April 1936, in "'As a Friend You Have Never Failed Me': The Fitzgerald–Murphy Correspondence," *Journal of Modern Literature*, 5

(September 1976), 375–76. Fitzgerald had asked for her comment, and for Gerald's, on his *Esquire* essays in a letter postmarked 30 March 1936, *Letters*, pp. 431–32.

15. John Dos Passos to F. Scott Fitzgerald, October (?) 1936, *Crack-Up*, p. 311.

16. John Dos Passos to F. Scott Fitzgerald, n.d., Fitzgerald Papers, Princeton University Library.

17. Marjorie Kinnan Rawlings to F. Scott Fitzgerald, n.d., Fitzgerald Papers, Princeton University Library.

18. Ernest Hemingway to F. Scott Fitzgerald, quoted in Arthur Mizener, *The Far Side of Paradise* (New York: Vintage, 1959), pp. 259–60.

19. Ernest Hemingway to Maxwell Perkins, quoted in A. Scott Berg, *Max Perkins: Editor of Genius* (New York: Thomas Gongdon Books/Dutton, 1978), p. 302.

20. Hemingway's remark is repeated in F. Scott Fitzgerald to Beatrice Dance, 15 September 1936, *Letters*, p. 542.

21. Westbrook Pegler, "Fair Enough," *New York World-Telegram* (26 December 1940), p. 17, partly quoted in Jackson R. Bryer, *The Critical Reputation of F. Scott Fitzgerald: A Bibliographical Study* (Hamden, Conn.: Archon Books, 1967), p. 206.

22. John Chamberlain, "The New Books," *Harper's*, 191 (September 1945), unpaged; Matthew J. Bruccoli, "The Perkins–Wilson Correspondence," *Fitzgerald/Hemingway Annual 1978*, ed. Matthew J. Bruccoli and Richard Layman (Detroit: Gale Research, 1979), p. 65.

23. *Dear Scott/Dear Max*, p. 227.

24. *Ibid.*, p. 228.

25. Gilbert Seldes to F. Scott Fitzgerald, 26 June 1936, Fitzgerald Papers, Princeton University Library.

26. Matthew J. Bruccoli, *Scott and Ernest* (New York: Random House, 1978), pp. 129–30; F. Scott Fitzgerald to Beatrice Dance, 15 September 1936, *Letters*, p. 542.

27. F. Scott Fitzgerald to Corey Ford, April 1937, *Letters*, p. 549.

28. Hamilton Basso to Edmund Wilson, 14 October 1944, Fitzgerald Papers, Princeton University Library.

29. Sheilah Graham and Gerold Frank, *Beloved Infidel: The Education of a Woman* (New York: Henry Holt, 1958), p. 237.

30. Edmund Wilson to Maxwell Perkins, 16 February 1941, in Edmund Wilson, *Letters on Literature and Politics 1912–1972*, ed. Elena Wilson (New York: Farrar, Straus and Giroux, 1977), pp. 337–38.

31. Edmund Wilson to John Biggs, 3 June 1943, Wilson *Letters*, p. 348.

32. F. Scott Fitzgerald to Zelda Fitzgerald, August 1939, *Letters*, p. 107.

33. Arnold Gingrich, "Publisher's Page—Will the Real Scott Fitzgerald Please Stand Up and Be Counted?" *Esquire*, 62 (December 1964), 12, 16.

34. Laura Guthrie, Memoir, Summer of 1935, p. 73, Fitzgerald Papers, Princeton University Library.

35. *Ibid.*, pp. 138–43.

36. *Ibid.*, p. 148.

37. Note, Fitzgerald Papers, Princeton University Library.

38. Lionel Trilling, "F. Scott Fitzgerald," *The Nation*, 166 (25 August 1945), 182.

39. Glenway Wescott, "The Moral of F. Scott Fitzgerald," in *Crack-Up*, pp. 323–37.

40. Andrews Warning, "Fitzgerald and His Brethren," *Partisan Review*, 12 (Fall 1945), 545.

41. Zelda Fitzgerald to F. Scott Fitzgerald, n.d., Fitzgerald Papers, Princeton University Library.

42. F. Scott Fitzgerald to Beatrice Dance, 15 September 1936, *Letters*, p. 543.

43. Alfred Kazin, "Fitzgerald: An American Confession," *Quarterly Review of Literature*, 2 (1945), 342.

44. Milton Hindus, in his chapter on *The Crack-Up* in *F. Scott Fitzgerald: An Introduction and Interpretation* (New York: Holt, Rinehart and Winston, 1968), elaborates on the shortage of specific detail: pp. 90–91.

45. Malcolm Cowley, introduction to *The Stories of F. Scott Fitzgerald* (New York: Scribner's, 1951), p. xxi; Wescott, pp. 327–28.

46. *Crack-Up*, p. 71.

47. V. A. Weaver to F. Scott Fitzgerald, 17 February 1936, Fitzgerald Papers, Princeton University Library.

48. George Martin to F. Scott Fitzgerald, 20 January 1937, Fitzgerald Papers, Princeton University Library.

49. George Martin to F. Scott Fitzgerald, February (?) 1937, Fitzgerald Papers, Princeton University Library.

50. *Crack-Up*, p. 89.

51. Typescript of "Early Success" with corrections, Fitzgerald Papers, Princeton University Library.

52. *Crack-Up*, pp. 71–72, 76–77.

53. Kenneth Eble, *F. Scott Fitzgerald* (Boston: Twayne, 1977), rev. ed., p. 141.

54. *Crack-Up*, pp. 73, 80; Mrs. E. H. Tyson to F. Scott Fitzgerald, n.d., Fitzgerald Papers, Princeton University Library.

55. William Barrett, "Fitzgerald and America," *Partisan Review*, 18 (May–June 1951), 349–50.

56. Kazin, p. 341.

57. *Crack-Up*, pp. 72–73.

58. *Ibid.*, pp. 78–79.

59. *Ibid.*, pp. 82–83.

60. *Ibid.*, p. 84.

61. Joan Didion, *Slouching Towards Bethlehem* (New York: Simon and Schuster, 1979 [1961]), pp. 147–48.

62. Quoted in Berg, p. 282; Burton Rascoe to F. Scott Fitzgerald, 10 February 1936, and Julian Street to F. Scott Fitzgerald, 12 February 1936, Fitzgerald Papers, Princeton University Library; F. Scott Fitzgerald to Julian Street, 24 February 1936, *Letters*, pp. 532–33.

63. *Crack-Up*, p. 84.

64. Robert Sklar, *F. Scott Fitzgerald: The Last Laocoön* (New York: Oxford University Press, 1967), p. 309.

65. F. Scott Fitzgerald to Mrs. Laura Feley, 20 July 1939, *Letters*, p. 589.

66. Trilling, p. 182.

JUDITH FETTERLEY

Who Killed Dick Diver?:
The Sexual Politics of Tender is the Night

I will probably be carried off eventually by four strong guards shrieking
manicly [*sic*] that after all I was right and she was wrong, while Zelda is
followed home by an adoring crowd in an automobile banked with
flowers, and offered a vaudeville contract.

(—F. Scott Fitzgerald, in *Zelda*)

At the heart of *Tender is the Night* is the anxiety-ridden perception that
culture, not biology, is destiny, that nothing protects a man from
experiencing the fate of woman in our society except his culturally
determined power to impose that fate on her. Profoundly autobiographical,
the novel has its source in the agonized complexity of the relationship
between Scott and Zelda. In what finally became a mutually antagonistic
struggle for survival, Scott based his claim to be the one "saved" on his role
as the professional writer and on the psychological and economic
consequences of that role. As the serious writer, whose seriousness is proved
by his being, as he once declared, "the highest paid short story writer in the
world"; as the wage-earner and caretaker, whose ability to perform those
functions is enabled by the "enormous prices" which he is paid; as the one
"integrated in spite of everything," whose integration is attested to by the
existence of stories which receive "enormous prices," Scott held the winning

From *Mosaic*, a journal for the interdisciplinary study of literature, Vol 17, Issue 1 (Winter 1984),
pp. 111–128. © 1984 Mosaic.

hand.[1] He did not see Zelda as different in kind from himself; in his fantasies she easily figures as the one "adored" and contracted, as the one saved. But holding the winning hand, filled with the trump cards of institutionalized sexism, made all the difference.[2] And quite a difference it was, as both Scott and Zelda knew.

Though at least one doctor involved in the "case" of Zelda Fitzgerald perceived Scott as equally sick and in need of treatment, and though he himself fantasized being mad, Scott had no intention of giving up in reality his claim to the role of "sane." Obvious, and crucial, advantages accompany the role of sane, as can be demonstrated by a brief comparison of the compositional facts of *Tender is the Night* and those of *Save Me the Waltz*. As recorded in Nancy Milford's biography of Zelda.

> On March 14 Scott wrote Dr. Squires in a fury. He had just received Zelda's manuscript. For four years, he wrote, he had been forced to work intermittently on his novel, "unable to proceed *because* of the necessity of keeping Zelda in sanitariums." Zelda had heard fifty thousand words of his novel and "literally one whole section of her novel is an imitation of it, of its rhythm, materials ... there are only two episodes, both of which she has reduced to anecdotes *but upon which whole sections of my book turn*, that I have asked her to cut. Her own material—her youth, her love for Josanne, her dancing, her observation of Americans in Paris, the fine passages about the death of her father—my criticisms of that *will* be simply impersonal and professional."
>
> ....
>
> The psychiatrists at Phipps were surprised by the vehemence of his reaction and could only apologize for having allowed Zelda to mail the novel to Scribner's without first gaining Fitzgerald's release. They wired him to say that she had switched addresses at the last moment without their knowledge. They promised it would not happen again, but clearly no one had anticipated his fury. (pp. 216–17)

Two primary assumptions emerge here. The first, contained in the reaction of the Phipps's psychiatrists, is that as husband, professional writer and "sane," Scott had the right to play the role of editor and authorizer in relation to Zelda's work. As wife, amateur and "crazy," Zelda not only had no right to an equivalent relation to Scott's work, she had no right to an equivalent relation to her own work; nothing of hers was to be released directly for publication; nothing of hers was to be published without Scott's having first edited and authorized it. That Scott himself assumed his right to this role, and its advantages, is equally clear.

His interference in the production of *Save Me the Waltz* was multiple. Not only did he edit it; he also tried to control the contractual context. Writing to Perkins, he asked him "to keep whatever praise he wished to give Zelda '*on the staid side*,' for Scott said it was important to the Doctors at Phipps that Zelda not be made to feel too jubilant about the fame and money that might come to her through publication.... His advice was given, he said, in order to protect Zelda's mental stability for fear of her 'incipient egomania ...'" (Milford, p. 225). In addition, the contract for *Save Me the Waltz* contained a clause that "stipulated that one-half the royalties earned would be retained by Scribner's to be credited against 'the indebtedness of F. Scott Fitzgerald', until a total of $5,000 had been repaid" (p. 226). With such a contract, it is quite unlikely that Zelda would ever earn those "enormous prices" which enable "sanity" and determine who is "saved."

Scott's fury reveals the second assumption—namely, that Zelda's madness is his material. Apparently for Scott, the role of being "sane" carried with it the right to appropriate for one's own purposes the experience of those who are "mad." The force of Scott's fury accurately measures the degree to which he had already imperialized Zelda's life. As Matthew J. Bruccoli has, demonstrated, *Tender is the Night* was a difficult book for Fitzgerald to write. It took him nine years and twelve drafts to complete. Significantly, the enabling event of the book was Zelda Fitzgerald's madness:

> The period of Mrs. Fitzgerald's treatment at Montreux, during which Fitzgerald did no writing on *Tender is the Night*, was probably the time when he conceived the Dick Diver version of the novel. Whether or not Fitzgerald's inability to complete the matricide story can be charged to the incompatibility of author and subject, it is certain that after April 1930 he had new material which he felt deeply. There was nothing bogus about Fitzgerald's anxieties for his wife; and when transferred to Dick Diver, they gave the new version an integrity which was missing in the matricide version.[3]

Thus at the very moment when Scott is consumed by fury at what he defines as Zelda's plagiarism, he is writing a book which will literally incorporate large sections of her letters to him; at the very moment when he is raging at

Zelda's use of anecdotes from their life together "upon which whole sections of my book turn," he is writing a book which literally turns upon the primary pattern of Zelda's life. The advantages of being "sane," of being defined as the professional writer and thus free to see things "impersonally," could hardly be made more clear.

Perhaps no moment in all of Milford's biography is so poignant as that which describes Zelda's reading of Scott's finally competed text: "'I have now got to the Rosemary–Rome episode. It makes me very sad—largely because of the beautiful, beautiful writing.... You know I love your prose style: it is so fine and balanced and you know how to achieve the emphasis you want so poignantly and economicly [*sic*]. It's a fine book ...'" (pp. 293–94). Zelda's praise presents a striking contrast to Scott's fury and provides the ultimate testament to his victory. For, however the struggle be formulated, Scott had won. And prime among the spoils of victory, prime among the reasons for wanting to win, was the advantage of being the one who gets to tell the story.

The story Fitzgerald told differs significantly from what actually happened. Indeed, it inverts the social and political reality which made its existence possible and by so doing serves to perpetuate the very reality it denies. Put simply *Tender is the Night* proposes that American men are driven "mad" by the feminization of American culture which forces them to live out the lives of women and which purchases the sanity of women at men's expense.[4] Playing out the proposition that nothing can save men from being "women" should women gain the cultural power so to define them, the novel could be described as an elaboration of the fantasy of Zelda the adored and Scott the manacled maniac.

To the degree that such a possibility is theoretically imaginable, the book is true; to the degree that such a fantasy stems logically from an opposite reality and is the predictable nightmare of those with power, the book is also true. Yet Fitzgerald asserts his content as neither theory nor fantasy but as historical fact and in this context *Tender is the Night* is radically dishonest. Clearly, the struggle between Scott and Zelda was fixed in his favor. Scott's ability to enforce the life of a woman on Zelda and to reserve to himself the role of "man" derived directly from his access to the various structures of power which a thoroughly masculinized America makes available to men, enabling them to remain "sane" while the women go mad. To write a book which asserts the opposite is self-serving at best. Yet there is perhaps a kind of honesty even in this inversion. The original impulse of *Tender is the Night* was matricidal; it began as a story about a boy who killed his mother. Though the matricidal plot has disappeared in the final version, the matricidal intent remains.[5] The enemy in the text is the American woman and the text does a job on her. To read *Tender is the Night* is to participate in the evocation of sympathy for Dick Diver, the victim of his culture, and to engage in the concomitant hostility toward that which has destroyed him. To the extent that our sympathies as readers affect other aspects of our lives, *Tender is the Night* intends toward the perpetuation of male power. Thus is Fitzgerald true: aware that what counts is power, he has written a book that counts.

*

The artistic instincts behind the original version of *Tender is the Night* were sure. Rosemary Hoyt serves not only as the catalyst which precipitates the decline of Dick Diver; she directs us to its source. First seeing Dick from the outside, through an other who is female, we brush against the novel's central fear—the fear of being object, not subject; of being image, not imagemaker; of being useful, not using; of being female, not male. Man-like, Rosemary comes to the Riviera for a brief vacation between jobs. Her work organizes and defines her life; her commitment to the job is sufficient to interrupt her holiday and take her off to Monte Carlo for a "contact." In contrast, Dick appears to be on a permanent holiday, defined by something other than work and potentially uncentered. When later we are given Dick's "heroic" period, we are in a position to grasp its significance:

> At the beginning of 1917, when it was becoming difficult to find coal, Dick burned for fuel almost a hundred textbooks that he had accumulated; but only, as he laid each one on the fire, with an assurance chuckling inside him that he was himself a digest of what was within the book, that he could brief it five years from now, if it deserved to be briefed. This went on at any odd hour, if necessary, with a floor rug over his shoulders, with the fine quiet of the scholar which is nearest of all things to heavenly peace....[6]

Complete absorption in work provides the heroism and perfection of this period in Dick's life. And in this perfect world, crucial to its perfection, women occupy a minor, carefully contained place: "With Elkins, second secretary at the Embassy, he shared an apartment, and there were two nice girl visitors—which was that and not too much of it" (p. 116). Dick meets Nicole in his heroic period, when, as he tells her, he is not "interested in anything except my work" (p. 142). The implicit connection between mental health, integration of personality, and commitment to work makes a deep impression on Nicole. Significantly, in the material which links the flashback of Book II to the contemporary present of Book I, Nicole soliloquizes: "And I'll look over the whole field of knowledge and pick out something and really know about it, so I'll have it to hang on to if I go to pieces again.... You've taught me that work is everything and I believe you. You used to say a man knows things and when he stops knowing things he's like anybody else ..." (pp. 161–62).

When Rosemary meets Dick, he is well on his way to being just "like anybody else." A crucial exchange occurs in Paris. In Abe North, the American composer, Fitzgerald creates a double for Dick, thus suggesting both the dimensions of the "problem" and its national origin. Though Dick has "long lost hope" in Abe, he assists in the effort to get Abe off the bottle, on the boat, and back to work. Yet, sensing in Dick the same "gigantic obscenity" that makes his own presence weigh the group down "like the wreck of a galleon," Abe attacks: "Something tells me I'll have a new score on Broadway long before you've finished your scientific treatise." "I hope so," Dick replies; "I hope so. I may even abandon what you call my 'scientific treatise,'" Mary's startled and shocked reply is "Oh, Dick!" (p. 62). Dick's announcement is clearly a detonation of major proportions. In her role as catalyst, Rosemary puts her finger on the "obscenity." Discovering that Dick is a doctor, she coos delightedly, "My father was a doctor too. Then why don't you—" (p. 63).

But if Dick is neither practising medicine nor working on his scientific treatise, what is he doing? Abe has his moment of truth before he disintegrates completely. In the station, waiting for the boat train, trying to find both reason and scapegoat for his collapse, he turns to Nicole; "'Tired of women's worlds,' he spoke up suddenly" (p. 81). The world Nicole inhabits, the world of the Riviera where Abe has spent his summer, the world Rosemary falls in love with, is the creation of Dick Diver and it is a woman's world. Our first view of Dick through Rosemary's eyes is emblematic: "After a while she realized that the man in the jockey cap was giving a quiet little performance for this group; he moved gravely about with a rake, ostensibly removing gravel ..." (p. 6). Dick's parody of work, reiterated in subsequent pictures of him—"he took his rake and began to work seriously at getting small stones out of the sand"—serves to focus our attention on his real activity creating forms which structure and make safe the days and nights, proving a sense of community which gives meaning to the lives and enhances the self-image of those included in it, pouring forth his energy and vitality to accomplish what Nicole has described as the ultimate business of women— that is, holding the world together. Dick's activity in carefully raking over his bit of beach is emblematic of his working over and ordering the human material which constitutes his community. Rosemary needs only one morning on the beach to discover that Dick Diver has created a world, to realize that those who are not part of it wish they were, and to long to become part of it herself. When Dick invites her to become part of his group, he does so with the knowledge that he is inviting her to join a world whose substance is ritual and community: "We go in, we take food and drink, so it's a substantial invitation" (p. 16).

Dick's capacity for creating such worlds is not limited to the setting of the beach. Dick—not Nicole—gives dinner parties. Dick orchestrates his dinner party from beginning to end, from the moment of invitation to the moment of departure, and the special feeling that the guests take away with them from the occasion is *his* gift. Dick's party recalls a similar event in Virginia Woolf's *To The Lighthouse*. The force of the comparison for our purposes resides, of course, in the degree to which it identifies Dick Diver as engaging in a quintessentially feminine activity. For Woolf's text is culturally accurate—women do give dinner parties; the daily round of meals and the sense of community and sociability associated with them are a part of women's "job," women's work. Woolf also recognizes that the threats to the community created through the art of female nurturance come from the ugly intrusion of various male egos all clamoring to be fed. In *Tender is the Night*, the reversal of roles is completed when Nicole emerges as the threat to the sense of community created by Dick. Her breakdown constitutes the ugly intrusion into his world, converting the delicate sense of communion which is his gift into the vulgarity of the consequent duel.

If Dick is engaged in feminine activity, he has the character traits which go with it—tact, delicacy of feeling, consideration for and sensitivity to others. His approach to warning Rosemary about the danger of sunburn on her first morning on the beach contrasts sharply with the crudeness of Mrs. Abrams' "we know who you are.... We wanted to warn you about getting burned the first day ... because *your* skin is important ..." (p. 7). Dick's tact, his politeness, his sensitivity is underscored later: "He managed the introduction so that her name wasn't mentioned and then let her know easily that everyone knew who she was but were respecting the completeness of her private life—a courtesy that Rosemary had not met with save from professional people since her success" (p. 16). Adept at the art of paying attention, Dick is able to make people feel special. He behaves quite differently from the heavily masculine Earl Brady who, sitting next to Rosemary at dinner and having been rebuffed in his effort to "monopolize her hand," spends the time talking shop, "or rather she listened while he talked shop" (pp. 31–32). Men talk and women listen, but Dick is not like most men.

This difference does not go unnoticed. Does not Tommy Barban like the Divers? "Of course—especially her—but they make me want to go to war" (p. 30). Surely Tommy's reaction has its origins in part in the same emotional repulsion which spawned Abe North's drunken insight about women's worlds. His response, like Abe's is compensatory, a necessary masculine balance to Dick's apparent femininity. Significantly, Tommy's response is markedly different, indeed oppositional, to that of the male homosexuals whom Dick has graced with an invitation. Meeting Dick several years later, one of them reminisces about "how nice you and your wife were," and recalls the evening as being "the most civilized gathering of people that I have ever known" (p. 246).

If the responses of men define Dick's femininity, so do those of women. Women respond to Dick as if he were a woman, or, perhaps more accurately, women treat Dick the way men usually treat women. Women appropriate Dick for his services and value him for his usefulness to them. His ability to handle the mess engendered by Abe North's unexpected, unannounced and drunken return to Paris saves Rosemary's reputation. Similarly, his final service, before dismissal, is undertaken to preserve the reputation of Mary North. And, of course, after his marriage his whole life is dedicated to the service of Nicole. Baby Warren lays it on the line with her talk about buying Nicole a doctor and with her casual evaluation of Dick's suitability for temporary service. More subtly, Mrs. Speers evaluates Dick's usefulness, giving Rosemary the go-ahead only after she has decided that Dick is the "real thing," capable of adding significantly to Rosemary's education and development, and not a "spurious substitute" who might damage her. Indeed, Mrs. Speers gladly places Rosemary in and on Dick's hands, anticipating the rest that will ensue for herself should her daughter's "exigent idealism ... focus on something" other than her mother. Thus, in his affair with Rosemary, Dick serves both mother and daughter. Of reciprocal concern for himself, there is none: "He saw that no provisions had been made for him ... in Mrs. Speers' plans" (p. 163).

Both Rosemary and Nicole fall in love with Dick at first sight; indeed, they fall in love with Dick in precisely the same way that Jay Gatsby falls in love with Daisy Buchanan: the first "nice" girl is simply transposed to the first "nice" man. The role reversal inherent in this parallelism receives its finishing touch from the fact that both Rosemary and Nicole remain curiously detached from the process of "falling in love" and essentially invulnerable to it. "Thus Rosemary's mother launches her on her affair with

Dick with the blessing, "You were brought up to work—not especially to marry.... Wound yourself or him—whatever happens it can't spoil you because economically you're a boy, not a girl" (p. 40). And at the end of the novel, it is Dick who is destroyed by love, not Nicole.

There is a moment in the novel when Dick confronts, head on, with a shock of recognition that is shared by the reader, the degree to which women view him as a woman. Dick, Nicole, Mary and Abe North have gone with Rosemary to see a private showing of her film, called, with excessive obviousness, "*Daddy's Girl.*" Fitzgerald belabors the point that the movies represent "women's worlds." They feature female characters played by female stars and their plots serve women's needs and present a "feminine" approach to life. Designed to make women "forget the dirty dishes at home and weep, even within the picture one woman wept so long that she almost stole the film away from Rosemary," *Daddy's Girl* embodies a fantasy of feminine power in a quintessentially feminine form: "Before her tiny fist the forces of lust and corruption rolled away; nay, the very march of destiny stopped; inevitable became evitable, syllogism, dialectic, all rationality fell away" (p. 69). Dick has just "winced for all psychologists at the vicious sentimentality" of the movie when Rosemary plays what she considers her trump card; she announces that she has arranged for a screen test for Dick: "Rosemary watched Dick comprehend what she meant, his face moving first in an Irish way; simultaneously she realized that she had made some mistake in the playing of her trump and still she did not suspect that the card was at fault" (p. 69).

Dick's protest is instinctively masculine, the Irish side of him serving here, as elsewhere, to symbolize his embattled masculine identity. Moments later the implicit becomes explicit: "I don't want a test.... The pictures make a fine career for a woman—but my God, they can't photograph me" (p. 70). But why not? Rosemary's instincts based on her apprehension of his essential femininity are accurate. In Dick's shock of recognition Rosemary completed her function as the catalytic agent in Dr. Diver's disintegration, revealing to him how far he has come from his heroic period and how insubstantial is his image of himself as an "old scientist all wrapped up in his private life" (p. 70).

*

The logical consequence of doing women's work and being perceived as a woman is living a woman's life. Though Rosemary's readiness to be "completed" may evoke echoes of Galatea, Dick Diver is no Pygmalion. Rather, he is merely a mother, whose substance is exhausted in the process of caring for others. Dick's "motherliness" constitutes a large part of both Nicole's and Rosemary's initial attraction to him. In the first flush of feeling, Rosemary gushes, "you like to help everybody, don't you? ... Mother likes to help everybody—of course she can't help as many people as you do" (p. 84). Similarly, Nicole's instincts lead her to Dick because he is "quieter than the others, all soft like a big cat. I have only gotten to like boys who are rather sissies. Are you a sissy?" (p. 121). And, like a mother, Dick's value lasts only as long as he nourishes. When he begins to "expect some nourishment from people now," he becomes both pitiful and dispensable. By the end of the novel Dick's milk is gone and Nicole is justified in her decision to "cut the cord forever": "Nicole could stand the situation no longer; in a kitchenmaid's panic she ran downstairs, afraid of what the stricken man above would feed on while she must still continue her dry suckling at his lean chest" (p. 279).

A scene prophetic of this termination occurs when Dick and Nicole return from Paris to the Riviera, alone. Wandering into the house, Dick sits down at the piano and starts to play: "Through the melody flowed a sudden realization that Nicole, hearing it, would guess quickly at a nostalgia for the past fortnight. He broke off with a casual chord and left the piano" (p. 170). Shaken by the realization that he "could no longer play what he wanted to play on the piano, it was an indication that life was being refined down to a point," Dick analyzes his situation: his "work" has become "confused with Nicole's problems; in addition, her income had increased so fast of late that it seemed to belittle his work" (pp. 171, 170). Without work of his own or economic independence, Dick's situation resembles that of a wife; thus what he wishes to play on the piano is not the point toward which his life is being refined. Emblematic of his inevitable deference and absorption is the name "Dicole," "the word with which he and Nicole had signed communications in the first days of love" and which he still uses, perhaps long after she has ceased to (p. 103). Nicole, on the other hand, is always Nicole, rarely, if ever, Mrs. Diver.

In his marriage to Nicole, Dick plays out the role of wife as mother, and the trajectories described by that relationship define the essence of the feminine career: namely, the giving over of energy, health, sanity, even identity, from the self to the other. Two carefully paralleled scenes demonstrate this process for us. The first occurs while Dick is still running the clinic with Franz. He, Nicole, and their two children set off for a day's outing at a carnival. What should be holiday turns into nightmare as Nicole has one of her "attacks." Arriving at the carnival, "Nicole began to run very suddenly," and when Dick finally catches up with her, she demands a brandy. Refusing her request, Dick gets her back in the car and starts home. Furious with Dick for being in control and able to control, Nicole literally tries to take the wheel into her own hands and drive him off the road and over the edge. Her suicidal and homicidal rage, twin products of her emptiness and sense of inferiority, turn after the event into contemptuous scorn: "You were scared, weren't you? ... You wanted to live!" (p. 192).

Near the end of the novel, Nicole and Dick, in an attempt to regain, among other things, their sense of fun, decide on the spur of the moment to visit a yacht anchored offshore. Once again what was intended as fun becomes nightmare, only this time Dick causes the transformation. Unable any longer to control his aggression, unable even to handle a dinner conversation, Dick is also no match for those whom he offends. During the evening, he disappears. Nicole, playing a game with Tommy, suddenly realizes that Dick is gone. When she finds him, "in the same slow manner he caught her wrist and drew her near.... Cold with terror she put her other wrist into his grip. All right, she would go with him—again she felt the beauty of the night vividly in one moment of complete response and abnegation—all right, then—" (pp. 273–74). Tommy's arrival interrupts Dick's suicidal and homicidal impulse, and Nicole is released—to discover how very much she now wants to live.

Nicole now enters *her* heroic period. Hers now is "the wide swell of fantasy" and hers the sense of possibility, luck, happiness; Dick has long since lost "the long ground-swell of imagination that he counted on for his judgements" and any luck that went with it (pp. 277, 86). Unable to function as a man, to be "beam and idea, girder and logarithm," Dick has become Nicole: "one and equal, not apposite and complementary; she was Dick too, the drought in the marrow of his bones. He could not watch her disintegrations without participating in them" (pp. 190–91). One final scene conveys the shift in positions. The morning after the night before, Tommy appears with a sore throat. Nicole diagnoses, prescribes and dispenses, while Dick weakly protests: "Say, there ... don't give Tommy the whole jar—it has to be ordered from Paris—it's out of stock down here" (p. 278).

*

By the end of *Tender is the Night*, the "degeneracy" of Dick's career is apparent. His final service is not different in kind from his earlier ones and it requires all the talents which have previously produced his finest moments. That Dick's career should culminate in the rescuing of two "degenerate" women from the sordid consequences of male impersonation records Fitzgerald's final estimate of it and identifies its essential immorality as, not surprisingly, nothing other than the fact that it fails to embody and re-enforce traditional sex roles. Thus the proposal that the less Dick acts like a woman the more admirable he is provides the corollary to the final revelation of rottenness at the core of his finest moments. To some degree, then, Dick's "disintegration" represents a more heroic state than his "integration." For think of it this way: were Dick Diver not male, there would be no story for Fitzgerald to tell. So the wife gives up a career in medicine and devotes herself to saving her husband; so she drinks a bit much; so she blurts things out at dinner parties and perhaps offends someone important; so she may eventually have to be dumped—so what? This is the stuff of soap opera, not great books. What gives *Tender is the Night* its scope and its tone, indeed its very idea, is the fact that this happens to a man.

Early in the novel a telling image occurs: "In a moment Nicole swam into his field of vision, whereupon he disappeared into his house and came out with a megaphone. He had many light mechanical devices. 'Nicole,' he shouted.... The ease with which her reply reached him seemed to belittle his megaphone ..." (p. 27). Dick's sense of proportion is clearly awry. He thinks that things, including himself, are larger than they really are. His reliance on "light mechanical devices" to create his sense of dimension marks him as a lightweight. Other images appear, emblematic of his lack of substance. There is, for example, that miniature briefcase—what can possibly be in it? The imagery accorded Abe North provides a striking contrast to the diminuitiveness of Dick's briefcase. As Abe exercises the masculine prerogative of "tearing things apart," he becomes a "gigantic presence" like "the wreck of a galleon," dominating the group with the "spectacle" of his "gigantic obscenity" (pp. 82, 83). And it is Abe, not Dick, who can convincingly impersonate General Pershing in the final gambit of the Paris party.

Spatial imagery helps place for us the relative weight of Dick Diver's behavior. In our final view, Dick has risen; he stands above the beach, looking down on it, and, separated from it, he blesses it as he departs. Though Dick is no longer "nice," is he not larger, better? For has he not discovered that "niceness" is the badge of faggotry, facilitating degeneracy? In talking with the "corrupt" Chilean boy, Dick comes to see that it is Francisco's charm that enables him "to perpetuate his outrages" (p. 254). To cease to be charming, then, has the value of masculine protest against the feminine emphasis on good manners. In an earlier confrontation with Baby Warren, Dick struggles against the suffocating force of niceness: "There's too much good manners.... My father had the kind of manners he inherited from the days when you shot first and apologized afterward" (pp. 177, 178). In ceasing to be nice, Dick has broken the stranglehold of women's values on him. Yet so feminized is America, so entrenched the power of "women's worlds," and so weakened is Dick from having lived so long within these worlds, that he has nothing to put in the place of these values.

Like so many other American "classics," *Tender is the Night* ends with its hero in a state of limbo, unable to go backward or forward and without a coherent, viable identity. And, like other American books, *Tender is the Night* traces the source of this state of limbo to a confusion in sex roles which in turn is connected to the peculiar nature of America. For here, as in *The Great Gatsby*, Fitzgerald indicts America, identifying the nation as female and blaming the woes of American men on the character of American women and on the feminization of American culture. If we ask what has caused Dick Diver to live out the life of a woman, the answer comes clear: America, his "gold-star muzzer," has done Dick Diver in, sacrificing him and all her sons on the altar of sexual warfare. Though the mourning mothers represent "all the maturity of an older America," that world is irreparably broken and the new world which they have brought into being is presented as matriarchal (p. 101).

That the new America is a world run for women is elaborated in a passage which describes Nicole:

> Nicole was the product of much ingenuity and toil. For her sake trains began their run at Chicago and traversed the round belly of the continent to California; chicle factories fumed and link belts grew link by link in factories; men mixed toothpaste in vats and drew mouthwash out of copper hogsheads; girls canned tomatoes quickly in August or worked rudely at the Five-and-Tens on Christmas Eve; half-breed Indians toiled on Brazilian coffee plantations and dreamers were muscled out of patent rights in new tractors—these were some of the people who gave a tithe to Nicole, and as the whole system swayed and thundered onward it lent a feverish bloom to such processes of hers as wholesale buying, like the flush of a fireman's face holding his post before a spreading blaze. (p. 55).

Not only is America run for women; it is also run by them. Daddy Warren is the last male tycoon; he has produced only daughters and in their hands is now concentrated the enormous wealth that he accumulated. Rosemary Hoyt is equally powerful for she sits at the center of the biggest business in America—the movies. A feminine medium, dominated by women, serving women's interests and reflecting feminine perceptions, the movies project powerful female images and images of women as powerful even into the heart of Europe. Thus Franz and his wife, Kaethe, carry out their argument over Dick and Nicole through references to the movies (pp. 239–40).

The feminization of America has produced a nation whose men "go to pieces." At lunch in Paris, Dick makes the claim that "no American men had any repose, except himself" (p. 51). The others, "seeking an example to confront him with," are in trouble: "not a man had come into the restaurant for ten minutes without raising his hand to his face.... A well-known general came in, and Abe, counting on the man's first year at West Point ... made a bet with Dick of five dollars" (pp. 51, 52). But even American generals are not what they used to be and this one, unlike Grant, "lolling in his general store in Galena ... ready to be called to an intricate destiny," finally, "with a touch of fury ... shot up his hand and scratched his gray immaculate head," thereby proving Dick's point (pp. 118, 52). Dick's father, himself of "tired stock," makes one last effort in bringing Dick up; thereafter, he emits only a faint presence. The absence of Dick's father contrasts markedly with the presence of fathers, and grandfathers, in the world of Franz Gregorovius, Dick's European partner and counterpart. Indeed, the character of Franz figures large in Fitzgerald's analysis of America. Looking at the relationship between Franz and Kaethe, one realizes that Franz has access to a dominance foreign to Dick's character and unavailable to him. Kaethe is wife as servant; she cleans the house, takes care of the children, brings on command "*noch ein Glas-Bier*," and perspires profusely. Subject to her husband's "quiet joke" of keeping news from her, she knows her place and she obeys.

The presence of fathers and grandfathers grounds Franz in reality and occasions him to respond with bemusement to Dick's observation that upon being released from the army he has only one plan: "to be a good psychologist—maybe the greatest one that ever lived." As Franz sees it, "That's very good—and very American.... It's more difficult for us.... I am continually confronted with a pantheon of heroes" (p. 132). Franz's experience of history as the substantial accumulation of male achievement exposes the illusory nature of Dick's pretensions. Like the typical American, Dick admits that he "was only talking big" because in America "everything's just starting over" (p. 132). However, when the sons of America talk big, the sons of Europe do not listen. Kaethe's final judgment that "Dick is no longer a serious man" is the logical outgrowth of his intellectual inheritance as an American (p. 241). When Dick reveals to Franz his plan of publishing everything he currently knows in pamphlet form, Franz is aghast: "Soon you will be writing little books called 'Deep Thoughts for the Layman,' so simplified that they are positively guaranteed not to cause thinking" (p. 138). His final acceptance of Dick's plans, however, is far more damning than his initial objections: "You are an American. You can do this without professional harm" (p. 138).

Fitzgerald wants there to be no confusion as to who or what is responsible for the flabbiness of American intellectual life or for the fact that Europeans do not take American men seriously. American men have learned to write shallow books at the movies, that art form dominated by the feminine and devoted to the sentimental, the irrational, the silly. The "American Woman" reigns and her "clean-sweeping irrational temper" has "broken the moral back of a race and made a nursery out of a continent" (p. 232). Even the mothers, representatives of an older America, are complicit. They are responsible for the Achilles' heels by which their sons ultimately perish—"the illusions of eternal strength and health, and of the essential goodness of people," illusions which lead the sons to believe they can be the "greatest one that ever lived" and to publish pamphlets stating all they know, "illusions of a nation, the lives of generations of frontier mothers who had to croon falsely, that there were no wolves outside the cabin door" (p. 117).

Even war cannot provide a compensatory influx of masculinity into the feminized American scene. Dick, awaiting his moment in Zurich, is no Grant awaiting his destiny in Galena. References to Grant, who in the pantheon of American heroes represents the masculine type—the man of war, strong, silent, dedicated, utterly serious and completely uncorrupted by charm— serve to underline the fact that the heroic and masculine age of America is a thing of the past. Such identity and career are not possible for Dick, who can only organize a party in which someone else gets to play General Pershing. Dick himself never saw action in the war, his work being "executive" rather than "practical," and thus his guided tour of one of the great battlefields outside Paris has something spurious about it. Nevertheless, his analysis is revelatory: "'Why, this was a love battle—there was a century of middle-class love spent here. This was the last love battle.' 'You want to hand over this battle to D. H. Lawrence,' said Abe" (p. 57). Abe's comment is pointed. For just as Dick can relate to the war only by turning a tour of the battlefield into a party, using the shards of masculine experience as the raw material for his feminine creation of community, so, in analyzing war as an act of love, he subsumes the masculine under the feminine and reveals the degree to which he has himself been feminized.

This process of feminization emerges additionally in Fitzgerald's reliance on military metaphors to describe Dick's career as a woman: "The enthusiasm, the selflessness behind the whole performance ravished her, the

technic of moving many varied types, each as immobile, as dependent on
supplies of attention as an infantry battalion is dependent on rations,
appeared so effortless that he still had pieces of his own most personal self
for everyone"; "he sometimes looked back with awe at the carnivals of
affection he had given, as a general might gaze upon a massacre he had
ordered to satisfy an impersonal blood lust" (pp. 77, 27). The absorption of
the masculine into the feminine is clearly documented, and such
documentation clearly reveals the lack of masculine alternative. Indeed, the
"tragedy" of Dick's life might well be described by the statement that no
other battle ground exists for him but that of love. For "it had early become
a habit to be loved, perhaps from the moment when he had realized that he
was the last hope of a decaying clan" (p. 302). Dick's capacity to live a
masculine life is undermined from the start; the exhausted male principle can
not overcome the dominance of the gold star muzzer who prepares her sons
to fight a women's war on women's grounds and thus inevitably to lose.

*

     Considerable critical attention has been given to Fitzgerald's choice of
Dick Diver's profession.[7] Faithful to the grand design of history, as many
critics have variously claimed, if not to its particular details, Fitzgerald
provides ample evidence within his text for the significance and validity of his
choice. The profession of psychiatry arose at precisely the point when,
through increasing economic and political opportunities, women threatened
seriously to challenge the destiny of their biology; and it arose precisely to
provide a counterforce adequate to meet and defeat this challenge. In the
struggle for dominance, the profession of psychiatry constitutes a major
weapon in the masculine arsenal. In a conversation with Franz, Dick
identifies the weakness of his profession as "its attraction for the man a little
crippled and broken. Within the walls of the profession he compensates by
tending toward the clinical, the 'practical'—he has won his battle without a
struggle" (pp. 137–38). For the man engaged in the losing battle described
above, the attractions of psychiatry are clear and the professional choice a
"natural" one. Under the guise of helping, the feminine cover of the career
of service, psychiatry affords such men large areas of dominance over
women, a dominance more insidious and far-reaching because so thoroughly
disguised. Through psychiatry, men can define both reality and sanity for
women.[8]
     Consider, for example, the situation of Nicole. Though raped by her
father, it is she, not he, who goes "mad," is incarcerated in a mental

institution and "treated." It is she, not he, who must be "re-educated." And what does "re-education" mean? It means that Nicole must understand that what happened to her has no political significance, no bearing on the relation between men and women. To get "well," Nicole must learn to trust men again; she must reject the idea that she had no "complicity" in her rape and abandon the "phantom world where all men, the more you liked them and trusted them, the more evil" they are (p. 131). Nicole is well when she is able to fall in love and thus to complete the process of "transferring" her "blocked" love for her father to another man. In a fictional world which insists on the sexual signification of even the slightest detail and which is thus saturated with "evidence" toward a theory of sex class-war, the value to men of a profession capable of obliterating in women the ability to develop such a theory is large.

The power afforded men by the psychiatric profession becomes richly palpable in one of the book's most painful scenes. A woman comes to Dick's clinic for "treatment," an American, a painter, who, by her own admission (perhaps she has already been "re-educated"), is "sharing the fate of the women of my time who challenged men to battle" (p. 184). This fate is appalling: "On her admittance she had been exceptionally pretty—now she was a living agonizing sore" (p. 183). Obviously the treatment has been unsuccessful. Indeed, one senses here an inadvertent and heavily disguised suggestion that "treatment" is in reality punishment. All the talent, equipment and training offered by this exemplary clinic can do nothing, to ease this woman's pain. So Dick offers explanation and understanding instead; and psychiatry legitimates and sacralizes his act. For the imprisoned and suffering patient, Dr. Diver defines reality; he tells her who she is and interprets the meaning, or, rather, non-meaning, of her experience. Re-enforcing the thought that treatment is really punishment, Dick's analysis strips the woman of heroic stature and strips her experience of symbolic significance, even though to accomplish this "cure" he must lie. Carefully, Dick reinterprets her own definition of her situation: "To your vast surprise it was just like all battles," and he adds, in a further elimination of the special, "You've suffered, but many women suffered before they mistook themselves for men" (p. 184). To her effort to attach significance to her suffering—"I am here as a symbol of something"—he replies, "mechanically," "You are sick" (p. 185).

In this role, Franz is comfortable. Dick, however, is not. More emerges here than the proposition that Dick as a feminized American male is simply not up to dominance. Indeed, what emerges here are the outlines of a subtext, subliminally interwoven with the dominant text, whose message contradicts and subverts that of the dominant text. For what saves this scene from a baldness of fantasy, a "sentimentality" so vicious as to make us wince for Fitzgerald, is its insincerity. Dick's statements to the woman appear flat, mechanical, uttered without conviction. At some point, Dick recoils from the possibilities of dominance offered him by his profession and resists the posture of definer of women's reality and policeman of sex-role boundaries. In this scene, one begins to sense and comprehend Dick's fatigue. In his last attempt to do his trick lift, we are given a powerful emblem of that fatigue:

> He could not rise. Nicole saw him shift his position and strain upward again but at the instant when the weight of his partner was full upon his shoulders he became immovable. He tried again—lifting an inch, two inches—Nicole felt the sweat glands of her forehead open as she strained with him—then he was simply holding his ground, then he collapsed back down on his knees with a smack, and they went over, Dick's head barely missing a kick of the board. (p. 284).

The sources of Dick's fatigue are obviously multiple. In addition to the exhaustion attendant upon several years of "women's work," there is the antecedent and perhaps continuing effort of being male. To be "beam and idea, girder and logarithm," to lift the load of female identity and suspend it from oneself, constantly to re-state the universe, re-define reality and re-educate women—in a word, to keep women down—is an exhausting enterprise. Of already exhausted stock, Dick is further exhausted by the effort to fight back the encroachments of "Amazons," by the need to do battle with the modern American woman who is no longer "happy to exist in a man's world," and who no longer seeks to preserve her "individuality through men and not by opposition to them" (p. 53).

Yet it would misrepresent the ambivalence and the complexity of the novel were we not to recognize the degree to which Dick's exhaustion testifies to his alienation from such work and to his preference for the woman's job. After all, Dick knows his lift is a "trick." To put it another way, Dick neither wishes to be Franz nor to marry Kaethe. Indeed, masculinity is not made attractive in *Tender is the Night*. Dick's dinner party is an event more highly valued in the novel than the duel which results from it—a non-event whose pointless stupidity presents a parody of masculine posturing. Similarly, though Dick professes to admire the manners of his father "inherited from the days when you shot first and apologized afterward," when he falls back on these manners and avails himself of "the honorable, the traditional resource of his land," what happens to him is "so awful that nothing could make any difference ... he was hopeless. He would be a different person henceforward ..." (pp. 178, 224, 233). Like the McKisco/Barban duel, Dick's brawl with the Roman police is stupid, unredeeming and unredeemable; Fitzgerald's text provides no glorification of the masculine recourse to violence. Tommy Barban, the professional fighter, instigator of duels, cool killer of communist border guards, may go to war, driven there by Dick, but he is not the novel's ideal. A barbarian, as his name suggests, he is a lower form of life than Dick, and when Nicole leaves Dick for Tommy, we perceive her choice as reversion. Though American women are blamed for Dick's destruction, still his "sickness" is more valuable than Tommy's "health." Thus Dick's final rising contains in the entirety of their tangled convolutions the novel's contradictions.

The negative attitude toward conventional masculinity is deeply embedded in the imaginative structure of *Tender is the Night*. On his way to trial for assaulting the Roman policeman, Dick passes through a courtyard: "a groaning, hissing, booing sound went up from the loiterers in the courtyard, voices full of fury and scorn. Dick stared about.... A native of Frascati had raped and slain a five-year old child and was to be brought in that morning—the crowd had assumed it was Dick" (p. 234). Though Dick is no literal rapist, it is not a case of mistaken identity ("I want to make a speech ... I want to explain to those people how I raped a five-year-old girl. Maybe I did"). Male sexuality and rape have been previously connected in the character of Nicole's father, Devereux Warren. And lying to his imprisoned patient, helpless beneath his definitions and manipulations, Dick may have glimpsed the idea that "re-education" is itself a form of rape. Thus doctor, father, husband, rapist all blend together in one hideous identity from which Dick turns and flees.

Profoundly autobiographical in its central impulses, *Tender is the Night* has buried at its heart Scott's awareness that his sanity and his career were purchased at the price of Zelda's and purchased by his manipulation of the power accorded men over women. For such knowledge, what forgiveness? From such guilt, what else but flight? Is it surprising, then, that at some level this text lacks all conviction, or that its imaginative life often contradicts its putative thesis?

For Scott chose to marry Zelda and Dick is not Franz, nor did he marry Nicole to make or keep her sick. He wishes her to be well. But his wish turns back upon himself, for in his world Nicole can become well only at his expense. Here, then, is the bitter source of the real tragedy behind and within this text—the metaphoric trap most thoroughly sprung. Fitzgerald's imagination cannot transcend the economic imagery which dominates it. In such a metaphoric system, the interests of men and women inevitably are oppositional, for given a limited quantity of sanity, integration, creativity, if one gets more, the other must get less. An economy of scarcity ensures the perception that only one of two can survive. Fitzgerald embodies this economic vision in a metaphor which occurs precisely at the moment when Dick commits himself to Nicole. Going up, up, up into the Alps, Dick reflects on the mechanism which is lifting him: "As water gushed from the chamber under the car, Dick was impressed with the ingenuity of the whole idea—a complimentary car was now taking on mountain water at the top and would pull up the lightened car up by gravity, as soon as the brakes were released. It must have been a great inspiration" (p. 147). Moments later, he encounters Nicole, seeing her for the first time outside of the institution, as a woman and not a patient: "The delight in Nicole's face—to be a feather again instead of a plummet, to float and not to drag" (p. 149). But who must get heavy so that she can float? The cable car image determines the trajectory of the text and as Nicole rises, Dick goes down.

Yet what are the choices? Fitzgerald's model allows no honorable solutions. If the novel has Gausse's kick at the ass of Lady Caroline Sibley-Biers at its emotional heart, still Fitzgerald does not want Dick to be the one who administers it. Is it not better to disappear into the obscurity of upstate New York than to mete out such chastisement to women? Is it not better to leave the battle than to take on the role of barbarian' warrior, re-educating doctor or rapist father? Perhaps if Fitzgerald himself had acted on the convictions embedded in his novel, we would be reading *Save Me the Waltz* instead of *Tender is the Night*. But the question would still be now, as then, why not both?

NOTES

1. Nancy Milford, *Zelda* (New York, 1970), pp. 270, 272, 273.

2. For a discussion of the way in which biographies of Scott Fitzgerald—and even to a point Milford's *Zelda* as well—reflect this view, see Anna Valdine Clemens, "Zelda Fitzgerald: An Unromantic Revision," *Dalhousie Review*, 62, 2 (1982), 196–211.

3. Matthew J. Broccoli, *The Composition of "Tender is the Night"* (Pittsburgh, 1963), p. 73.

4. For an interpretation of the novel with a similar vision of its essential point, yet with a very different attitude toward that point, see Milton R. Stern, The Golden *Moment: The Novels of F. Scott Fitzgerald* (Urbana, 1970), pp. 289–462.

5. In addition to retaining the matricidal intent, the final version of the novel may also be seen to retain the motivation for that intent. The initial matricidal plot, as Broccoli has pointed out, was based on a newspaper account of a sixteen-year-old girl who killed

her mother. In Fitzgerald's early version this was transformed into the story of a son whose homicidal rage and self-defeating violence derive from both his mother's opposition to his career and the feminine nature of that career. The situation, in short, centers in the issues of gender power and gender privilege—which is precisely the point of the final version.

6. F. Scott Fitzgerald, *Tender is the Night* (New York, 1934), p. 116.

7. See, for example, Henry Dan Piper, *F. Scott Fitzgerald: A Critical Portrait* (London, 1965), pp. 222–23, who argues "that Dick is not at all a convincing psychiatrist"; and Jeffrey Berman, "*Tender Is the Night*: Fitzgerald's *A Psychology for Psychiatrists*," *Literature and Psychology*, 29 (1979), 34–47, who contends, among other things, that as readers "we suspect that Dick has become a psychiatrist to hold in check those inner forces which ultimately lead to his ruin."

8. Clemens explores this form of "psychiatric" dominance with respect to Zelda's treatment, and she relates it further to the choice of Zelda's doctors: not Carl Jung, "an expert on neurosis and a proponent of the healing and regenerative powers of the creative impulse" but instead Bleuler, an expert on schizophrenia: "Was the choice of doctor simply a matter of money and medical etiquette as Milford states, or could it have been a matter of seeking out the man most likely to give the preferred diagnosis?" (p. 297).

ROBERT GIDDINGS

The Last Tycoon:
Fitzgerald as Projectionist

Please do not turn on the clouds until the show starts. Be sure the stars
are turned off when leaving.
> —Notice on the backstage switchboard of the Paradise Theatre,
> Farubault, Minnesota. Quoted in Ben M. Hall, *The Golden Age
> of the Movie Palace: The Best Remaining Seats* (1961)

Irving Thalberg carried with him the accoutrements of an artist; hence
he was unique in the Hollywood of the period. I don't know of anyone
else who has occupied the position. He was like a young pope.
> —Budd Schulberg

1

It has become widely accepted that Fitzgerald was at his best when writing
about experiences known and observed first-hand. In no respect has this been
more alleged than in the matter of the Jazz Age, Fitzgerald as its celebrant
and victim and in whose 'Jazz Age' fiction and essays (especially as collected
in *The Crack-Up*) the very essence of American history, the decades of the
1920s and 1930s at least, apparently had been caught on the wing. This may
have started out as a way of praising Fitzgerald, but it has produced its
problems. Was Fitzgerald the master or the servant of his materials? Other

From *Scott Fitzgerald: The Promises of Life*, A. Robert Lee, ed. pp. 74–93. © 1989 Vision Press.

than in *The Great Gatsby* (1925), by common agreement his one sure masterpiece, did he in truth write as more than the chronicler, the historical painter of his period? And more to immediate purposes, when the issue is *The Last Tycoon*—admittedly unfinished at his death in 1940—which so conspicuously takes for its central figure of Monroe Stahr a model literally as large (if not more so) as life, the studio mogul Irving Thalberg (1899–1936), can it be said that Fitzgerald not only kept but mastered his imaginative distance?

Arthur Mizener usefully sets out Fitzgerald's own exhilaration at the prospect of writing *The Last Tycoon*:

> Less than a year before his death, when he began the actual writing of *The Last Tycoon*, he was filled once more with the old, irrepressible excitement; you can hear it in the letter he wrote his daughter: 'Scottina: ... Look! I have begun to write something that is maybe *great*.... It may not *make* us a cent but it will pay expenses and it is the first labor of love I've undertaken since the first part of "Infidelity!"' [1]

Mizener goes on to speak of *The Last Tycoon* as indeed fulfilling Fitzgerald's hopes, and essentially because, as always with Fitzgerald at his best, it offers not 'social history or even nostalgically evocative social history' but 'the history of a consciousness'. Fitzgerald, in other words, whatever the temptation to see this last novel as overwhelmingly tied only to its time and place and Hollywood materials, manages infinitely more. A torso only *The Last Tycoon* may be, but on my estimate at least, it truly ranks among Fitzgerald's most glittering prizes, and precisely in how it takes the 'life' figure of Thalberg, whose mogulship Fitzgerald had every occasion to observe in his Hollywood script-writing days, and transforms aspects of him into Monroe Stahr. So that one immediately says yes, Monroe Stahr *is* Irving Thalberg, but yes, also, and mercifully, he is so much more, a portrait—a fiction—indeed as 'maybe great' as Fitzgerald so fervently hoped he had it within him to create. And one also says that *The Last Tycoon* goes beyond even that, beyond any one figure or phase of American history, into a vision of how Art, as Fitzgerald conceived it, might 'project' History itself.

But to return first to Thalberg: his life has not wanted for documentation. Witness, for example, Samuel Marx, *Mayer and Thalberg: The Make-Believe Saints* (1975), Bosley Crowther, *Hollywood Rajah: The Life and Times of Louis B. Mayer* (1960) and Bob Thomas, *Thalberg: Life and Legend* (1969). It all makes for fabulous reading. It is openly acknowledged that although Thalberg's name was technically not part of the company's title, he was the real driving force and elemental genius which made Metro-Goldwyn-Mayer the prosperous empire which it had become by the opening years of the 1930s.

And what an empire it was! It was the largest of the 124 subsidiaries owned by the huge conglomerate founded by Marcus Loew, the Australian-American tycoon, Loews Incorporated. Its plant in Culver City, California, covered fifty-three acres and was valued at $2,000,000. Its stars were paid $6,000 a week. It boasted the highest paid writing staff in the business with a payroll of $40,000 a week. Its parkland could be turned into anything required from battlefields to palace gardens. It had twenty-two sound stages and twenty-two projection rooms. Its films made the most money in the trade, each movie costing on average about $500,000. A billion people annually paid some $100,000,000 worldwide to go and see the products turned out by Metro-Goldwyn-Mayer. It could boast it had more stars than there were in Heaven—including Greta Garbo, Clark Gable, John Gilbert, Spencer Tracy, Lewis Stone, Laurel and Hardy, the Barrymores, Lon Chaney, Wallace Beery, Joan Crawford, William Powell, the Marx Brothers, Franchot Tone and Norma Shearer—and among its most famous productions were *The Big Parade*, *Anna Christie*, *Grand Hotel*, *Ben Hur*, *The Thin Man* and *Mutiny on the Bounty*. These were not all produced during Irving Thalberg's period with Metro-Goldwyn-Mayer. He died in 1936, before the making of such money-spinning commodities as *Goodbye Mr. Chips* and *The Wizard of Oz*, which are such typical products of Culver City's active imperialism.

The company originated from Loew's which was initially an exhibiting company which bought into Metro Pictures in 1920. Immediately afterwards it produced two extremely successful films—*The Four Horsemen of the Apocalypse* in 1921, directed by Rex Ingram, which introduced Rudolph Valentino as a star, and *The Prisoner of Zenda* in the following year, again directed by Rex Ingram, with Lewis Stone and Ramon Navarro. By 1925 it had merged with the Goldwyn production company and been joined by Louis B. Mayer Pictures. Mayer epitomized the American dream. He was a Jewish refugee from Russian persecution who had crawled from the very bottom of the pile to the very top of executive power. Early in his career he had sold junk and this was a reputation he was to carry with him forever, whether deserved or not. He said himself, 'Look out for yourself or they'll pee on your grave', but he probably would accept Bob Hope's famous comment as his most fitting epitaph: 'Louis B. Mayer came west in the early days with twenty-eight dollars, a box camera, and an old lion. He built a monument to himself—the Bank of America.' Herman Mankiewicz, the scriptwriter immortally associated with *Citizen Kane*, was less generous: 'There but for the grace of God, goes God.' Nevertheless with Mayer as its production head the company thrived, though stories of his tyranny are infamous, including his physical violence upon the persons of Charlie Chaplin, Robert Taylor and John Gilbert, and his emotional violence upon the likes of Myrna Loy, for whom he faked a heart attack in order to blackmail her into playing a particular rôle. He lay on the floor murmuring: 'No ... no.... Don't play the part, Myrna.... I understand. Please don't play the part.... I understand.... People will only say you played it so as to please a sick man.' She went on her knees to him and begged to be allowed the role she had originally refused. He reluctantly gave in as a doctor was called to his side. When she had left his office, Mayer leaped up from the floor and yelled 'Well, who's next?' and continued to keep his business appointments. Mayer dominated Metro-Goldwyn-Mayer for a quarter of a century. But this was the strange business world into which the frail but determined Irving Thalberg, original of Scott Fitzgerald's Monroe Stahr, entered as a young man. He was to provide the artistic flair, the cultivated and sophisticated tone, to counterbalance Mayer's shrewd understanding of mass public appetites.

2

During the early years of the decade following the Wall Street crash it has been estimated that Irving Thalberg was paid $500,000 a year, partly the result of a generous bonus system on Metro-Goldwyn-Mayer's productions. He worked very hard for it. His business methods and habits were strange, but they earned huge dividends. The Metro-Goldwyn-Mayer executive offices were a white wooden building, and Thalberg's office was on the second floor. He had a private projection room which had three desks, a couple of pianos and about thirty armchairs. He was seldom there before 10 a.m. But once there he devoted all his energies into ensuring that the company produced the best films in the world. His life story is another version of the American myth of the ordinary guy who makes it to the top of the tree. After leaving high school in Brooklyn, he worked as an office boy in Universal Pictures, where he had been 'discovered' by Carl Laemle, Snr., who was an executive producer, associated particularly with the success of *All Quiet on the Western Front* in 1930.

Thalberg's major business activity seemed to be talk and he used words quietly, sacredly and preciously, almost like a poet. He was fragile in appearance and less than 5'2" in height. He used his hands to great effect when he spoke and was given to pacing up and down his office with his hands clasped behind his back when deep in thought. His voice was always calm and contained, as if he was determined to be sparing in its use. The items noticeable on his desk were his dictaphone, a large box of cigarettes which he never opened, plates of apples and dates which he frequently dipped into and many bottles of medicine. He did not give out the impression of massively good and robust health.

All those who have written about the professional qualities possessed and employed by Irving Thalberg agree that two particular qualities were outstanding: his ability to deal thoroughly with all aspects of motion picture production, and his ability to come up with ideas. To an outsider the activities of a typical day in Thalberg's working life might seem to lack cohesion and purpose. But he knew what he was doing, and the industry knew that he knew. Mae D. Huettig gives a reasonable account of what he actually seemed to do for a living:

> There is naturally no chance that Mr. Thalberg's activities will fall into routine. His efforts follow no pattern whatsoever, except that they consist almost exclusively of talk. He deals with actors, whose simple wants of avarice or vanity he finds it easy to appease. He deals with writers, with whom he seldom commits the unpardonable blunder of saying: 'I don't like it, but I don't know why.' He is ceaselessly aware of Delores Del Rio's gifted husband, Cedric Gibbons, who designs MGM scenery, and of the tall, twittering hunchback Adrain, who drapes MGM's loveliest bodies. He deals with M. E. Greenwood, the gaunt studio manager, who used to be an Arizona faro dealer and now tells MGM's New York office how much the company has spent every week and how much to place on deposit for MGM's account at the Culver City branch of Bank of America. Through Mr. Greenwood, and sometimes more directly, Irving Thalberg observes the two thousand of the skilled but unsung: 'grips', assistant cameramen, 'mixers', cutters, projectionists, carpenters, unit managers, artisans, seamstresses, scene painters. Often he calls a group of these underlings into the projection room to consider pictures with him.[2]

But none of this Thalberg-supervised activity would have existed had it not been for the ideas which were the genesis of all movies. Here Thalberg's genius was even more apparent, his mind a seeming fount of good basic scripting ideas as well as brilliant ideas about points of detail.

Thalberg could sense the basic need at the very core and centre of a movie; it was his idea to borrow Tallulah Bankhead from Paramount to give much needed zest to *Tinfoil*. *Rasputin and the Empress* (1932) gave Lionel Barrymore one of his biggest and best rôles, but it was Thalberg's idea to have the movie directed by Richard Boleslavsky, the Polish stage director who came to Hollywood in 1930 from the Moscow Arts Theatre (he went on to direct *The Painted Veil*, *Clive of India* and *Les Misérables*). It was Thalberg who recognized and exploited the particular gifts of Howard Hawks, who had been in the industry since 1918 and who had become a household name certainly from *Scarface* 1932 on; Hawks had a penchant for grainy realism and action-packed drama as well as very polished and professional comedies. (He made *The Criminal Code* for Thalberg in 1931.) He encouraged the very cosmopolitan talents of Sidney Franklin, who directed *Beverly of Graustark* (1926), *The Last of Mrs. Cheyney* (1929), *Private Lives* (1931), *Smiling Through* (1932), *The Guardsman* (1932) and *The Barretts of Wimpole Street* (1933) and went on to produce the immortal *Mrs. Miniver* in 1942. The many-sided W. S. Van Dyke was another director in Thalberg's stable, whose films included *White Shadows in the South Seas* (1928), *Trader Horn* (1931), shot on safari in Africa, *Tarzan the Ape Man* (1932), which introduced the greatest of all ape-men, the former Olympic athlete Johnny Weissmuller, *Manhattan Melodrama* (1934) and the still very impressive disaster movie prototype, *San Francisco* (1936). Sam Wood, director of *A Night at the Opera* and *A Day at the Races*, who had a gift for football and college pictures and left his mark on *Goodbye Mr. Chips* (1939) and directed the future president of the United States in *Kings Row* in 1942, was another of Thalberg's favourites. Edgar Selwyn, master of soggy melodrama, who directed such films as *Night Life of New York*, *The Girl in the Show*, *War Nurse*, *The Sin of Madelon Claudet*, *Turn Back the Clock* and *The Mystery of Mr. X*, is additional evidence of Thalberg's range of interests, as was Tod Browning, who made his name directing early masterpieces of the cinema's gothic horrors: *The Unholy Three*, *London After Midnight*, *Dracula* and *Freaks*.[3] A director whose talents and inclinations might have seemed the most suited to Thalberg's taste was Clarence Brown, who specialized in rather fussy period subjects—*The Last of the Mohicans*, *Anna Christie*, *Anna Karenina*—but who showed a very sure touch in such dramas as *Goosewoman* (1925), which is still considered a picture of immense stature and authority and contains a brilliant performance by Marie Dressier as a retired opera singer who unwittingly implicates her own son in a murder case. Irving Thalberg seemed able to work harmoniously with these versatile creative talents.

But as well as exercising his diplomacy in dealing with these lofty persons, he could also deal with minute details of finance, committee work, casting, preparing and supervising scripts, conferring with his team of writers and resolving the numerous minor and not so minor industrial disputes between personnel during day-to-day production activities. All this was done with little external sign of anxiety or neurosis. He briefly developed one irritating habit which was soon cured. His therapeutic rolling of a twenty-dollar gold coin on his desk top during discussions was immediately cured by ridiculous satirical imitation by his colleagues.

Notoriously, Thalberg's day did not end at 5 p.m. The day's toiling over, the bargains all struck (J. B. Priestley wanted $50,000 for *The Good Companions*—Thalberg got it off him for half the price), Irving Thalberg drove back to his mansion at Santa Monica overlooking the Pacific Ocean where he pored over scripts and watched Metro-Goldwyn-Mayer movies in his sitting room. He lived and died for the movies and nothing else seemed to interest him very much. He was married to Norma Shearer, star of *The Barretts of Wimpole Street* and *Romeo and Juliet*. His dying words seem humdrum enough: 'Don't let the children forget me.' But we shall not look on his like again. As Gene Fowler remarked: 'On the way down, I saw Thalberg's shoes in the hall, and no one has filled them.'

The remarkable thing about his treatment at the hands of Scott Fitzgerald in *The Last Tycoon* is the fact that very little of this is captured at all in the character of Monroe Stahr. What Fitzgerald preferred to do was to focus exclusively on just one or two aspects of Thalberg's character as far as it was revealed in his professional life and to work these facets up into very high definition. His identification of these particular aspects of Thalberg's personality, considering that he knew the Hollywood tycoon personally and professionally, tells us a great deal about Fitzgerald, even though the book may in fact do less than justice to Irving Thalberg.

3

The Last Tycoon is not a thinly disguised biography of Irving Thalberg. Although it deals with a leading figure in the motion picture industry, it is not even really about films. To read *The Last Tycoon* properly we must be careful not to mistake the evidence, impressive and convincing though much of it is, for the case Fitzgerald wanted to present. This fragment may only partially be described as 'his unfinished novel of Hollywood'.[4] For this mistaken emphasis, among several other things, we have Edmund Wilson to thank.[5] It is certainly the case that we are led into the novel's major themes

by means of constant references to an omnipresent Hollywood right from
the start:

> Though I haven't ever been on the screen I was brought up in
> pictures. Rudolph Valentino came to my fifth birthday party—or
> so I was told. I put this down only to indicate that even before the
> age of reason I was in a position to watch the wheels go round.
>
> I was going to write my memoirs once, *The Producer's Daughter*,
> but at eighteen you never quite get round to anything like that.
> It's just as well—it would have been as flat as an old column of
> Lolly Parsons'. My father was in the picture business as another
> man might be in cotton or steel ... I accepted Hollywood with the
> resignation of a ghost assigned to a haunted house. I knew what
> you were supposed to think about it but I was obstinately
> unhorrified.[6]

Thus (and more) Cecilia Brady, college educated daughter of Monroe Stahr's
partner in Hollywood. At the opening of the book we are given the
traditional stereotypical view of the Hollywood producer. It is significantly
embedded in an anecdote of Wylie White's:

> Listen, Cecilia: I once had an affair with the wife of a producer.
> A very short affair. When it was over she said to me in no
> uncertain terms, she said: 'Don't you ever tell about this or I'll
> have you thrown out of Hollywood. My husband's a much more
> important man than you!'[7]

We cannot help but contrast this with the first impression of Monroe
Stahr we are given only a few pages on. He is not presented as a money-mad
mogul, crazy with his own power, but as a man with an almost magnetically
spiritual quality about him. Cecilia falls over him accidentally, but there is a
symbolic dimension here. She would easily fall for him. He was a man, she
says, that any girl would go for with no encouragement at all. They would
not be able to help it. They would be drawn to him. As his dark eyes look at
her she wonders what they would look like if he was to fall in love:

> They were kind, aloof and, though they often reasoned with you
> gently, somewhat superior. It was no fault of theirs if they saw so
> much. He darted in and out of the rôle of 'one of the boys' with
> dexterity—but on the whole I should say he wasn't one of them.

But he knew how to shut up, how to draw into the background, how to listen. From where he stood (and though he was not a tall man, it always seemed high up) he watched the multitudinous practicalities of his world like a proud young shepherd to whom night and day had never mattered....[8]

Stahr is a mysterious figure. Initially he hides himself behind the mundane name 'Smith', but this only temporarily masks his star quality. Fitzgerald is at pains when introducing him to stress his superior attributes: he seems tall, even though he may not be; he has dark, mysterious eyes; qualities of gentle superiority are emphasized; he is in the world, yet not really part of it as he watches the multitudinous practicalities proudly like a shepherd. He has a god-like indifference to night and day as he seems removed from the passing of time which affects other mortals. As he twists the ring on his finger it seems to have a magical effect on Cecilia, who comes to believe that she has been rendered invisible. She can barely summon the power to address so charged a being: 'I never dared look quite away from him or quite *at* him ... and I knew he affected many other people in the same manner.'[9]

His figure is a strange combination of the ethereal and the pugnacious. She reflects how the bulky ring on his finger contrasts with his delicate fingers and slender body. He has a slender face and arched eyebrows. His hair is dark and curly:

> He looked spiritual at times, but he was a fighter—somebody out of his past knew him when he was one of a gang of kids in the Bronx, and gave me a description of how he walked always at the head of his gang, this rather frail boy, occasionally throwing a command backward out of the corner of his mouth.[10]

Monroe Stahr is a Prince, an aristocrat among robber barons and warlords. He seems to stand for a particular set of values which include personal courage, skills and expertise, professionalism and ambition combined, but buffed and polished with sophistication, delicacy and refinement. He has all the American virtues, but they are refined to an almost aristocratic essence. But there is a very important element in this aristocratic personality as presented in Scott Fitzgerald's hero: he is not a patron of the arts, he is a creative person. This seems to interest Fitzgerald very much in his portrait of the last tycoon. Yes, it is undeniable that Stahr works for the motion picture industry, whose job it is to provide entertainment for the masses, but he is emphatically not presented to us merely as an executive of the industry. He is a man who expresses the essence of himself in what he does: he is an artist. Much of the essential Monroe Stahr is revealed in his relationship with the writer, George Boxley. This is particularly true of the scene where Stahr explains to Boxley how films tell stories and indicates that film is not a narrative medium which apes printed literature; it is a language of its own, with its own vocabulary, grammar and syntax, *its own way of telling you things*.

Significantly, Boxley is British, with all the associations of history, tradition and an old-fashioned way of doing things which far too many Americans mistake automatically for 'class' and 'quality'. Typically, Boxley the novelist tends to despise the modern means of cultural production which feeds him and pays his mortgage and his other living expenses. Boxley feels that he is the victim of a conspiracy, that the 'hacks' who work with him on film scripting have a vocabulary of a mere few hundred words. Stahr tells him that the trouble with what he writes is that it is not appropriate to the medium he is writing for: 'it was just talk, back and forth ... Interesting talk but nothing more.'

Boxley finds this insulting. How dare this American film executive, this example of the senior management whose concern is the proper control of finance and budgeting, tell him, the established British novelist, how to write?

> I don't think you people read things. The men are duelling when
> the conversation takes place. At the end one of them falls into a
> well and has to be hauled up in a bucket.[11]

Monroe Stahr rightly perceives that Boxley would consider writing for the movies cheap and vulgar, something beneath his real dignity as a *writer*. Part of the trouble is that Boxley himself does not even go to the movies. Why does he feel that about the movies? Because people are always duelling and falling down wells 'and wearing strange facial expressions and talking incredible and unnatural dialogue'. But Stahr has brought Boxley to Hollywood because he wants his films to be properly written. He is employing him as a professional writer, but he must not be so proud as to feel superior to the very matter he is expected to write:

> Slip the dialogue for a minute.... Granted your dialogue is more
> graceful than what these hacks can write—that's why we brought
> you out here. But let's imagine something that isn't either bad

dialogue or jumping down a well. Has your office got a stove in it that lights with a match?

Boxley seems to think that it has, but he never uses it. Never mind, says Stahr, imagine that you are in your office:

> You've been fighting duels or writing all day and you're too tired to fight or write any more. You're sitting there staring—dull, like we all get sometimes. A pretty stenographer that you've seen before comes into the room and you watch her—idly. She doesn't see you, though you're very close to her. She takes off her gloves, opens her purse and dumps it out on a table—.[12]

Stahr stands up and tosses his key-ring on the desk. Boxley listens as he goes on:

> She has two dimes and a nickel—and a cardboard matchbox. She leaves the nickel on the desk, puts the two dimes back into her purse and takes her black gloves to the stove, opens it and puts them inside. There is one match in the matchbox and she starts to light it kneeling by the stove. You notice that there's a stiff wind blowing in the window—but just then your telephone rings. The girl picks it up, says hello—listens—and says deliberately into the phone, 'I've never owned a pair of black gloves in my life.' She hangs up, kneels by the stove again, and just as she lights the match, you glance around very suddenly and see that there's another man in the office, watching every move the girl makes—[13]

Here Monroe Stahr pauses again, and picks up his keys and puts them in his pocket. Boxley is really interested now and asks what happens next? Stahr replies: 'I don't know ... I was just making pictures.' Boxley then attempts to indicate that he was not really interested, merely curious. It was just 'melodrama' he says. Stahr replies:

> Not necessarily ... In any case, nobody has moved violently or talked cheap dialogue or had any facial expression at all. There was only one bad line, and a writer like you could improve it. But you were interested.[14]

This is a key moment in Fitzgerald's portrait of Stahr. It gives Stahr the artist, the creator, the man who makes things. It is of overriding importance to grasp this point as it is vital in the character construction of the leading figure in *The Last Tycoon*, and the novelist's investigation of the value system he has undertaken depends wholly on the use he makes of particular qualities selected from his observations of 'the boy wonder'— Irving Thalberg. Monroe Stahr is a man who is clearly aware that in his daily work as a man who wants to make motion pictures of quality for the mass market which depends on the Hollywood studio system, he must negotiate the best relationship he can between the creative and the productive elements of the industry. Fitzgerald establishes this as a central problem for Monroe Stahr, as it was to him and as it was to Shakespeare, and Dickens and Trollope and D. H. Lawrence and the entire host of imaginative and sensitive and insightful storytellers before Scott Fitzgerald's time.

The writer—like the film maker—is immediately faced in modern times with a complex of relationships between himself and what he wants to tell the world (the stuff of literature) and the means of literary production— economic, technical, cultural and social—which have to be resolved as harmoniously as possible. No modern writer is able directly to address his audience. Monroe Stahr, the great film tycoon, stands emblematically for the figure of the storyteller in his relationship with the means of production and distribution on which the survival of literature depends. The strength and fascination of Fitzgerald's Monroe Stahr is the result not of his having based him on Irving Thalberg whom he knew in Hollywood, etc., etc. but in what Stahr stands for. This conversation with George Boxley brilliantly demonstrates Stahr's understanding of how manmade art works on the imagination. But he also understands, as a later discussion with Boxley shows, how important is the relationship between the artist and the means of production. These matters cannot be left to chance. The artist must understand them if he is fully to realize himself as an artist. It is no good feeling superior to them. The economics and the technology of artistic production are as important as the creative and imaginative aspects of art. In the greatest art, they become one and the same thing, and the greatest writers understand this—to the positive advantage of their development as artists in realizing the potential of the means to communicate what they have to say.[15]

Monroe Stahr puts this case to Boxley in the hope that the novelist will understand what motion pictures can do: suppose you were in a chemist's shop, buying medicine for a relative who was very ill, then whatever caught your attention through the window and distracted you would be material for pictures. Such as a murder outside the window, asks Boxley. Stahr implies that in motion pictures there is not always the necessity to pile into melodrama at the first possible opportunity. It might be a spider, working on the pane:

> 'Of course—I see.'
>
> 'I'm afraid you don't, Mr. Boxley. You see it for *your* medium, but not for ours. You keep the spiders for yourself and you try to pin the murders on us.'
>
> 'I might as well leave,' said Boxley. 'I'm no good to you. I've been here three weeks and I've accomplished nothing. I make suggestions, but no one writes them down.'
>
> 'I want you to stay. Something in you doesn't like pictures, doesn't like telling a story this way—'
>
> 'It's such a damn bother,' exploded Boxley. 'You can't let yourself go—'[16]

As he speaks, Boxley realizes that Stahr was a helmsman with many matters to take into account in steering a true course. He senses the stiff wind that must be sensibly battled against and the creaking of the rigging of a ship sailing in great awkward tacks along an open sea. Another analogy Fitzgerald uses is the feeling Boxley has that they are in a huge quarry where even the newly cut marble bears the tracery of old pediments and half-obliterated inscriptions from the past:

> 'I keep wishing you could start over,' Boxley said. 'It's this mass production.'
>
> 'That's the condition,' said Stahr. 'There's always some lousy condition. We're making a life of Rubens—suppose I asked you to do portraits of rich dopes like Billy Brady and me and Gary Cooper ... when you wanted to paint Jesus Christ! Wouldn't you feel you had a condition? Our condition is that we have to take people's own favourite folklore and dress it up and give it back to them. Anything beyond that is sugar. So won't you give us some sugar, Mr. Boxley?'[17]

This seems to me a very good summing up of the assumptions Irving Thalberg had about the motion picture industry. He once said: 'The medium will eventually take its place as art because there is no other medium of interest to so many people.'[18] These are qualities of an ideal nature which Fitzgerald strongly indicates in his portrait of Monroe Stahr, and make him at once a powerful and vigorous figure, yet one prone to destruction. It is important to note the symbolic use Fitzgerald makes of leading figures taken from American history in this novel as well as in others—*Tender is the Night*, for example, with its echoes of Ulysses Grant.[19]

Fitzgerald was considerably influenced by his reading of the historical works of Henry Adams (1838–1918) whom the novelist knew personally. Adams was educated at Harvard and studied law in Germany. He taught history at Harvard for a time and published *The History of the United States During the Administration of Thomas Jefferson and James Madison* (1889–91). In much the same way as another major American writer—T. S. Eliot—Adams found modern times disturbing and believed civilization was about to disintegrate. Like Eliot he, too, looked to the Middle Ages for that harmony and permanence he found lacking in the twentieth century. This is the essential theme of Adams's *Mont-Saint-Michel and Chartres* (1904). General Grant was Adams's hope for maintaining liberalism, virtue and humanism in modern America. Grant was elected president, Adams believed, because he stood for moral order against the rising tide of greed, mammonism and anarchy. Adams came to see in Grant's two terms of office—1868–72 and 1872–76—a surrender of moral and political virtue to those very forces of materialism and corruption that he so feared would destroy the American nation. It is of considerable significance that Fitzgerald compares Dick Diver to Grant, and shows that he, like Adams's failed hero, succumbed to temptation when he found himself surrounded with the wealthy and socially distinguished. Like Grant, Diver is a dreamer destroyed by realities which he is too frail to combat.[20] In the character of Monroe Stahr Fitzgerald again draws on American history to provide symbolic texture to his themes.

4

Two other outstanding figures from the nation's history in this respect add conspicuous gravity to the thematic structure of *The Last Tycoon*: Andrew Jackson and Abraham Lincoln. Jackson is introduced quite early in the book as the group of ill-assorted characters stranded by transport problems go to visit the home of Old Hickory. In the zappy words of Wylie White:

> Just in time ... The tour is just starting. Home of Old Hickory—
> America's tenth president. The victor of New Orleans, opponent
> of the National Bank, and inventor of the Spoils System.

Making allowances for the Hollywood scriptwriter's shorthand this does summarize the values and associations of Andrew Jackson (1767–1845).

Jackson was, in fact, the seventh president, but in essence the career given here does embody the major features of his folkloric reputation. Andrew Jackson fought in the War of Independence and was captured by the British. He helped to frame the constitution of Tennessee and represented the state in Congress in 1796 and in the Senate in 1797. He was a judge of the supreme court of Tennessee.

He became a national hero during the 1812 war with the British after a series of brilliant victories against the Indians and defeating Sir Edward Michael Pakenham's army of 16,000 veterans at New Orleans. Jackson was governor of Florida and ran for the presidency in 1825 as a Democrat against John Quincy Adams, W. H. Crawford and Henry Clay. Jackson had the highest number of popular votes but not a majority. In 1828 he was elected with a majority of electoral votes. The strength of Jackson's image in popular history is to be located in the values he stood for: he was a genuine self-made man, a product of the socioeconomic and political philosophy on which the United States was founded, he was courageous and he was a man of principle.

He was re-elected in 1832. To get things done he swept great numbers of officials from office and replaced them with his own partisans, coining the phrase, 'To the victor belong the spoils', to cover these actions. But it meant that he got things done. In spite of the censure of the Senate he broke the power of the Bank of the United States, asserting that it had too much power and was a corrupting element in American political life. During his second administration the national debt was fully paid and the surplus was distributed to the several states of the union. He retired at the end of his second term and died at his house, the Hermitage, Nashville, Tennessee. In *The Last Tycoon* the stranded party look at Jackson's house:

> It was still not quite dawn. The Hermitage looked like a nice big white box, but quite a little lonely and vacated after a hundred years. We walked back to the car....[21]

One member of the party considers that even if people do not know much about Jackson or why he is important in American history, there must be something significant about him, if they have preserved his house all these years, and that Jackson must have been 'some one who was large and merciful, able to understand'. At both ends of life man needed nourishment: 'a breast—a shrine'. Significantly the visiting party are unable to gain access to the Hermitage, the house is locked. It is as if the values Jackson stood for are no longer available to these representatives of a more rapacious America in the twentieth century.

Monroe Stahr is directly associated with Abraham Lincoln. It is George Boxley who recognizes:

> that Stahr like Lincoln was a leader carrying on a long war on many fronts; almost single-handed he had moved pictures sharply forward through a decade, to a point where the content of the 'A productions' was wider and richer than that of the stage. Stahr was an artist only, as Mr. Lincoln was a general, perforce and as a layman.[22]

There is another important reference to Lincoln, seen through the eyes of a distinguished visitor to the studios, the Danish Prince Agge, who is described in Scott Fitzgerald's list of characters as an 'early Fascist'.[23] Agge obviously believes in the superiority of some races to others:

> He was hostile to Jews in a vague general way that he tried to cure himself of. As a turbulent man, serving his time in the Foreign Legion, he thought that Jews were too fond of their own skins. But he was willing to concede that they might be different in America under different circumstances....[24]

But the panoramic view he gets of the crowded film studios is like the Melting Pot of Nations itself.

> Coming out of the private dining room, they passed through a corner of the commissary proper. Prince Agge drank it ineagerly. It was gay with gipsies and with citizens and soldiers, with sideburns and braided coats of the First Empire. From a little distance they were men who lived and walked a hundred years ago, and Agge wondered how he and the men of his time would look as extras in some future costume picture.
> Then he saw Abraham Lincoln, and his whole feeling suddenly changed. He had been brought up in the dawn of Scandinavian socialism when Nicolay's biography was much read. He had been told Lincoln was a great man whom he should admire, and he hated him instead, because he was forced upon him....[25]

But now that he sees Lincoln before him he cannot help staring at him. The actor sits there, with his legs crossed, his kindly face fixed on his forty-cent dinner, 'including dessert', with a shawl wrapped round his shoulders to protect himself from the erratic air-conditioning: 'This then, was Lincoln....' Agge realizes that this is what they all meant to be. Much to his surprise this glimpse into the inner meaning of things in this new society, this man-made nation, is shattered as the living presence from the past of American history, the great and good Abraham Lincoln, father of the new nation state, unexpectedly raises his hand and stuffs a triangle of pie into his mouth. In the United States the extraordinary and the ordinary are all mixed up together, and the best and the brightest can be seen rising from humble origins and at the same time reasserting absolute ordinariness; the historic and the humdrum are one and the same. It is the dynamic of this society which has created Monroe Stahr, and as Fitzgerald's plans for *The Last Tycoon* survive to indicate, it was these same forces which would threaten and destroy him.[26]

5

As Charles E. Shain opines, *The Last Tycoon* has the mark of the '30s on it as surely as the early fictions had taken the American boom as their theme: 'The subject was Hollywood as an industry and as a society, but also as an American microcosm.'[27] But there is mercifully more to it than that. *The Last Tycoon* is an impressive and moving fragment, not just because it is a faithful portrait of the motion picture industry at a particular period of its development—to say that is to mistake the Hollywood for the trees—but because Fitzgerald convincingly uses this material to explore some of his driving interest in the creative processes and their relationship with industry and mass society. As a creative artist himself he could not fail to be interested in the compromise and negotiation which must take place between the various stages of the processes between ideas and conception, on the one hand, and production and consumption on the other. Had he lived to finish it, our impression of *The Last Tycoon* might well be gloomier. As it stands it remains a brilliant and dazzling achievement. The novel was filmed in 1976 with Robert de Niro as Monroe Stahr. It was not a very good movie, but its weaknesses are significant. It saw itself as part of a particularly strong tradition in film-making—the movie about movie-making, sardonically lifting the lid on the whole business. This line stretches back from *Sunset Boulevard* in 1950, through *The Star*, *The Barefoot Contessa*, *Hollywood Boulevard*, the various versions of *A Star Is Born*, *The Day of the Locust* and *The Carpetbaggers*. Its period detail was excellent, and the recreation of the industry's technology and management was impressive. But its focus was awry. It was like a bad cake made with the best ingredients. *The Last Tycoon* is not about films. It is about art. Scott Fitzgerald wrote in his notebook:

'There never was a good biography of a good novelist. There couldn't be. He's too many people if he's any good.'[28] But *The Last Tycoon* is very nearly a great novel about a maker, unfinished as indeed it is.

NOTES

1. Arthur Mizener, *Introduction, F. Scott Fitzgerald. A Collection of Critical Essays* (New Jersey: Prentice-Hall, 1963), pp. 3–4.

2. Mai D. Hueling, 'Fortune-Metro-Goldwyn-Mayer', in Tino Balio (ed.), *The American Film Industry* (Madison, Wisconsin: University of Wisconsin Press, 1976), p. 259.

3. *Freaks* was completed in 1932 but was withheld from public showing by censorship for thirty years. It is a circus melodrama featuring genuine freaks. An odd movie to have been sponsored by the fastidious Irving Thalberg.

4. Marcus Cunliffe, *The Literature of the United States* (Harmondsworth: Penguin, 1968), p. 292.

5. For a discussion of *The Last Tycoon* as 'Hollywood novel' see Arthur Mizener, 'The Maturity of Scott Fitzgerald', in the *Sewanee Review*, LXVII (Autumn 1959), 658 ff.

6. F. Scott Fitzgerald, *The Last Tycoon*, in *The Bodley Head Scott FitZgerald* (London: Bodley Head, 1966), Vol. 1, 167.

7. *The Last Tycoon*, ibid., p. 175.

8. Ibid., p. 180.

9. Ibid., p. 180.

10. Ibid., p. 181.

11. Ibid., pp. 197–98.

12. Ibid., p. 198.

13. Ibid., p. 198–99.

14. Ibid., p. 199. This is, in fact, an excellent account of how stories are told in pictures, and suggests that F. Scott Fitzgerald learned much from his days in Hollywood— cf James Monaco: *How to Read a Film: The Art, Technology, History and Theory of Film and Media* (New York: Oxford University Press, 1981), pp. 125 ff; J. Dudley Andrew, *The Major Film Theories* (New York: Oxford University Press, 1976), pp. 220 ff.; Robert Scholes's essay 'Narration and Narrativity in Film' in Gerald Mast and Marshall Cohen (eds.), *Film Theory and Criticism: Introductory Readings* (New York: Oxford University Press, 1979), pp. 417–33, and Robert Richardson, *Literature and Film* (Bloomington, Indiana: University of Indiana Press, 1969), pp. 65 ff.

15. An obvious example would be Dickens, who seized the opportunities of reaching a growing readership by means of serial publication. *Bleak House, Great Expectations* and *Our Mutual Friend* are not masterpieces in spite of the mass production of literature in mid-Victorian Britain; they are masterpieces because of the means of production available to Dickens at that time.

16. F. Scott Fitzgerald, *The Last Tycoon*, op. cit., pp. 277–78.

17. Ibid., p. 278.

18. Quoted in John Robert Columbo (ed.), *Wit and Wisdom of the Moviemakers* (London: Hamlyn, 1979), p. 116.

19. C. W. E. Bigsby, 'The Two Identities of F. Scott Fitzgerald' in Malcolm Bradbury and David Palmer (eds.), *The American Novel and the Nineteen Twenties* (London: Edward Arnold, 1971), pp. 142 ff.

20. The case is persuasively argued by C. W. E. Bigsby, see 'The Two Identities of F. Scott Fitzgerald', ibid., pp. 14 ff.

21. *The Last Tycoon*, op. cit., p. 178.

22. *The Last Tycoon*, ibid., pp. 278–79.

23. Ibid., p. 211.

24. Ibid., p. 213.

25. Ibid., pp. 216–17.

26. Ibid., pp. 303–8.

27. Charles E. Shain, 'F. Scott Fitzgerald', in *Seven Modern American Novelists: An Introduction*, edited by William Van O'Connor (Minneapolis: University of Minnesota Press, 1964), p. 116.

28. Quoted in *The Bodley Head Scott Fitzgerald*, op. cit., p. 7.

JOHN F. CALLAHAN

F. Scott Fitzgerald's Evolving American Dream: The "Pursuit of Happiness" in Gatsby, Tender is the Night, and The Last Tycoon

Since the first stirrings of the F. Scott Fitzgerald revival in the 1940s, readers have been fascinated by the oppositions in his work and character. Critics from several different generations have noted how Fitzgerald used his conflicts to explore the origins and fate of the American dream and the related idea of the nation.[1] The contradictions he experienced and put into fiction heighten the implications of the dream for individual lives: the promise and possibilities, violations and corruptions of those ideals of nationhood and personality "dreamed into being," as Ralph Ellison phrased it, "out of the chaos and darkness of the feudal past."[2] Fitzgerald embodied in his tissues and nervous system the fluid polarities of American experience: success and failure, illusion and disillusion, dream and nightmare.

"I did not care what it was all about," Hemingway's Jake Barnes confessed in *The Sun Also Rises*. "All I wanted to know was how to live in it."[3] Fitzgerald, who named and chronicled that brash, schizophrenic decade, was no stranger to the dissipation of values and the pursuit of sensation in the Jazz Age of the 1920s. But for all that, he strained to know what life is all about *and* how to live in it. To him, Hemingway's it was not simply existence and the soul's dark night of melancholia and despair. It also stood for an American reality that, combined with "an extraordinary gift for hope" and a "romantic readiness,"[4] led to the extravagant promise identified with

From *Twentieth Century Literature* Vol 42, No. 3 (Autumn, 1996), pp. 374–395. © 1980 Hofstra University.

America and the intense, devastating loss felt when the dream fails in one or another of its guises.

Face to face with his own breakdown, Fitzgerald traced his drastic change of mind and mood in his letters and *Crack-Up* pieces. From the conviction during his amazing early success in his 20s that "life was something you dominated if you were any good,"[5] Fitzgerald, at the end of his life, came to embrace "the sense that life is essentially a cheat and its conditions are those of defeat, and that the redeeming things are not 'happiness and pleasure' but the deeper satisfactions that come out of struggle."[6] Abraham Lincoln was Fitzgerald's American exemplar of this "wise and tragic sense of life" (Turnbull, *Letters* [*L*] 96). And in *The Last Tycoon* (*LT*) he associates Monroe Stahr's commitment to lead the movie industry closer to an ideal mix of art and entertainment with Lincoln's creative response to the contradictions of American democracy embodied in the Union.

Fitzgerald's invocation of Lincoln recalls the proud and humble claim he made to his daughter from Hollywood. "I don't drink," he wrote; then, as if freed from a demon's grasp, he recounted the inner civil war he fought to keep his writer's gift intact: "I am not a great man, but sometimes I think the impersonal and objective quality of my talent and the sacrifices of it, in pieces, to preserve its essential value have some sort of epic grandeur." "Some sort" he qualifies, as it! preparing for the ironic, self-deflating admission in the next sentence. "Anyhow after hours I nurse myself with delusions of that sort" (*L* 62, 61). But Fitzgerald did preserve the "essential value" of his talent; the pages he left confirm that. Like Lincoln who lived only long enough to sketch out what a truly reconstructed nation might look like, Fitzgerald was defeated in his attempt to finish his last novel. Yet what he wrote is all the more poignant because, finished, *The Last Tycoon* might have recast and reformulated the intractable oppositions of *The Great Gatsby* and *Tender Is the Night*.

"The test of a first rate intelligence," Fitzgerald wrote in *The Crack-Up* (Wilson, *CU*), that posthumous collection full of his sinewy, mature, self-reliant thought, "is the ability to hold two opposed ideas in the mind at the same time and still retain the ability to function" (*CU* 69). By function, Fitzgerald means more than cope; he's affirming that readiness to act in the world with something approaching one's full powers—"a willingness of the heart" combined with enabling critical intelligence. Fitzgerald's fictional alter egos, Jay Gatsby and Dick Diver, lost this stance of simultaneous detachment and engagement, if they ever possessed it, for they could live in the world only with a single, consuming mission. In his life, Fitzgerald, too, had to steel himself against the tendency toward Gatsby's self-destroying romantic obsession, and like Diver, he had to wrench free from the opposed, complimentary shoals of identification and alienation in his marriage with Zelda.

After *Tender Is the Night* and before his fresh start in Hollywood in 1937, Fitzgerald reflected on his earlier search for an equilibrium of craft, reputation, and power as expressed in the literary vocation and his large personal ambition. "It seemed," he remembered,

> a romantic business to be a successful literary man—you were not ever going to be as famous as a movie star but what note you had was probably longer-lived—you were never going to have the power of a man of strong political or religious convictions but you were certainly more independent.

To the end, like the vivid, still-evolving Monroe Stahr in *The Last Tycoon*, Fitzgerald stays in motion, keeps the dialectic between life and craft going, if not to resolution—"Of course within the practice of your trade you were forever unsatisfied" (*CU* 69–70)—at least in pursuit of new and unrealized novelistic possibilities. "But I, for one, would not have chosen any other" (*CU* 69–70), he concludes, and keeps faith with his vocation by writing about craft and character in the life of a gifted movie man, whose form Fitzgerald feared might subordinate the novel, "which at my maturity was the strongest and supplest medium for conveying thought and emotion from one human being to another," to "a mechanical and communal art that, whether in the hands of Hollywood merchants or Russian idealists, was capable of rendering only the tritest thought, the most obvious emotion" (*CU* 78).

Meeting Irving Thalberg, Fitzgerald becomes more open to the craft of the movies as practiced in Hollywood. Like Fitzgerald the novelist, Monroe Stahr produces movies, not opportunistically (for the most part) but from within. There is a fluidity to Fitzgerald's conception of Stahr missing from Gatsby and his dream, so ill defined in its worldly guise, so obsessive and absolute in its fixation on Daisy; and missing also from the aspiring hubris of Dick Diver, trapped by his misguided, innocent mingling of love and vocation in his dream of personality in *Tender Is the Night*. Stahr, like the writer who created him, learns that daring to function can be a first step toward loosening the paralyzing grip of "opposed ideas."

Fitzgerald's characters, like the seismograph alluded to in *Gatsby*, register changes in his sensibility. Not that Monroe Stahr is Fitzgerald; like the others, he is a composite character. "There never was a good biography of a good novelist," Fitzgerald wrote in his notebook. "He's too many people if he's any good." Nevertheless, Fitzgerald put into Stahr's character much of the awareness he came to have in the melancholy troubled years after *Tender Is the Night*. "Life, ten years ago," he wrote in 1936, "was largely a personal matter." Without telling how that's changed but making it clear that it has, Fitzgerald confronted his present imperative:

> I must hold in balance the sense of the futility of effort and the sense of the necessity to struggle; the conviction of the inevitability of failure and the determination to "succeed"—and, more than these, the contradiction between the dead hand of the past and the high intentions of the future. (*CU* 177, 70)

To be sure, Fitzgerald did not always hold these contradictions of mind and will, memory and imagination, in equilibrium. But increasingly, as he worked on *The Last Tycoon* during his last year and a half in Hollywood, he sensed a progression from his earlier novels—enough that he strove to set a standard mingling intelligence with "a willingness of the heart." Intelligence identifies and holds in suspension "opposed ideas," but the "ability to function" in the midst of what Keats called "uncertainties, mysteries, doubts"[7] follows from that "willingness of the heart" Fitzgerald identified as a peculiarly intense American urge to do something about one's condition, to take risks for a better self, a better life, a better nation. "For example," Fitzgerald wrote, illustrating his embrace of contradiction, "one ought to be able to see that things are hopeless and still be determined to make them otherwise" (*CU* 64). So he was. And as a writer, until the end of his life, Fitzgerald linked his pursuit of craft and personality, if not any longer simply happiness—"the natural state of the sentient adult is a qualified unhappiness" (*CU* 84)—with the unfolding story of America.

Perhaps because of Fitzgerald's struggles and his paradoxical, sometimes exhilarated serenity alongside the pain and loss reflected in the diminishing hourglass of his life, in *The Last Tycoon* he was able at least to break the stalemate between previously opposed ideas. For this reason, Fitzgerald's passing before he could finish *The Last Tycoon* is an incalculable loss, only to be guessed at from the drafts he left, however much in progress, and his rich, copious notes, charts, and outlines. With Hollywood as milieu and the producer Stahr as protagonist, the American dream becomes even more identified with the urge to integrate private and public pursuits of happiness than in Fitzgerald's other novels.

In *The Last Tycoon* Fitzgerald does for the American dream what Ralph Ellison argues every serious novel does for the craft of fiction. Even as a fragment, the work extends the range of idea and phenomena associated with the dream. As a man and a writer, he became at home in that country of discipline and craft he had discovered but, later lamented, did not truly settle down in until it was too late. As he wrote to his daughter Scottie, a student and aspiring writer at Vassar, I wish I'd said "at the end of *The Great Gatsby*: 'I've found my line—from now on this comes first. This is my immediate duty—without this I am nothing'" (*L* 79). In 1939 and 1940, *The Last Tycoon* did come first. But burdened with expenses, lacking the quick, lucrative *Saturday Evening Post* markets of his youth, lacking in any case the "romantic readiness" to write stories with happy endings, and in sporadic, failing health, Fitzgerald had to balance his novel with other work, and eke it out in pieces. Nevertheless, he ended up a writer's writer. From that single window, he looked beyond his circumstances and saw the American dream not as a personal matter and no longer a nostalgic, romantic possibility but as a continuing defining characteristic of the American nation and its people. Far from being behind him, as Nick Carraway had claimed in *The Great Gatsby*, the dream, refigured in *The Last Tycoon*, is a recurring phenomenon in each phase, place, and guise of Fitzgerald's imagination of American experience.

The American story, Fitzgerald wrote late in life, "is the history of all aspiration—not just the American dream but the human dream...."[8] The story that Fitzgerald told was his version of a dream hauntingly personal and national. "When I was your age," he wrote his daughter in 1938, "I lived with a great dream. The dream grew and I learned how to speak of it and make people listen." Like Keats, who, Fitzgerald imagined, was sustained to the end by his "hope of being among the English poets" (*CU* 81), Fitzgerald aspired to be among the novelists. But, as he confessed to his daughter in a bone-scraping passage, he compromised his artist's dream by indulging the very thing that inspired it—romantic love. Of his marriage to Zelda, he wrote in retrospect, "I was a man divided—she wanted me to work too much for her and not enough for my dream" (*L* 32). The imbalance Fitzgerald attributed to Zelda was also his own tension and tendency. Nevertheless, what gave his life and work such fascination was exactly that dream of mingling craft and accomplishment with love—first with Zelda, and at the end in more muted fashion with Sheilah Graham, his companion in Hollywood.

In its American guise, the dream Fitzgerald sought to realize flowed from that most elusive and original of the rights proclaimed by the

Declaration of Independence. Framed as an "unalienable" right by Thomas Jefferson and espoused by the other founders of this revolutionary nation, the "pursuit of happiness" magnified the American dream into an abiding, almost sacred promise. Going back to that scripture of nationhood, it is striking to note that although Jefferson amended John Locke's "life, liberty, and property or estate" to "life, liberty, and the pursuit of happiness," neither he nor any other signatory explained or remarked in writing on the change. But naming the "pursuit of happiness" an unalienable right confirmed the newly declared American nation as an experimental, necessarily improvisational society dedicated to the principle that every human personality is sacred and inviolable. Yes, blacks, women, Native Americans, and even indentured servants were excluded, but excluded *then*, not forever. For as Lincoln was to imply in the Gettysburg Address, the Declaration's eloquent language strained toward the proposition that all persons were free, and, therefore, implicated in and responsible for the nation's destiny. And the idea and covenant of American citizenship required that all individuals make themselves up in the midst of the emerging new society. And the process of creation would be vernacular, arising from native ground, the weather, landscape, customs, habits, peoples, and values of this new world in the making.

That was and remains the promise of America. But, Fitzgerald's novels remind us, things were never this simple. And as the late Ralph Ellison, who seems closer and closer kin to Fitzgerald, put it, "a democracy more than any other system is always pregnant with its contradiction."[9] One such contradiction unresolved by the Declaration or the ensuing Constitution, and played out since in national experience and Fitzgerald's novels, is between property and the "pursuit of happiness." Certainly, as Eugene McCarthy has noted, the third unalienable right "undoubtedly included the right to pursue property as a form of happiness, or as 'a happiness.'"[10] For some the "pursuit of happiness" was simply a euphemism for property. Officially, the tension went unresolved and scarcely acknowledged until the 14th Amendment forbade the states to "deprive any person of life, liberty, or property, without due process of law." The less concrete, more elusive "pursuit of happiness" went unmentioned except by implication. Yet, for over 200 years, before and after passage of the 14th Amendment, Americans have sought to balance property's material reality with the imaginative possibilities hinted at in the phrase the "pursuit of happiness."

What if we were to read *Gatsby*, *Tender Is the Night*, and *The Last Tycoon* as projections of that sometime struggle, sometime alliance between property and the pursuit of happiness? As human impulses, property and the pursuit of happiness are sometimes contradictory, sometimes complementary metaphors for experience. Let property stand for the compulsion to divide the world and contain experience within fixed, arbitrary boundaries. And let the "pursuit of happiness" become imagination's embrace of the complexity, fluidity, and possibility open to human personality. In Jefferson's time, if not so strongly in Fitzgerald's or our own, the "pursuit of happiness" also implied individual responsibility for the "spirit of public happiness" that John Adams felt so strongly in the colonies, which he judged the American Revolution won almost before it began. Jefferson did not include the word *public*, but his phrase implies the individual's integration of desire with responsibility, self-fulfillment with the work of the world. In short, in this promissory initial American context, the pursuit of happiness was bound up with citizenship, and citizenship with each individual's responsibility for democracy.

The first thing to be said about Fitzgerald's novels is that these enactments of the American dream are expressed in the love affairs and worldly ambitions of Jay Gatsby, Dick Diver, and Monroe Stahr. In *The Great Gatsby* (*TGG*), *Tender Is the Night*, and *The Last Tycoon*, the matrix of the dream differs, but in each case, the hero is, like Fitzgerald, "a man divided," yet he seeks to integrate love of a woman with accomplishment in the world. Telling his story to Nick Carraway after he has lost Daisy Fay for the second and last time, Gatsby remembers that when he first met her, he felt like the latest plunderer in the line of Dan Cody, his metaphorical father, and a mythical figure who, in Fitzgerald's interpretation, "brought back to the Eastern seaboard the savage violence of the frontier brothel and saloon." Sensitive to the demarcations of background, money, and status, Gatsby

> knew he was in Daisy's house by a colossal accident. However glorious might be his future as Jay Gatsby, he was at present a penniless young man without a past, and at any moment the invisible cloak of his uniform might slip from his shoulders.

Meanwhile, "he had deliberately given Daisy a sense of security; he let her believe he was a person from much the same stratum as herself." Jay Gatsby pursues Daisy knowing that her sense of happiness and the good life depends on money and property. Nevertheless, "he took what he could get, ravenously and unscrupulously—eventually he took Daisy one still October night, took her because he had no real right to touch her hand" (*TGG* 76, 113). Ironically, Gatsby's lieutenant's uniform allows him proximity to Daisy simply as a man long enough to seduce her.

Until Gatsby makes love to Daisy, he projects little soul or feeling, only a self-absorbed passion mixed up with his urge to defy American boundaries of class, status, and money. The experience of love deeply moves and changes Gatsby, but so pervasive is the culture of material success that his new reverence and tenderness toward her are inseparable from money and possessions, and perhaps from Carraway's image of Daisy "gleaming like silver, safe and proud above the hot struggles of the poor"—Gatsby's struggles, maybe, as a boy and penniless young man in North Dakota and Minnesota. Earlier that same day in 1922, Gatsby calls Daisy's voice a voice "full of money." But his subsequent words to Carraway about that experience of love in wartime 1917, a time that obscured boundaries of class and background in favor of a seemingly all-powerful fluidity and equality, convey the mystery and tenderness of his earlier emotion. "I can't describe to you how surprised I was to find out I loved her, old sport," Gatsby tells Carraway in his sometimes too well-chosen words whose tone nonetheless carries a touch of wonder. "I even hoped for a while that she'd throw me over, but she didn't, because she was in love with me too." The more vividly Gatsby remembers, the more the tricks of his voice yield to the feeling underneath. "She thought I knew a lot because I knew different things from her.... Well, there I was, way off my ambitions, getting deeper in love every minute, and all of a sudden I didn't care" (*TGG* 114, 91, 114).

Gatsby discovers that Daisy loves him because of his different experience, not despite it as he feared. He surrenders his ambitions, as yet inchoate, unfocused, adolescent, to his intense feeling for Daisy. But their love is an interlude, happening "in the meantime, in between time." More vividly alive because of his love for Daisy, Gatsby "did extraordinarily well in the war," becoming a captain and, following the Argonne, a major given "command of the divisional machine guns" (*TGG* 72, 114). He emerges as a leader. Although his ambitions are vague, thinking of other American trajectories, a pioneering future in politics or in some other new venture, aviation, say, or advertising, might have awaited Gatsby if Daisy had stayed true to her love for him.

Instead, Daisy Fay turns fickle and self-indulgent. Desperate for Gatsby to return, impatient and petulant over his mistaken assignment to Oxford, she must have her life "shaped now, immediately—and the decision must be made by some force—of love, of money, of unquestionable practicality—that was close at hand" (*TGG* 115). Daisy's pursuit of happiness in the form of her dangerous, defiant love for Gatsby surrenders to the palpability of a safe, material, unequal propertied union with Tom Buchanan. Afterwards, on his forlorn lover's progress through the streets of Louisville,

Daisy's hometown and scene of their love, Gatsby understands: To win Daisy he gathers money and property, the latter transient and garish, in the quick and illegal ways open to him—Meyer Wolfsheim and the rackets. After another interval of love inspired by the possibilities of human personality— remember, Daisy sees Gatsby's possessions for the Horatio Alger emblems that they are and responds only to the passion, will, and tenderness that lie behind them—the struggle over Daisy (and, parabolically, America) is fought on the field of property. Whose money is solid wealth, whose possessions land, oil, and the like? And whose property stays in the same hands for generations?

In *Gatsby*, sooner or later human feelings are negotiated in relation to property or some other form of material reality subject to ownership. Gatsby's wonder of discovery, Daisy's magic of "bringing out a meaning in each word that it had never had before and would never have again" (*TGG* 82), these unanticipated, intense moments of experience recede before Tom Buchanan's relentless revelation of the shady transience of Gatsby's wealth. But perhaps Gatsby, too, gives Daisy little choice between two opposed fixed ideas. When Tom Buchanan forces a showdown with Gatsby at the Plaza Hotel, the two men turn Daisy into a prized possession to be fought over on the basis of social and economic conventions. In effect, Buchanan invokes the *droit du seigneur*. He is the lord, Gatsby the serf, Daisy the woman belonging to the vast American estate. Contending on that ground, Gatsby may well pay an emotional tithe to the poor boy from North Dakota, and again feel he has no right to touch Daisy's hand. In any case, the scene at the Plaza is an acrimonious "irritable reaching after fact or reason"[11] without love. Who can blame Daisy for withdrawing after her perspective goes unheard by both men? On this occasion, Gatsby is no more able than Buchanan to consider Daisy a woman in her own right, a unique and equal person whose voice has had the power to give the words she sings singular feeling and meaning. For each man, Daisy is a possession; for Buchanan material, for Gatsby ideal. So Daisy, the actual woman, the flawed and vulnerable human personality, flees. Held to no standard of decency or accountability by either man after her hit- and-run killing of Myrtle Wilson, she once again chooses the conventional, worldly protection of Tom Buchanan.

Gatsby's dream of love corroded to nightmare, the passion ebbs from his work, such as it is. And no wonder. His flimsy network of "gonnegtions" and sinister underworld deals in booze and bonds were all for love of Daisy. When she returns to Tom Buchanan and their leisure-class world, partly because of Gatsby's desperate bargain with the American underworld, and partly because of his narcissistic, romantic inability to comprehend her attachment to Buchanan, Gatsby is emptied of love and ambition alike. The heart and wonder are gone from him; there is no happiness to pursue. His time of love and "aesthetic contemplation" passed, Gatsby, Nick imagines, sees around him only a frightening physical landscape—"a new world, material without being real" (*TGG* 123), an American world bleaker and, for all its glut of accumulations, more insubstantial than the spare, monotonous prairie James Gatz started from in rural North Dakota. For all his romantic gifts of personality, lacking a discerning critical intelligence, Gatsby seems destined to have served that same "vast, vulgar meretricious [American] beauty" of which Dan Cody is the apotheosis (*TGG* 75).

"France was a land, England was a people, but America, having about it still that quality of the idea, was harder to utter." In this passage from "The Swimmers," a 1929 story later distilled into his *Notebooks*, Fitzgerald evokes the anguished intense patriotism he finds in American faces from Abraham Lincoln's to those of the "country boys dying in the Argonne for a phrase that was empty before their bodies withered" (*CU* 197). For Fitzgerald that American "quality of the idea" finds most worthy expression in the impulse to offer the best of yourself on behalf of someone or something greater than yourself. Directed toward the world, a "willingness of the heart" intensifies the individual's feelings and experience. In *Tender Is the Night* (*TITN*) as in *Gatsby*, the dream of love and accomplishment is distorted by the values of property and possession. Like Gatsby, Dick Diver has large ambitions: "... to be a good psychologist—maybe to be the greatest one that ever lived."[12] Dick's colleague, the stolid Swiss, Franz Gregorovius, stops short hearing his friend's pronouncement, as did the aspiring American man of letters, Edmund Wilson, when the undergraduate Fitzgerald declared: "I want to be one of the greatest writers who have ever lived, don't you?"[13] Like Fitzgerald, Diver mingles love with ambition, though passively, almost as an afterthought: "He wanted to be loved too, if he could fit it in" (*TITN* 23).

Reminiscent of Gatsby, Diver's dream resides initially in a masculine world in which one man's ambition and achievement are measured against another's. But, as with Gatsby, experience changes the values implicit in Diver's equation. Stirred by professional curiosity, he meets Nicole Warren. Because of her youth and beauty, the patient becomes in Diver's eyes primarily a woman, though a woman imagined as "a scarcely saved waif of disaster bringing him the essence of a continent." To the inexperienced Diverge—"only hot-cheeked girls in hot secret rooms" (*TITN* 27)—Nicole is a figure for the romantic possibility of an America that, like the "fresh green breast of the new world" whose "vanished trees ... had made way for Gatsby's house" (*TGG* 137) is, though violated and compromised, suggestive of innocence, vitality, and possibility, and above all, still worthy of love.

So Dick Diver gambles his "pursuit of happiness" on marriage to Nicole. But his desire to be loved—"I want to be extravagantly admired again," Fitzgerald said as he was writing *Tender*—seduces him away from his scholarly writing as a psychiatrist. Once diverted from his work, he does not find happiness as curator of the leisure-class expatriate American world he and Nicole create on the Riviera, or as psychiatrist in charge of the clinic bought with Warren money, or as Nicole's husband, or, finally, "wolf-like under his sheep's clothing" a pursuer of women more in mind than in actuality. For Diver, like Gatsby, the pursuit of happiness becomes personally hollow in love, and professionally so in his work. Again, perhaps like Gatsby, only more so, Diver is more responsible than he knows for the dissolution of his dream of love and work.

For her part, Nicole, like Daisy, only more poignantly, veers between two selves. Cured, she embraces her heritage as her robber baron grandfather Warren's daughter; her white crook's eyes signify a proprietary attitude toward the world. More vividly and knowingly than before, she becomes the goddess of monopoly and dynasty described early in the novel. "For her sake trains began their run at Chicago and traversed the round belly of the continent to California." Nicole, "as the whole system swayed and thundered onward," is, in Europe, remote product and beneficiary of her family's multinational corporate interests. Like Daisy, Nicole "has too much money"; like Gatsby, Dick Diver "can't beat that" (*TITN* 113, 311).

Yet in *Tender Is The Night*, the matter is not so simple. Marrying Nicole, Dick takes on a task demanding a heroic and perhaps a too stringent discipline and self-denial. After the most violent and threatening of Nicole's schizophrenic episodes, he realizes that "somehow [he] and Nicole had become one and equal, not opposite and complementary; she was Dick too, the drought in the marrow of his bones." Her personality reinforces rather than compensates for what is missing in him. Even more fatal for Diver's balance between husband and psychiatrist, "he could not watch her disintegrations without participating in them" (207). Underneath the historical overtones of the American dream gone terribly, incestuously, wrong, Fitzgerald explores the strained and, finally, chilling intimacy of a marriage turned inward against the autonomy and independence of each person. With slow excruciating inevitability, Diver's "willingness of the heart," so catalytic to his imagination, charm, and discipline, deserts him.

She went up to him and, putting her arm around his shoulder and touching their heads together, said:

"Don't be sad."
He looked at her coldly.
"Don't touch me!" he said. (*TITN* 319)

Diver has come so far from his former love for Nicole, "a wild submergence of soul, a dipping of all colors into an obscuring dye" (*TITN* 235), that he now recoils from her touch. The Divers are no longer man and woman to each other. In truth, the conditions and pathology sustaining the marriage are played out. Nicole is rid of her incestuous dependence on Dick, and Dick seeks to recover the independence he sacrificed as Nicole's husband, doctor, and, above all, protector.

Discipline, spirit, and imagination attenuated if not broken, Diver returns to America a stranger. With Nicole now acting as Fitzgerald's chronicler, the last news of Diver tells of the "big stack of papers on his desk that are known to be an important treatise on some medical subject, almost in process of completion." So much for his craft; as for the dream of love, he becomes "entangled with a girl who worked in a grocery store" (*TITN* 334). Homeless in spirit, Diver drifts from one lovely, lonely Finger Lakes town to another, and whatever dreams he has, he dreams in oblivion without his former promise and intensity of feeling and action.

Fitzgerald created his deepest, most realized novel out of his own predicament. His dissipation and need to write short stories for the *Saturday Evening Post* to sustain his and Zelda's standard of living seduced him away from his craft and to some extent his dream of love. Still, Fitzgerald bled out *Tender Is the Night* at La Paix—"La Paix (My God!)" (*L* 345)—in Rodgers Forge outside Baltimore. He brought his "big stack of papers" to completion. But when reviews were mixed and sales modest, also perhaps because, exhausted, he had no new novel taking shape in his mind, only the early medieval tale of Phillippe or *The Count of Darkness*, with its curiously anachronistic tilt toward Ernest Hemingway's modern code of courage, Fitzgerald sank deeper into drink and depression. Finally, as Scott Donaldson observes, Asheville, Tyron, and other North Carolina towns became suspiciously like the small towns of Diver's self-imposed exile at the end of *Tender Is the Night*.[14]

For more than three years after publication of *Tender Is the Night*, Fitzgerald continued to imitate the desolate trajectory he'd projected for Dick Diver.

Everything was a struggle. Perhaps "to preach at people in some acceptable form" (*L* 63) and to show himself an unbowed Sisyphus, without the camouflage of fiction, he dove into the confessional *Crack-Up* pieces. To the chagrin of those who wished him well, and even some who did not, he wrote an even more exposed confession of faith than *Tender Is the Night*. His low point came with the appearance of "The Other Side of Paradise," a portrait of the novelist as a broken-down man and a failed writer that appeared on his fortieth birthday in the New York Post in September of 1936. "A writer like me must have an utter confidence, an utter faith in his star," he told the reporter. "But through a series of blows, many of them my own fault, something happened to that sense of immunity, and I lost my grip."[15] The reporter featured the empty bottles and the desolate hotel room more than Fitzgerald's words, however, and the self-inflicted blow of humiliation Fitzgerald absorbed seeing the piece in print prompted him to make an abortive gesture at suicide.

Only an offer from Hollywood less than a year later broke the pattern of waste, the spell of despair, and roused Fitzgerald from his uneasy, purgatorial hibernation. Slowly, tortuously, he came back to life as a man and a novelist. Taking another crack at Hollywood, where the "inevitable low gear of collaboration" (*CU* 78) had twice mocked his sense of artistic vocation, Fitzgerald renewed his "pursuit of happiness." His theme was another variation of the American dream. For as a place and an industry, Hollywood was at once the consequence and the purveyor of the dream, often an eager expression of the culture's lowest common denominator. Unlike his earlier moves, to the south of France to write Gatsby in 1924 and Baltimore to write *Tender* in 1932, Fitzgerald saw going to Hollywood as a lucky last chance to recoup his fortunes. He had a screenwriter's contract; perhaps if he got himself together another novel would take shape. In the meantime, riding west on the train in July 1937, Fitzgerald welcomed the chance to pay his debts, educate Scottie, care for Zelda, and keep himself. And Hollywood also offered a fresh start. "Of all natural forces," he had written in *The Crack-Up*, "vitality is the incommunicable one" (*CU* 74). And he did not flinch from taking stock of his condition. "For over three years," he wrote his cousin Ceci, "the creative side of me has been dead as hell" (*L* 419). So, he might have added, was the side of him that lived in relationships at a high pitch of intensity.

In Hollywood almost two years, Fitzgerald pursued once more his dream of love and craft. Cherished by Sheilah Graham who had her own life and ambition, Fitzgerald felt alive enough in his pores to revive the dream of being truly among the novelists. "Look," he wrote his daughter late in

October 1939 with a surge of the old vitality and self-confidence, "I have begun to write something that is maybe great." And he went on to tell her with touching understatement: "Anyhow I am alive again" (*L* 61). In the last year of his life, Fitzgerald poured into Monroe Stahr and *The Last Tycoon* the sense that life was ebbing and his resolve to pursue happiness as a writer and a man to the end. Into Stahr he put exhaustion—the sense of death in the mirror—and readiness for love—"the privilege of giving himself unselfishly to another human being," Fitzgerald's words for a love more mature than romantic. Into his new book, he put the passion to make *The Last Tycoon* "something new" that could "arouse new emotions, perhaps even a new way of looking at certain phenomena."[16] For him the "pursuit of happiness" now meant, in Francis Kroll Ring's words, "the pursuit of the limits of his craft," which she, who knew him well, notes that he felt "he had not reached."[17]

Fitzgerald did not speak directly of the dream in *The Last Tycoon* as he had in *Gatsby*, *Tender Is the Night*, and, with occasional bitter nostalgia, the *Crack-Up* essays. But it was there in Monroe Stahr's pursuit of private and public happiness, there with a measure of caution and maturity as well as a dangerous, consuming intensity. Monroe Stahr is both outside and inside the mold of Fitzgerald's previous heroes. Like Gatsby, Stahr is self-made, a leader of men in Hollywood as Gatsby briefly had been in France during the Great War. But Stahr's ambition and creative power fuse with the public good; he does not become a crook or a gangster to advance his ideal, romantic pursuit of happiness. Neither does he confuse love with vocation. No,

> Stahr like Lincoln was a leader carrying on a long war on many fronts; almost single-handedly he had moved pictures sharply forward through a decade to a point where the content of the "A productions" was wider and richer than that of the stage.

Like Dick Diver, Stahr's mind puts him in select company, and also like Diver, Stahr is a man with a strong, specific sense of vocation. But unlike Diver, Stahr distills his passion into a sustained, disciplined appetite for his work. Stahr is also a Jew, whose identity as an American outsider is more fully, consciously felt and put to more palpable professional use than had been the case with either Gatsby or Diver.

Stahr makes it to the pinnacle in Hollywood—a world open to and largely created by Jews—by virtue of his brains, judgment, leadership, taste, and sense of craft and quality possible in the medium of film with its democratic accessibility and mass appeal. Compared to Lincoln by

Fitzgerald, Stahr believes he's about to take a call from President Roosevelt in front of the woman he's just recently met and is fast coming to love. "I've talked to him before," Stahr tells Kathleen before the phone call turns out to be from an agent whose orangutan is "a dead ringer for McKinley" (*LT* 83). But Fitzgerald, always sensitive to the feel of a decade's turning points, implies parallels between Stahr's protective role in the movie industry and Roosevelt's in government. "There is no world but it has its heroes," he writes, "and Stahr was the hero." He evokes Stahr's staying power during the evolving phases of the movies, as well as in the making of an individual picture. "Most of these men had been here a long time—through the beginnings and the great upset, when sound came, and the three years of depression, he had seen that no harm came to them." Stahr was perhaps a paternal employer, as Roosevelt was a paternal, protective President. Both men preside over transitional circumstances in ways more evolutionary than revolutionary by force of character and impersonal compassionate intelligence, and by taking a personal interest in the problems of their constituencies. "The old loyalties were trembling now," Fitzgerald concludes in the passage describing Stahr mingling with those who work for him at the end of a day at the studio: "There were clay feet everywhere; but still he was their man, the last of the princes. And their greeting was a sort of low cheer as he went by" (*LT* 27).

Stahr dreams of and attains knowledge and success in Hollywood's ambiguous, often insincere world of entertainment, art, and profit, the solitary, Cartesian way. He "did his reasoning without benefit of books—and he had just managed to climb out of a thousand years of Jewry into the late eighteenth century." About the past, Fitzgerald notes that Stahr "could not bear to see it melt away" (*LT* 118). Reading this you can't help recall Fitzgerald's elegiac prose about the early promise of America "where the dark fields of the republic rolled on under the night" (*TGG* 137), or those pioneering Virginia "souls made of new earth in the forest-heavy darkness of the seventeenth century" (*TITN* 222). In a word, Fitzgerald continues, Stahr "cherished the parvenu's passionate loyalty to an imaginary past" (*LT* 118). But, having faced Stahr's and his own nostalgia, Fitzgerald invokes checks and balances against the romantic pull of the past. Stahr invents a peculiar, involuntary collaboration among the screenwriters, and his broader accomplishment as producer—"I'm the unity"—comes from his radical pragmatic courage to grasp and implement innovations. In short, Stahr is able "to retain the ability to function" amidst the contradictions of democracy and corporate power and property. Fitzgerald, too, wanted to achieve in *The Last Tycoon* what he felt he and his contemporaries so far had not done with the novel. "I want to write scenes that are frightening and inimitable,"[18] he writes in one of his notes.

Both Fitzgerald and Stahr are men whose creative powers flow more richly into the world when they are involved in a satisfying, intimate relationship with a woman. For all of Stahr's love affair with an "imaginary past," Kathleen awakens his passion for life in the present. Despite his "definite urge toward total exhaustion," when he and Kathleen touch, Stahr feels the abiding elemental world again; at the coast he comes alive to the rhythms of land and sea and sky. After he and Kathleen make love at his unfinished Malibu beach house—"It would have been good anytime, but for the first time it was much more than he had hoped or expected"—they watch countless grunion fish come to touch land "as they had come before Sir Francis Drake had nailed his plaque to the shore" (*LT* 92, 108, 152).

Stahr's love for Kathleen intensifies his confidence about his gifts and worldly aspirations in a way reminiscent of Fitzgerald. "I used to have a beautiful talent once, Baby," Fitzgerald told young Budd Schulberg during the Dartmouth Winter Carnival debacle. "It used to be wonderful feeling it was there."[19] Page by page, Fitzgerald ekes out *The Last Tycoon*, his physical stamina no longer able to keep up with his mind. Nor keep up with his will. As Frances Kroll Ring, Fitzgerald's then 20-year-old secretary tells it, he'd take a weekend off when he needed money to pay bills. With single-minded discipline fired by a desire to have the coming week free for his novel, he would plot and write a Pat Hobby story for *Esquire*.[20] But always the dream of realizing his promise as a pioneering American novelist was there, perhaps made more palpable by his love affair with Sheilah Graham and his dedication to her education, and, for that matter, to his daughter Scottie's education. The latter is especially poignant, for Scottie, of the same generation as Fitzgerald's narrator, Cecilia Brady, and his contemporary and intellectual conscience, Edmund Wilson, were Fitzgerald's two imagined readers of *The Last Tycoon*, and that connection kept him going on more than one desolate, discouraging occasion.

In the novel, Fitzgerald does not leave the connection between love and craft to speculation. While the grunion flop at their feet on the Malibu shore, Stahr and Kathleen encounter a black man who tells Stahr he "never go[es] to movies" and "never let[s his] children go" (*LT* 92). Later, at home alone, Stahr recalls the man—"He was prejudiced and wrong, and he must be shown somehow some way." The man had been reading Emerson, and for Stahr he becomes the representative responsible good citizen whose allegiance Stahr must win for his soul's sake, the movies' sake, and the sake of American culture, of which Stahr sees himself a guardian. "A picture,"

Stahr thinks, "many pictures, a decade of pictures, must be made to show him he was wrong." And Stahr immediately commits himself to a specific action. "[H]e submitted the borderline pictures to the Negro and found them trash. And he put back on his list a difficult picture that he had tossed to the wolves, ... to get his way on something else. He rescued it for the Negro man" (*LT* 95). Here Stahr puts his corporate property and producer's power in service of a higher common good—democratic (e)quality. Here the "pursuit of happiness" expresses his best potential and the best of American popular culture. What's more, Stahr's responsiveness to the black man's criticism is bound up with his passionate and tender love for Kathleen. His power to act as a public man is perhaps brought to brief, occasional fullness by the experience of love and intimacy.

Yet Stahr, Fitzgerald takes pains to observe, was not born to love and intimacy. He worked hard to shape the raw materials of his personality into a sensibility capable of an intimate relationship. "Like many brilliant men, he had grown up dead cold." Looking over the way things were,

> he swept it all away, everything, as men of his type do; and then instead of being a son-of-a-bitch as most of them are, he looked around at the bareness that was left and said to himself, "This will never do." And so he had learned tolerance, kindness, forbearance, and even affection like lessons. (*LT* 97)

Not surprisingly, Stahr's impulses toward the private happiness of intimacy are not as natural or sure-handed as his pursuit of public happiness in the world in the form of work and power, competition and money.

For all his mingling of love and craft in what seems a mature pursuit of happiness, Stahr hesitates with Kathleen. Perhaps Fitzgerald would have changed somewhat the terms of his story; we do not know. What we do know is that Stahr waits, fatally it turns out, though he is sure in his heart and his mind. "He could have said it then, said, 'It is a new life,' for he knew it was, he knew he could not let her go now, but something else said to sleep on it as an adult, no romantic" (*LT* 115). What Stahr and Kathleen do not know is that outside forces are closing in. The man Kathleen calls "The American," who rescued her from her old life's quagmire in London, is already speeding toward Los Angeles and the marriage ceremony they've agreed to, his train hours early. If there's something hasty, even amateurish about this twist of Fitzgerald's plot, so be it. To say he might have changed it or refined the terms is to remember that he too, like Stahr, did not have the luxury of time.

In what Fitzgerald did write, Stahr says good night to Kathleen, but keeps his feelings to himself. "We'll go to the mountains tomorrow," he tells her with the public voice of the man in charge, the producer, as if that were all. For his part, Fitzgerald the novelist, unable to resist one of those asides that mark his relations with his characters, especially those he loves, reflects on Stahr's temporizing judgment: "You can suddenly blunt a quality you have lived by for twenty years" (*LT* 116).

This line does not belong entirely to Fitzgerald but to Cecelia Brady, his narrator, who also loves Stahr, and in the way of a woman, not a novelist. Here, too, Fitzgerald was breaking new and different ground from that traversed in previous novels. He gambled that this young woman, "at the moment of her telling the story, an intelligent and observant woman" (*LT* 140), could reveal Stahr's complexity as well as her own and that of Hollywood and American society in the transitional time of the Depression and the coming of the Second World War. Through Cecelia's sensibility as insider and outsider, Fitzgerald registers changes in what Ellison has called the American social hierarchy.[21] In *The Last Tycoon*, Stahr, a Jew not far from the shtetl, makes a black man his moviemaker's conscience, falls in love with an Irish immigrant, and has his story told by another woman, a young Irish American who, by virtue of her father's Hollywood money and her intelligence and grace, moves among the well-to-do on both coasts.

In Fitzgerald's fascinating, fragmentary notes and sketches for the novel's ending—three teenagers' discovery of the fallen plane and the personal effects of Stahr and other passengers—and epilogue—Stahr's lavish Hollywood funeral full of hypocrisy and intrigue—the dream fights on in life-affirming, life-denying variations. Whatever Fitzgerald might have done, we glimpse in Stahr what might unfold if the pursuit of private and public happiness were to fuse in a common responsiveness. The one transforms and intensifies the other; the self trembles, now fully alive.

Stahr, whether in conversation or the act of love with Kathleen, or in his renewed sense of aesthetic possibility in response to a black man's rejection of the movies, comes to know that his vitality depends on mingling passion and tenderness toward Kathleen with the pragmatic imagination of his producer's craft. Without one, the other falters, as Fitzgerald shows in his draft of the last episode he wrote and his notes for the novel's succeeding chapters. In the last months of his life, Fitzgerald struggled toward the same equilibrium beyond Stahr's grasp, but not his imagination, in his settled relationship with Sheilah Graham and the steadfastness with which he pursued the limits of his craft. Despite his efforts to finish *The Last Tycoon*, Fitzgerald left a fragment that is, for all its promise, as Richard Lehan put it, "a brilliantly incomplete work that has all the limitations of being a draft and thus never fully conceptualized and polished by revision, where Fitzgerald always did his best work."[22] Nevertheless, Fitzgerald's fragment is a palpable reminder, at once mocking and reassuring, about his novelist's dream and the American theme.

"So we beat on," to echo and recast Gatsby's ending, not necessarily "borne back ceaselessly into the past" (*TGG* 137). For in *The Last Tycoon*, there is a fluidity and ambiguity about property and the "pursuit of happiness" missing from the social structures underlying Gatsby and *Tender Is the Night*. Even more than *Tender Is the Night*, in its protean state *The Last Tycoon* appears a work of ceaseless fluctuations. Unlike *Tender*, *Tycoon*'s unfolding and denouement were to be governed by a moral and aesthetic principle underscored in Fitzgerald's notes. ACTION IS CHARACTER, he wrote in large block letters, and they are the last words in Edmund Wilson's edition of the fragment. As Fitzgerald's notes and outlines reiterate, Monroe Stahr was to struggle until the end. He would not await his fate passively like Gatsby or, like Dick Diver, abdicate to a private corner of America. Fitzgerald imagines Stahr a player to the last and only the ironic contemporary deus ex machina of a plane crash would interfere with his decision to call oft a retaliatory murder he's arranged in sick desperation. Gatsby operates in the shadows of American violence and power; Diver becomes a sleepwalking Rip van Winkle in a time of transition, but Stahr lives in the glare never believing that "things are [entirely] hopeless." Rather, he is "determined [to the end] to make them otherwise." Such, at least, is the impression conveyed by Fitzgerald's posthumous, very much in-progress fragment of a novel.

In Stahr's case and Fitzgerald's, the choices are contingent and pragmatic rather than ideal. It is no longer the case, as Fitzgerald once believed, that "life was something you dominated if you were any good" (*CU* 69). This romantic categorical imperative is long gone from his life and burned oft the pages of *The Last Tycoon*. By 1940, life was the pursuit of equilibrium, and the dream has become an ability to put previously opposed ideas into relationship, what D. H. Lawrence, in praise of the novel, called "the trembling instability of the balance."[23] Perhaps this is why Fitzgerald, and his evolving patriot parvenu, Monroe Stahr, come to the American dream still with a "willingness of the heart." Its promise was not happiness at all, as Jefferson and Adams realized so long ago, but the pursuit of happiness. The American experiment looked toward an ideal of individuals straining for self-realization with every nerve and muscle, every thought and feeling, in order to create what Ellison identified as that "condition of being at home in the world which is called love and which we term democracy."[24] For Fitzgerald the pursuit of happiness and the American Dream were inseparable. Digging deeply into his experience and the nation's, Fitzgerald made Monroe Stahr's story and character express the complexity of American life, its contradictions and possibilities alike. "The writing gave him hope," Frances Ring remembers from Fitzgerald's last months, "that something good was happening, that he was whole again."[25]

Perhaps the sense of his powers returning prompted Fitzgerald's note to himself near the end. "I am the last of the novelists for a long time now,"[26] he wrote, and who can know what he meant? Could he have meant that he was the last of his generation to keep faith with the nineteenth-century view of the novel as a testing ground for the experiment of American culture and democracy? Could he have meant his remark as a challenge to succeeding writers to pick up where he left oft in exploring the American theme? Whatever he meant, even unfinished, *The Last Tycoon* has had the effect of leading readers and writers back to Fitzgerald's work knowing, as he knew, that the story of America has an endless succession of takes, but no final script.

Notes

1. For a sense of Fitzgerald criticism over the past 4-1/2 decades, see Jackson R. Bryer's "Four Decades of Fitzgerald Studies: The Best and the Brightest" and Sergio Perosa's "Fitzgerald Studies in the 1970s," both in *Twentieth Century Literature*, 26 (1980). Also see *Critical Essays on The Great Gatsby*, ed. Scott Donaldson, and Critical Essays on *Tender Is the Night*, ed. Milton R. Stern.

2. Ralph Ellison, *Invisible Man*, 433.

3. Ernest Hemingway, *The Sun Also Rises*, 148.

4. *The Great Gatsby*, 4. Henceforth *The Great Gatsby* will be cited in the text as *TGG*.

5. *The Crack-Up*, ed. Edmund Wilson, 69. Henceforth *The Crack-Up* will be cited in the text as *CU*.

6. Andrew Turnbull, ed., *The Letters of F. Scott Fitzgerald*, 96. Henceforth the *Letters* will be cited in the text as *L*.

7. Letter to George and Thomas Keats, 21 Dec. 1817, in Rollins, ed., 193.

8. Quoted by Andrew Turnbull in *Scott Fitzgerald*, 307.

9. Ralph Ellison, *Going to the Territory*, 251.

10. Eugene McCarthy, *Complexities and Contraries: Essays of Mild Discontent*, 112.

11. Keats, 193.

12. *Tender Is the Night*, 22. Henceforth *Tender Is the Night* will be cited in the text as *TITN*.

13. F. Scott Fitzgerald as quoted by Edmund Wilson in "Thoughts on Being Bibliographed," 54.

14. Scott Donaldson, "The Crisis of Fitzgerald's 'Crack-Up,'" 185.

15. Michel Mok, *New York Post*, 25 Sep. 1936.

16. *The Last Tycoon*, 139, 141. Henceforth *The Last Tycoon* will be cited in the text as *LT*. (Matthew J. Bruccoli, editor of *The Love of The Last Tycoon* [1993] is correct to say that Edmund Wilson assigned the title of *The Last Tycoon*. Nevertheless, Bruccoli's evidence for his title is less than convincing; thus my decision to use the 1941 Wilson edition.)

17. Letter from Frances Kroll Ring to the author.

18. F. Scott Fitzgerald's Notes as quoted by Matthew J. Bruccoli in *The Last of the Novelists: F. Scott Fitzgerald and The Last Tycoon*, 156.

19. F. Scott Fitzgerald to Budd Schulberg as quoted by Arthur Mizener in *The Far Side of Paradise*, 317.

20. Frances Kroll Ring, *Against the Current: As I Remember F. Scott Fitzgerald*, 52–55.

21. This is a recurring phrase and theme of Ellison's, found in *Shadow & Act*, *Going to the Territory*, and in some of his unpublished or uncollected pieces included in *Collected Essays*.

22. Richard Lehan, letter to the author.

23. D. H. Lawrence, *Phoenix: The Posthumous Papers of D. H. Lawrence*, 528.

24. Ralph Ellison, *Shadow & Act*, 105–06.

25. Frances Kroll Ring, unpublished remarks delivered at the Fitzgerald–Hemingway International Conference in 1994.

26. Bruccoli, op. cit., 156.

WORKS CITED

Bruccoli, Matthew J. *The Last of the Novelists: F. Scott Fitzgerald and The Last Tycoon*. Carbondale: Southern Illinois UP, 1977.

Bryer, Jackson R. "Four Decades of Fitzgerald Studies: The Best and the Brightest." *Twentieth Century Literature* 26 (1980): 247–67.

Donaldson, Scott. "The Crisis of Fitzgerald's "Crack-Up," *Twentieth Century Literature* 26 (1980).

———, ed. *Critical Essays on The Great Gatsby*. Boston: Hall, 1984.

Ellison, Ralph. *Collected Essays of Ralph Ellison*. New York: Random, 1995.

———. *Going to the Territory*. New York: Random, 1986.

———. *Invisible Man*. New York: Random, 1952.

———. *Shadow & Act*. New York: Random, 1964.

Fitzgerald, F. Scott. *The Great Gatsby*. In *Three Novels*. New York: Scribner's, 1953.

———. *The Last Tycoon*. In *Three Novels*. New York: Scribner's, 1953.

———. *Tender Is the Night*. In *Three Novels*. New York: Scribner's, 1953.

Hemingway, Ernest. *The Sun Also Rises*. New York: Scribner's, 1926.

Keats, John. *The Letters of John Keats, 1814–21*. Ed. Edward Rollins. Vol. 1. Cambridge: Harvard UP, 1958.

Lawrence. D.H. *Phoenix: The Posthumous Papers of D. H. Lawrence*. New York: Viking, 1968.

Lehan, Richard. Letter to the author. 25 May 1995.

McCarthy, Eugene. *Complexities and Contraries: Essays of Mild Discontent*. New York: Harcourt, 1982.

Mizener, Arthur. *The Far Side of Paradise*. Boston: Houghton, 1965.

Mok, Michel. "The Other Side of Paradise." *New York Post* 25 Sep. 1936.

Perosa, Sergio. "Fitzgerald Studies in the 1970s." *Twentieth Century Literature* 26 (1980): 222–46.

Ring, Frances Kroll. *Against the Current: As I Remember F. Scott Fitzgerald*. Berkeley: Creative Arts, 1985.

———. Letter to the author. 7 Sep. 1994.

———. Unpublished remarks delivered at the Fitzgerald–Hemingway International Conference, Paris, 8 July 1994.

Stern, Milton R., ed. *Critical Essays on Tender Is the Night*. Boston: Hall, 1986.

Turnbull, Andrew, ed. *The Letters of F. Scott Fitzgerald*. New York: Scribner's, 1963.

———. *Scott Fitzgerald*. New York: Scribner's, 1962.

Wilson, Edmund, ed. *The Crack-Up*. New York: New Directions, 1965.

———. "Thoughts on Being Bibliographed," *Princeton University Library Chronicle* (Feb. 1944).

NANCY P. VAN ARSDALE

Princeton as Modernist's Hermeneutics: Rereading This Side of Paradise

Princeton, not Amory Blaine, is the center of *This Side of Paradise*. Although many critics tend to analyze the text as a bildungsroman, an episodic accounting of a young man's maturation, this first book is better understood as the author's effort to interpret what he had personally signified as the symbol of symbols, Princeton University. F. Scott Fitzgerald presented the institution as far more than a setting; indeed it became his center of the universe. Princeton must be analyzed as a modernist's paradise temporarily gained, inevitably lost, never forgotten. Readmission remains Amory's secret hope, as it was for Adam, Eve, and Scott. Contemplating the concept of a modernist's paradise within a hermeneutical framework that has evolved from traditional biblical study through American Puritanism, romanticisms, and realism leads us to the modernist's redefinition of Eden in this work: Princeton is the new religious, national, and social hermeneutics, an architectural and systematic text through which Fitzgerald interpreted his twentieth-century world.

How far should we stretch the idea of hermeneutical interpretation when examining the book of an atheist? In *Inventions: Writing, Textuality, and Understanding in Literary History*, Gerald L. Bruns argues that modern judicial, literary, and social concepts, in addition to traditional scriptural tenets, must be incorporated in a contemporary study of hermeneutics.

From *F. Scott Fitzgerald: New Perspectives*, Jackson R. Bryer, Alan Margolies, and Ruth Prigozy, ed. pp. 39–50. © The University of Georgia Press.

Sacvan Bercovitch has studied how the hermeneutical interpretation of America as paradise has undergone ideological shifts through the centuries, yet remains fundamental to our national literature. In "The Image of America: From Hermeneutics to Symbolism," Bercovitch traces the hermeneutic tradition from Puritanism to the American Renaissance: "The American strategy undertakes to unite both of these developments, national and spiritual. In effect, it yokes together the internal and external Kingdom of God by asserting the simultaneity of a geographical locale, America, and a mode of vision." The poetry of Edward Taylor, for example, clearly reveals the minister's ambition to guide and steer his congregation, in effect *his* America, according to his imaginative application of scriptural tenets.[1]

More than a century after Puritanism had faded, American romantics continued to believe firmly in the idea of America as a reality, as a promised land, an earthly paradise provided by God. Bercovitch finds writers such as Hawthorne, Thoreau, Emerson, and Melville repeatedly re-creating in their work the *religious* experience of encountering a promised land. Such an experience leads to failure or expulsion, whether the setting is Melville's tumultuous and vast seas or Thoreau's *Walden Pond*. God is found in both the infinite and the infinitesimal, as these American allegories and parables explore the spiritual dimensions of nature in men's encounters with greater forces.

When we bring the Kingdom of God into Fitzgerald's modern world, the atheist dismisses the divine but nonetheless clings to a belief in the mythic Kingdom—Kingdom of *something*. Identifying that something becomes the challenge. America as an image of paradise is transmuted into the Ivy League campus in Fitzgerald's book, a place fraught with the symbolism of at least a higher culture even if the belief in a higher heaven has been relinquished. John Aldridge suggests that Amory Blaine is disappointed ultimately in Princeton's imperfection, but perhaps Fitzgerald was more disappointed in his own weakness, in his inability to be good enough to remain in paradise.[2]

In his later fiction, Fitzgerald distanced himself a little bit at least from his central characters by placing them at Yale and occasionally at Harvard, instead of Princeton, as Arthur Mizener has observed.[3] Nevertheless, Fitzgerald's earliest attempts to fictionalize the impact Princeton was having on him can be traced to his own undergraduate days there. In 1916, he published "The Spire and the Gargoyle" in the *Nassau Literary Magazine*, quite a bit of which, including the story's title as a chapter heading, was recycled in the final published version of *This Side of Paradise*. The features of the Gothic ornamentation on campus reveal the adolescent's first effort at adapting for literary purposes the architectural symbols of spiritual aspiration in the spire and human limitation in the gargoyle. Although the preliminary draft of the novel was titled "The Romantic Egotist," referring directly to his main character with his self-centered idealism, the final title returns to the evocation of place with a modernist's twist to the biblical reference; does the story take place outside of paradise from beginning to end, or does Amory find himself on "this side" after he leaves Princeton?

A close analysis of "The Spire and the Gargoyle" supports the latter idea, that Princeton is itself paradise and the world outside its gates is exile. Fitzgerald never even bothered to name his protagonist in the story, instead devoting his energies to signifying the architectural symbols that were, for the novice author, more important than the characters. In both the story and the novel, the architectural features can be symbolically interpreted as forces at odds with one another; this fact is essential to the story but is less effective in the novel. The spires represent academic achievement and ambition. The gargoyles are the narrow-minded preceptors and uninspiring instructors. The spires, like church steeples, point to the open sky, heaven, the divine; education can open up the human mind to infinite realms. In contrast, the gargoyles are small, frightening creatures—devils in stone. The two images thus juxtapose the concept of knowledge as liberation with the idea of institutional education as an evil, limiting process.

For the most part, both the story and the novel use poetic language to evoke Princeton as an intensely romantic setting. Its architecture is, in the eyes of the undergraduate, inspirational. Beautiful spring days transform the campus into a heavenly place, where the voices of singing seniors replace any need for choruses of angels on high. Scott Donaldson suggests that the "physical beauty of the place ... helped to arouse the lyrical strain in Fitzgerald."[4] Fitzgerald apparently considered the spirit of the campus his own divine and personal muse.

The theme of "The Spire and the Gargoyle" focuses on personal responsibility. The main character, a student, has been under the delusion that acceptance to Princeton is a final goal. He has not been successful in terms of academic standards, cutting classes excessively. The tension of the first segment of the story revolves around a last-chance, make-up examination. If he fails, the student will be banned from Princeton, "his college days faded out with the last splendors of June."[5]

Before establishing the main character's character and predicament, Fitzgerald devotes much attention to presenting the campus and its effect on the student's imagination. The first sentences of the story depict the setting: "The night mist fell. From beyond the moon it rolled, clustered about the spires and towers, and then settled below them so that the dreaming peaks seemed still in lofty aspiration toward the stars" (105). Although the symbolic interpretations of the towers are clichés, they reveal Fitzgerald's attitude that a character cannot be separated from his environment. The student, now up in his room, reflects on his fate at the university:

> In view of his window a tower sprang upward, grew into a spire, yearning higher till its uppermost end was half invisible against the morning skies. The transiency and relative unimportance of the campus figures except as holders of a sort of apostolic succession had first impressed themselves on him in contrast with this spire. In a lecture or in an article or in conversation, he had learned that Gothic architecture with its upward trend was peculiarly adapted to colleges, and the symbolism of this idea had become personal to him. Once he had associated the beauty of the campus night with the parades and singing crowds that streamed through it, but in the last month the more silent stretches of sward and the quiet halls with an occasional late-burning scholastic light held his imagination with a stronger grasp—and this tower in full view of his window became the symbol of his perception.... To him the spire became an ideal. He had suddenly begun trying desperately to stay in college. (106–7)

Much of this architectural description reappears, virtually as is, in *This Side of Paradise*. Because considerably more effort has been put into Amory's characterization, the reader of the novel may miss the spire's significance to the student. To succeed at Princeton is to be admitted to the realm of higher spirituality pointed out by the spire. The temptation offered by the tree of knowledge of Eden is reinterpreted by Fitzgerald in both the story and the novel as a final examination. In the story, the role of the serpent is given to the preceptor who administers the exam; yet he is not represented in the novel. Ultimately, Fitzgerald must have decided that the preceptor was too obvious a depiction of the student's enemy; in *This Side of Paradise*, Amory's only enemy is Amory himself. Still, Fitzgerald handles the preceptor in "The Spire and the Gargoyle" once he, like the student, is forced to operate outside of paradise. The second part of the story takes place several years later when the student, who did fail the examination, meets the preceptor in New York at a museum. Again, the setting is used symbolically to identify the protagonist's current dilemma. The class and style of Fifth Avenue are juxtaposed with the masses and tackiness of Broadway. Although we are not informed of his current occupation, the protagonist obviously aspires to belong to the upper classes of the Avenue. He quests for a modernist's holy grail in a time when science has undermined religious faith: "Always a symbolist, and an idealist, ... he sought around him in his common life for something to cling to, to stand for what religions and families and philosophies of life had stood for" (109).

The student has lost the one institution he did believe in: Princeton. He is surprised to learn, during tea conversation, that the preceptor has also left Princeton, at least for the moment. The preceptor explains that the needs of his growing family forced him to leave the college for a better-paying teaching position in Brooklyn. They both find a common bond in shared memories of the college's spires.

The third part of the story takes place months later, when the protagonist coincidentally meets the preceptor on a train to Princeton. The preceptor is visiting his brother, an instructor at Princeton, and he still hopes to return to his position there. The protagonist realizes that the preceptor, in spite of his financial difficulties, belongs to the place much more than he does: "The gargoyle, poor tired little hack, was bound up in the fabric of the whole system much more than he was." In contrast, the protagonist is struck by his own "complete overwhelming sense of failure" (114), his detachment from all places. Without even leaving the station, he catches the next train back to the city.

Although in part I the student seemed willing to blame the preceptor for failing his examination, he now recognizes the failure as exclusively his own. This may sound like a simple, adolescent experience—accepting one's own failures, recognizing there are consequences to one's own actions and negligence. Yet the plight of the protagonist is so integrated with the symbolism of Princeton, Broadway, and Fifth Avenue that Fitzgerald returned to all three sections of the story to borrow ideas for his first novel. In his essay "The Romantic Self and the Uses of Place," Richard Lehan correlates the story's outcome to that of the novel: "As in *This Side of Paradise*, the story ends with a sense of all that impedes the self-creating imagination. Whatever its limitations, and there are many, 'The Spire and the Gargoyle' reveals that very early in his career Fitzgerald had connected a sense of self with a sense of place, and both of these with a sense of destiny."[6]

In *This Side of Paradise*, Fitzgerald does a far superior job of developing the principal character, here named Amory Blaine; the novel also attempts to put the realm of responsibility and the significance of a social institution into a larger context than that of just the individual. Its final chapter, regardless of its weaknesses, focuses on a character who has changed personally and who wants to see society change as well. Although the book's final views are poorly presented, what is critically important is that Amory gives his lecture on socialism while returning to the towers and spires of Princeton. If "The Spire and the Gargoyle" focuses on how a place can influence an individual's fate, *This Side of Paradise* attempts to state that individuals should change the places and institutions of society. Specifically, paradise must be reclaimed when the academic community and society together redefine the mission of Princeton as an educational institution.

While Fitzgerald was expanding the core of the story into the first draft of a novel-length version, *The Education of Henry Adams* was circulating in a privately published and distributed edition (1918). Adams's text struggles to come to terms with the American educational experience in a period far removed from Puritanical religious conviction; in his case, Adams rejects the significance of Harvard classrooms as having any true positive influence on a young modernist's mind. Fitzgerald's novel similarly criticizes Princeton as an institution of higher learning, but like Adams, the young writer attempts to find grounds for modern morality in a world with "all Gods dead, all wars fought, all faiths in man shaken."

Fitzgerald's spiritual and cultural advisor, Father Sigourney Fay, the prototype for the novel's Monsignor Darcy, personally knew Adams and had perhaps discussed the autobiographical work with his young friend. Whereas Adams's treatise concludes with a comparison of the thirteenth-century Virgin and the twentieth-century Dynamo, *This Side of Paradise* ends with Amory, in a car heading back toward Princeton, lecturing to a deus ex machina on socialism. Adams tries to focus on technology as the substitute for religion; the young Fitzgerald attempted to focus on Marxist politics as a better institution for modern America than either the church or Princeton. But why does Amory take this stance en route to the university? In the final lines of his Harvard chapter, Henry Adams concludes: "As yet he [Adams, the new Harvard graduate] knew nothing. Education had not begun."[7] In effect, Amory returns to Princeton in the last pages, having realized how his formal educational experiences as well as his chance at paradise have been utter failures. But his return also represents his effort to bang on paradise's gates and seek admission on new grounds. Amory seeks the higher realm of justice, knowledge, and morality locked within Princeton's world as defined by its architecture.

What are Amory's reasons for *initially* choosing to go to Princeton? Temptations of the most superficial kind attract him: it "drew him most ... with ... its alluring reputation as the pleasantest country club in America."[8] Amory devotes his first two years at Princeton, before the critical examination, to the university's social traditions, specifically its clubs and organizations. From the beginning, he is a freshman advocate of the Princeton tradition. When he first develops an acquaintance with the boys in his house, he "spread the table of their future friendship with all his ideas of what college should and did mean," especially the "intricacies of the social system" (48). Yet even in these first descriptions of Amory's freshman year, Fitzgerald suggests that the true purpose of Princeton has only been partially sensed. From his first days there, Amory "loved Princeton—its lazy beauty, its half-grasped significance" (47).

The campus poet, Thomas Park d'Invilliers, first opens Amory's eyes to another side of Princeton. Based on John Peale Bishop, d'Invilliers is an avid writer and reader. Andrew Turnbull refers in his biography to the uniqueness of such literary interests: "Part of the Princeton code was not to appear to take one's studies too seriously and Bishop had an unmistakable aura of bookishness."[9] The English professors at Princeton may fail to inspire enthusiasm about poetry or modern writers, but Tom teaches Amory to enjoy reading—and writing. Several of Amory's friends, including Tom, question the Princeton social system long before Burne Holiday leads his rebellion during junior year. At one point, Tom informs Amory that he is tired of "the snobbishness of this corner of the world." He wonders if graduation from Princeton will ruin his natural intellectual curiosity: "I've learned all that Princeton has to offer. Two years more of mere pedantry and lying around a club aren't going to help me." Amory argues not why Tom must stay, but that it is useless to leave. The school has already placed its mark on the boys. As Amory explains, "For better or worse we've stamped you; you're a Princeton type!" (92).

Amory rates his own success based on his efforts outside of the classroom. The first acknowledgment of his social stature on campus is the invitation to join the staff of the newspaper: "Amory, by way of the *Princetonian*, had arrived" (78). Subsequent achievements include his admission to Cottage Club and his writing for the Triangle Club. For a while, Amory gets away with cutting class, ridiculing his professors, sleeping during lectures, and failing examinations. Of course, such a poor academic record will finally have an impact on Amory's life at Princeton. But note that it is a girlfriend, not someone on campus, who first suggests that Amory's view of Princeton is warped. The young woman is Isabelle, one of the first females to engage the young romantic's imagination. During a visit to her parents' house, Isabelle finally rejects Amory. She has grown weary of all his talk of Princeton and his self-importance: "Oh, you and Princeton! You'd think that was the world, the way you talk!" (102).

Then comes the critical examination. Fitzgerald transformed the consequences of this test from "The Spire and the Gargoyle" to *This Side of Paradise* so the focus centers on social rather than academic objectives. In the story, failing leads to banishment from Princeton. In the novel, failing results in being cutoff from club memberships. The test is given during September of Amory's junior year. Completely bored with the preparation classes, Amory contemplates his relationship with Isabelle and his life as a student: "Somehow, with the defection of Isabelle the idea of undergraduate success had loosed its grasp on his imagination, and he contemplated a possible failure to pass off his condition with equanimity, even though it would arbitrarily mean his removal from the *Princetonian* board and the slaughter of his chances for the Senior Council" (105–6). Alec, one of Amory's friends, warns him unequivocally what failing the examination will mean to his social status: "Your stock will go down like an elevator at the club and on the campus" (106).

When Amory receives his examination results in the mail, it is fitting that he chooses to open the envelope in front of an audience. His manner is most sarcastic when he informs his peers that the slip is "Blue as the sky, gentlemen" (107). Universal possibilities, at least according to the social standards so important to Amory, are now shut off to him. In effect, the failed examination results shatter his world, just as they did the protagonist's in "The Spire and the Cargoyle." He has failed Princeton.

Indeed, Fitzgerald attempts to show that this is the first time in Amory's life where he recognizes how environments have affected his identity. The writer employs the device of a list in a most unusual way for this purpose. The passage reads:

1. The fundamental Amory.
2. Amory plus Beatrice.
3. Amory plus Beatrice plus Minneapolis.

Then St. Regis' had pulled him to pieces and started him over again:

4. Amory plus St. Regis'.
5. Amory plus St. Regis' plus Princeton.

That had been his nearest approach to success through conformity. The fundamental Amory, idle, imaginative, rebellious, had been nearly snowed under. He had conformed, he had succeeded, but as his imagination was neither satisfied nor grasped by his own success, he had listlessly, half-accidentally chucked the whole thing and become again:

6. The fundamental Amory. (108–9)

Although the list acknowledges a person's influence, his mother's, the primary influences on his life have been places, not people: Minneapolis, St. Regis', Princeton. Essentially without those places, exiled from those places, Amory is nothing.

During Amory's subsequent time at Princeton he witnesses a body of students on campus who rise up together, questioning and refusing to join the clubs. The novel is weakened because Fitzgerald failed to intertwine sensitively the two kinds of introspections, Amory's own personal ones and Princeton's institutional ones. Amory remains only a passive observer of the revolutionary students. Then in the novel's last chapter, Amory suddenly identifies himself with a much larger rebellion—socialism. The connection between the microcosm of society at the university and society at large is loosely made at best.

Fitzgerald strove to show that art itself can be a rebellion too, but he did not let the character of Amory adequately represent this notion either. After failing the examination in his junior year, Amory grows more interested in poetry, or, in hermeneutical terms, the Word of meaning; it is, in effect, his new extracurricular activity. Amory writes, but his poems are mostly satirical commentaries on the more boring faculty members around campus. He reads more too. It is at this time that he discovers the poetry of Rupert Brooke. The novel's title and epigraph are borrowed from Brooke and highlight Amory's predicament at Princeton: "Well this side of Paradise! ... / There's little comfort in the wise." Amory also commences a campus-wide search for other poets: "Together with Tom d'Invilliers, he sought among the lights of Princeton for someone who might found the Great American Poetic Tradition" (116). Although Amory's appreciation for poetry increases during this period, he realizes his own talents are limited. He decides he does not have what it takes to be a poet, a modern artist whose words truly represent "the Word" of the twentieth century.

When war breaks out and many students enlist as soldiers, they do so because that is what is expected of Princeton men, of any college men for that matter. Only Burne Holiday, the book's true political rebel, takes a different point of view. His own choice, extremely radical for the period, is to be a pacifist. Amory has a difficult time understanding how Burne can choose this course. The Germans are such an obvious enemy, in his and most

of America's eyes. But even more important, Amory has a harder time
accepting Burne's fervent belief in his personal ability to make such a
decision. Burne leaves Princeton on a humble bicycle. Amory feels he is
"leaving everything worth while" (163) because he is choosing to leave
Paradise behind. Yet as Amory watches Burne depart, he doubts his own
ability to make a personal decision that goes against the grain of the
establishment: "as he saw Burne's long legs propel his ridiculous bicycle out
of sight beyond Alexander Hall, he knew he was going to have a bad week.
Not that he doubted the war—Germany stood for everything repugnant to
him; for materialism and the direction of tremendous licentious force; it was
just that Burne's face stayed in his memory and he was sick of the hysteria he
was beginning to hear" (163).

Just as Amory acknowledges Burne's transformation, he is also
conscious that the mood of the times is changing. Princeton has done its best
to shelter its students from the modern world, but Amory nonetheless
detects that even Princeton will finally have to make accommodations to
modernity: "The war seemed scarcely to touch them and it might have been
one of the senior springs of the past, except for the drilling every other
afternoon, yet Amory realized poignantly that this was the last spring under
the old regime" (166). The socially conscious boy is becoming a man who
recognizes that the religious beliefs and comfortable social networks of the
past may no longer work in this new era. But what will replace those
networks? Amory leaves Princeton in the acceptable fashion, as a soldier. But
does he ever really let go of the idea of Princeton as a paradise-on-earth for
the upper classes?

The correspondence between John Peale Bishop and Fitzgerald,
when both were soldiers, sheds light on this question. In a letter dated
December 27, 1917, Bishop justified the war. He told Fitzgerald that he
personally was "fighting simply to keep the old way of things ... fighting
for Princeton, I suppose, for in spite of all its faults it somehow represents
all that I want to hold on to."[10] Fighting for Princeton? Yes, because
Princeton's social system may have been challenged, but the sense of
Princeton as the closest-place-to-perfection on earth never fades.
Although the act of publishing *This Side of Paradise* caused Princeton to
exile Fitzgerald a second time, his later prose shows he never abandoned
his vision of the place as paradise.

The football game sometimes represents the equivalent of a religious
icon or ritual in Fitzgerald's hermeneutic of Princeton. He exploits the
symbolic possibilities in both the 1927 essay "Princeton" and the 1928
Saturday Evening Post story "The Bowl." Whereas the story refers to specific

Yale–Princeton games, the essay elevates the language of signification and equates such games with the indescribable meaning of modern life: "For at Princeton, as at Yale, football became, back in the nineties, a sort of symbol. Symbol of what? Of the eternal violence of American life? Of the eternal immaturity of the race? The failure of a culture within the walls? Who knows? It became something at first satisfactory, then essential and beautiful."[11]

Fitzgerald attempted to present the central importance of Princeton to the universe in a football song for the school. In a letter addressed to Brooks Bowman, who had written a successful Triangle production song called "East of the Sun," Fitzgerald advised the songwriter to revise the song's lyrics in the following pattern so it could be used as a Princeton cheer:

> East of the sun, west of the moon
> *Lies Princeton*,
> South of the south, north of the north
> *Lies Princeton*....[12]

Ironically, Fitzgerald was scribbling notes about college football on a Princeton newsletter when he died.

Perhaps the hermeneutical significance of Princeton to Fitzgerald is best revealed in "Princeton," an essay he wrote for *College Humor*. It reflects on his undergraduate experiences, but certain passages recall the tone of invocation in the Princeton descriptions of *This Side of Paradise*. His prose is lyrical, impassioned, philosophical at times, because the author continued to be an ardent worshiper at Princeton's altar. Fitzgerald satirically noted that paradise was certainly out of place in New Jersey; he called it "a green Phoenix" rising "out of the ugliest country in the world." It is located in the East, but it is not of the East: "The busy East has already dropped away when the branch train rattles familiarly from the junction."[13]

The concluding paragraph of the essay in particular emphasizes how beautiful—and elusive—Princeton remains as time moves the student further and further away from his days there: "Looking back over a decade one sees the ideal of a university become a myth, a vision, a meadow lark among the smoke stacks. Yet perhaps it is there at Princeton, only more elusive than under the skies of the Prussian Rhineland or Oxfordshire; or perhaps some men come upon it suddenly and possess it, while others wander forever outside. Even these seek in vain through middle age for any corner of the republic that preserves so much of what is fair, gracious, charming in American life."[14]

Fitzgerald critics have for too long focused on the New York City and Long Island of *Gatsby* as the geographic key to his interpretation of American life. When we look at Princeton as the place that transformed him into a writer, we discover Fitzgerald's central hermeneutic. Princeton and the Ivy League remained a key symbol of higher order, purpose, and meaning to Fitzgerald throughout his life. He would repeatedly refocus on Princeton, not as a setting, but as a signifier of the divine, a social and institutional construction containing the highest truth, a symbol more crucial in his early work than even the individual self.

NOTES

1. Bruns, *Inventions*, 112–13; Bercovitch, "Image of America," 158.
2. Aldridge, "Fitzgerald," 33.
3. Fitzgerald, *Afternoon of an Author*, 70.
4. Donaldson, *Fool for Love*, 35.
5. Kuehl, *Apprentice Fiction*, 106. All subsequent page references to "The Spire and the Gargoyle" are to this edition and appear parenthetically in the text.
6. Lehan, "Romantic Self," 5.
7. Adams, *Education of Henry Adams*, 64.
8. Fitzgerald, *This Side of Paradise*, 40. All subsequent page references to *This Side of Paradise* are to the 1920 edition and appear parenthetically in the text.
9. Turnbull, *Scott Fitzgerald*, 52.
10. Donaldson, *Fool for Love*, 35.
11. Fitzgerald, *Afternoon of an Author*, 72.
12. Donaldson, *Fool for Love*, 34.
13. Fitzgerald, *Afternoon of an Author*, 71.
14. Ibid., 79.

WORKS CITED

Adams, Henry. *The Education of Henry Adams*. 1918. New York: Modern Library, 1931.
Aldridge, John. "Fitzgerald: The Horror and the Vision of Paradise." In *F. Scott Fitzgerald: A Collection of Critical Essays*. Ed. Arthur Mizener. Englewood Cliffs, N.J.: Prentice-Hall, 1963. 32–42.
Bercovitch, Sacvan. "The Image of America: From Hermeneutics to Symbolism." In *Early American Literature: A Collection of Critical Essays*. Ed. Michael T. Gilmore. Englewood Cliffs, N.J.: Prentice-Hall, 1980. 159–67.
Bruns, Gerald L. *Inventions: Writing, Textuality, and Understanding in Literary History*. New Haven, Conn.: Yale University Press, 1982.
Donaldson, Scott. *Fool for Love: F. Scott Fitzgerald*. New York: Congdon & Weed, 1983.
Fitzgerald, F. Scott. *Afternoon of an Author: A Selection of Uncollected Stories and Essays*. Ed. Arthur Mizener. New York: Scribners, 1958.
———. *This Side of Paradise*. New York: Scribners, 1920.

Kuehl, John, ed. *The Apprentice Fiction of F. Scott Fitzgerald: 1909–1917*. New Brunswick, N.J.: Rutgers University Press, 1965.

Lehan, Richard. "The Romantic Self and the Uses of Place in the Short Stories of F. Scott Fitzgerald." In *The Short Stories of F. Scott Fitzgerald: New Approaches in Criticism*. Ed. Jackson R. Bryer. Madison: University of Wisconsin Press, 1982. 3–21.

Turnbull, Andrew. *Scott Fitzgerald*. New York: Scribners, 1962.

MEREDITH GOLDSMITH

White Skin, White Mask: Passing, Posing, and Performing in The Great Gatsby

The scandal of Jay Gatsby's success can only be described, it seems, through a series of ethnic and racial analogies. In the bewildered eyes of Nick Carraway, Jay Gatsby could have sprung more easily from "the swamps of Louisiana or from the lower East Side of New York" than alighted fully formed on the shore of Long Island Sound with no family, history, or origins (54). Later in *The Great Gatsby*, Tom Buchanan engages in the same comparative logic, characterizing Gatsby's wooing of Daisy as tantamount to "intermarriage between black and white" (137). For both Tom and Nick, racial miscegenation and immigrant ethnic assimilation provide models of identity formation and upward mobility more easily comprehensible than the amalgam of commerce, love, and ambition underlying Gatsby's rise. Framing the revelation of Gatsby's past with African-American and ethnic comparisons, F. Scott Fitzgerald reveals a lacuna in the narration of white, working-class masculinity.

If the scandal of Gatsby's success lies in his ambiguously ethnic, white, working-class origins, the success of his scandalous behavior resides in his imitation of African-American and ethnic modes of self-definition. In this essay, I argue that Gatsby's mode of self-invention may be fruitfully read against those of the protagonists of Harlem Renaissance and Americanization fiction of the late teens and twenties. In the works of

From *Modern Fiction Studies* 49, 3 (Fall 2003) pp. 443–468. © 2003 for the Purdue Research Foundation by the Johns Hopkins University Press.

177

African-American novelists such as James Weldon Johnson, Walter White, and Nella Larsen and such Jewish-American writers as Abraham Cahan, Anzia Yezierska, and Mary Antin, racial and national identities become objects of imitation, appropriated by parvenu protagonists through the apparatus of speech, costume, and manners. I should make clear that it is not my intention to subsume the differences between the narrative strategies or political contexts of these two genres. While the protagonists of passing narratives usually succeed by concealing the past, often at the risk of violent retribution, the *telos* of the immigrant narrative typically demonstrates an ambivalent integration of the ethnic past and the American present. Despite their differences, passing and Americanization fiction provide examples of the theatrical character of assimilation, as do Gatsby's parties, largely bypassed in Fitzgerald scholarship. Paralleling the Jewish actors of early Hollywood film, who, according to Michael Rogin's thesis, appropriated American identities through the vehicle of blackface, the performers at Gatsby's parties craft social personae through the appropriation of African-American cultural forms into their acts.[1] However, *The Great Gatsby*'s explosion of the dialectic between imitation and authenticity, which Miles Orvell has argued is characteristic of the modernist era, transcends the novel's concerns with performance, ethnicity, and race.[2] The "commodity aesthetic"—what Jean-Christophe Agnew has characterized as a mode of identity formation that "regards acculturation as if it were a form of consumption and consumption, in turn, not as a form of waste or use, but as deliberate and informed accumulation" (135)—that all the characters in this novel exercise implicates them in the logic of imitation, even those who struggle most forcefully to protect themselves from it. Demonstrating the complicity of the Anglo-Saxon leisure class with the cultures of consumerist, racial, and performative imitation (usually considered the prerogative of parvenus and outsiders), Fitzgerald refutes the possibility of any identity, whether racial, class, or ethnic, as "the real thing."[3]

STAGING SOCIAL MOBILITY: RACE, ETHNICITY, AND IMITATION

The masculine *bildungsroman* of the Harlem Renaissance and ethnic immigration provide a new entry point into *The Great Gatsby*, demonstrating the unspoken affinity of Fitzgerald's narrative with these genres. Jimmy Gatz's failed transformation into Jay Gatsby incorporates elements of both, initially suppressing Gatsby's past in the tradition of passing fiction and finally locating the roots of his success in his Franklinesque immigrant ambition. Reading *Gatsby* in tandem with James Weldon Johnson's

Autobiography of an Ex-Coloured Man (1912; 1927) and Abraham Cahan's *The Rise of David Levinsky* (1917)—pivotal examples of the passing and Americanization genres, respectively—illuminates Fitzgerald's tacit dialogue with the African-American and ethnic literary context of the era. Like Gatsby, Johnson's ex-coloured man and Cahan's Levinsky perceive "personality" as an "unbroken series of successful gestures" (*Gatsby* 6), gaining access to leisure-class America by adapting their appearances and manners to an Anglo-American ideal. Cahan's novel traces the rise of a working-class Jewish immigrant to a powerful position in the garment industry; the hero of Johnson's novel, the light-skinned son of a biracial union, embraces the economic and social mobility whiteness offers. Like Gatsby, each hero fetishizes success in the American marketplace and achieves economic success through unscrupulous means. Each mobilizes the romance plot as a source of social mobility; as Gatsby idealizes Daisy's "beautiful white girlhood" (24), Johnson's narrator weds a white woman and cuts himself off from his past, and Levinsky uses a series of women as stepping stones for his rise to power. In addition, all three heroes violate masculine heterosexual norms. Johnson's ex-coloured man notes his own extreme beauty and is mentored by a probably gay white man, David Levinsky enjoys a fervent same-sex friendship with a boyhood friend, after which future heterosexual relations pale in intensity, and Gatsby acts as a vessel for Nick's ambiguously homoerotic attentions.[4] Despite the readily available similarities between *The Great Gatsby* and these texts of black and ethnic mobility, however, scholars have continued to treat the African-American, ethnic, and Anglo-American traditions discretely, as does Gerald Bergevin, who writes that *The Great Gatsby* "takes place in a suburban world that operates as if the simultaneous Harlem Renaissance did not exist" (21). In contrast, this essay claims that modernist urban difference thoroughly saturates the largely suburban world of *The Great Gatsby*, as Fitzgerald's oblique sampling of the discourses of black and ethnic mobility of the era reveals.

Fitzgerald situates Gatsby in the context of early-twentieth-century literary models of black and ethnic self-invention as Nick and Gatsby cross the Queensboro Bridge on their first trip to New York. As Fitzgerald writes, Nick and Gatsby encounter

> A dead man ... in a hearse heaped with blooms, followed by two carriages with drawn blinds and by more cheerful carriages for friends. Their friends looked out at us with the tragic eyes and short upper lips of south-eastern Europeans and I was glad that

the sight of Gatsby's splendid car was included in their somber holiday. As we crossed Blackwell's Island a limousine passed us, driven by a white chauffeur, in which there sat three modish Negroes, two bucks and a girl. I laughed aloud as the yolks of their eyeballs rolled toward us in haughty rivalry.

"Anything can happen now that we've slid over this bridge," I thought; "anything at all ..."

Even Gatsby could happen, without any particular wonder. (73)

As Nick structures the scene, the "negroes" and immigrants gaze at him, rather than he at them or they at each other. Obsessed with the alternately "tragic" and "haughty" eyes of these others—directed toward himself and Gatsby—his own gaze disappears. Nick's inductive reasoning positions immigrant and African-American mobility as a precedent for the strange miracle of Gatsby's existence; Gatsby appears less as a man than as something of an event (something that could "happen"), existing as a shadowy aftereffect of the models of racial and ethnic self-invention on the bridge.

The "modish Negroes" and melancholic immigrants on the bridge provide one example of how racial and ethnic paradigms of identity formation irrupt into *The Great Gatsby*; however, they are hardly alone. The Jewish Meyer Wolfsheim, the novel's most apparent vestige of the Americanization fiction of the 1920s, corroborates Daniel Itzkovitz's reading of representations of Jewish men in early twentieth-century America: the Jewish male, Itzkovitz writes, "was American but foreign; white but racially other; consuming but nonproductive. He was an inauthentic participant in heterosexuality, and inauthentically within the walls of high culture. In all of these cases the Jewish male was imagined to be a secret perversion of the genuine article" (177). Nick first characterizes Wolfsheim in the vocabulary of inauthenticity, asking upon their first meeting, "Who is he anyhow—an actor?" (77). In the manuscript version of the novel, Tom evinces a similar anxiety about the residents of West Egg: "These theatrical people are like Jews," Tom asserts. "One Jew is all right but when you get a crowd of them—" (*The Great Gatsby: A Facsimile* 171). Tom never gets to finish his point, but it seems clear that he associates Jews with the propensity to mass, challenging the singularity of the Anglo-American aristocracy. Like the "old Yiddish comedians" (68) that Gloria Gilbert disparages in Fitzgerald's *The Beautiful and Damned* (1922), Wolfsheim appears dominated by one characteristic, his nose, which, as Sander Gilman notes, served as the "central locus" of Jewish difference in the anti-Semitic imagination (180). Wolfsheim's nose overcomes the rest of his face, "covering Gatsby" with its "expressive" (74) qualities and later "trembling" "tragic[ally]" (77). Physiognomy substitutes for character, in Fitzgerald's closest echo of the scientific racist thought of his day.[5]

If Fitzgerald's ambivalence toward ostensible ethnic vulgarity and actual ethnic success marks his representation of Jews, his depictions of African Americans in the mid-1920s place his readers on much less comfortable ground.[6] In a letter to Carl Van Vechten praising *Nigger Heaven* (1926), for example, Fitzgerald's enthusiasm for the novel that outraged W. E. B. Du Bois underscores Bergevin's point. As Fitzgerald writes, "[Your novel] seems ... to sum up subtly and inclusively, all the *direction* of the northern nigger, or rather, the nigger in New York. Our civilization imposed on such virgin soil takes on a new and more vivid and more poignant horror as if it had been dug out of its context and set down against an accidental and unrelated background" (490). Despite Fitzgerald's deeply offensive language, this unguarded comment deepens the analogy between the "modish Negroes" on the Queensboro Bridge, Gatsby, and Fitzgerald himself. The product of a cross-class and cross-regional marriage, Fitzgerald considered himself something of an aberrant hybrid.[7] As seen here, he reads both Gatsby and the "negroes" on the bridge as such: the first a product of the melding of the decadent culture of the East Coast elite and the midwestern post-immigrant working class and the second the unfortunate imposition of "our civilization" on ostensibly unspoiled black culture. The letter also figures African Americans prior to the Great Migration as a feminized national body, in a parallel fantasy to that of the unspoiled continent, the "fresh, green breast of the new world" Nick envisions at *The Great Gatsby*'s conclusion (189). As Carraway's gaze comes to parallel Fitzgerald's, urban Northern African Americans, the working-class man turned leisure-class dandy, and the product of a cross-class and cross-regional alliance mirror and model the nation itself.

THE PERFORMATIVE APPARATUS OF AMERICANIZATION

Fashion makes explicit the imitative trajectories of narratives of both passing and Americanization. In *Autobiography of an Ex-Coloured Man*, the gift of tailor-made clothing allows the ex-coloured man to reconstitute himself as white, while Cahan's David Levinsky "was forever watching and striving to imitate the dress and the ways of the well-bred American merchants with whom [he] was, or trying to be, thrown" (260). The imitative qualities of Gatsby's clothing—like that of the novel's other sartorial social climbers—

ironizes his efforts at originality. As Gatsby exposes the contents of his armoire to Daisy, for example, his clothing compensates for his lack of familial lineage. Figuring his closet as a kind of Fort Knox, with "bricks" of shirts "piled a dozen feet high," Gatsby appropriates images of might to mask the deficiencies of his origins. If in his "hulking cabinets" Gatsby attempts to approximate Tom Buchanan's brutish economic and physical mastery, Gatsby's acquisition of his clothes signals his alienation from it. Significantly, Gatsby is unaccountable for his own sartorial style, relegating the job to a middleman: "I've got a man in England who buys me clothes. He sends over a selection of things at the beginning of each season, spring and fall" (97). Allowing Dan Cody to outfit him with a new set of clothes, Gatsby, like Levinsky and the ex-coloured man, capitalizes on his homosocial, professional, and personal associations to facilitate his social mobility.[8]

Like his clothing, Gatsby's efforts to transform his physical appearance also suggest his bodily alienation from the Anglo-American leisure class. We remember that Gatsby watches mesmerized as Daisy raises his "pure dull gold" brush to her blonde hair. The monosyllabic description of the brush, with its lack of serial commas, suggests an inimitable quality ostensibly matching Daisy's own perfection. But as Gatsby notes to Nick, "It's the funniest thing, old sport ... I can't—when I try to—" (97). Gatsby's near-speechless moment as he watches Daisy brush her hair, emphasized by its dashes, calls attention to hair itself, another link between *Gatsby* and the fiction of passing and Americanization. Hair lies on a bodily boundary, occupying a liminal position between self and world, and alterations to male hair certify the self-transformation in narratives of both passing and Americanization. For example, the loss of David Levinsky's sidelocks on his first day in America effects his symbolic transformation into an American (Cahan 101). When the ex-coloured man vows to live as a white man, he claims that he will "change his name, raise a mustache, and let the world take [him] for what it would" (Johnson 190). As a child, the narrator exploits the light/dark contrasts of his skin and hair to convince himself that he is white: upon learning of his mother's blackness, the ex-coloured man "notice[s] the softness and glossiness of [his] dark hair that fell in waves over my temples, making [his] forehead appear even whiter than it really was" (Johnson 17). Fitzgerald's depiction of Gatsby's hair casts class mobility in the terms of the manipulation of both self- and external perception both Johnson and Cahan's narratives suggest. While Gatsby's hair "looks as if it were trimmed every day" (54), Nick accentuates the continuities between Gatsby's body and the objects around him, noting that his own lawn has been "well-shaved" by Gatsby's gardener (93). During Gatsby's tenure as Dan Cody's assistant, he styles his hair in a dashing pompadour (99), making himself "just the sort of Jay Gatsby that a seventeen year old boy would be likely to invent" (104). Like Cahan's David Levinsky and Johnson's ex-colored man, Gatsby's changes to his hair style encode his efforts at self-revision on the body for the external gaze.

In the *Gatsby* manuscripts, Fitzgerald underscores the class and gender implications of hairstyle, linking Gatsby's style choice more closely to those of Daisy's. At Gatsby's second party, Daisy and Tom encounter the Star. The Star's eagerness to copy Daisy's haircut flatters Gatsby; Daisy, refusing to be "the originator of a new vogue," claims that being imitated would "spoil it for me" (*Great Gatsby: Revised* 102). Reversing the norms of fandom, in which audiences yearn to resemble those on screen, here the star yearns to appropriate Daisy's perfection. However, for the working actress to imitate the woman of leisure threatens the boundary between the classes that the Buchanans deem essential: the Star is sustained by publicity, from which Daisy must protect herself to preserve her class position. The circulation of men's images may enhance their reputation, while it threatens those of women: the reproduction of Gatsby's image, whether through news, rumor, or legend increases his power; Tom's scandals land him in the papers but fail to unseat him from his class position. However, the circulation of the female image harbors particular dangers, evoking the historical connection between public women, actresses, and prostitutes (Gallagher 47).[9] Fitzgerald links Daisy and the Star through parallel kissing scenes: when Gatsby recalls kissing Daisy on the Louisville street in 1917 (117), the author uses the same images of whiteness, moonlight, and flowers that he distributes around the director's embrace of the Star (113). For Daisy to admit such parallels, however, is impossible: the circulation of Daisy's image would force her into uneasy familiarity with the actress, endangering both her class and sexual position.

While Fitzgerald might be expected to draw a contrast between those aspects of "personality" (6) that may be externally manipulated—like possessions, clothes, and hair—and those more ostensibly a function of the body—like physical characteristics, Fitzgerald renders just such characteristics the function of imitation and repetition. While Gatsby's smile, for example, first appears to harbor singularity, Fitzgerald ultimately reveals it too as a reproducible commodity:

He smiled understandingly—much more than understandingly. It was one of those rare smiles with a quality of eternal reassurance in it, that you may come across four or five times in life. It faced—or seemed to face—the whole external world for an instant, and then concentrated on *you* with an irresistible prejudice in your favor. It understood you just so far as you wanted to be understood, believed in you as you would like to believe in yourself and assured you that it had precisely the impression of you that, at your best, you hoped to convey. (52–53)

The passage enacts the movement from mass audience to individual viewers; metonymizing the smile until it stands in for Gatsby, Nick allows himself to bask in its glow. Stepping out of the role of mass viewer for a moment, Nick experiences a moment of communion with Gatsby, feeling that their relationship, like Gatsby's with Daisy, is "just personal" (160), liberated from the realm of objects.

However, Gatsby's smile works as a commodity that extends his social power, recalling that of David Levinsky, who develops a "credit face" to solicit investments despite his own lack of capital (Cahan 202). Like Levinsky, Gatsby's smile enables him to elicit trust, facilitating his economic rise. Like an advertisement in its use of the second person, the passage reports Nick's seduction by Gatsby's charisma, marketing Gatsby's smile to the reader as if it were a commodity. In the manuscript, however, Fitzgerald transformed Gatsby's face into an art object: "He was undoubtedly one of the handsomest men I had ever seen—the dark blue eyes opening out into lashes of shining jet were arresting and unforgettable" (*The Great Gatsby: A Facsimile* 53). The transition from the language of art—with its aura intact—to that of reproducible object or advertisement suggests Fitzgerald's increasing awareness of the problem of commodity aesthetics. As Daisy remarks later in the novel, Gatsby "resemble[s] the advertisement of the man" (*Gatsby* 125), although Tom prohibits her from telling us precisely which one. In her identification of Gatsby's nonspecificity, Daisy gets it closer to right than she knows: even Gatsby's seeming uniqueness is bound up with his likeness to a set of commodified representations.

Fitzgerald's collapsing of the boundary between the frankly imitative and the ostensibly authentic links the character at the very top of the novel's economic and racial hierarchy—Daisy—with Wolfsheim, who resides on or near the bottom. *The Great Gatsby* links Daisy and Wolfsheim by contrasting the ostensibly innate class superiority of her voice with the openly imitative aspects of both his and Gatsby's. Most memorably, of course, Daisy's voice metaphorizes the seeming innateness of her class position, while Gatsby's near-Victorian formality recalls the immigrant struggle to master American speech and etiquette, poignantly presented in Cahan's *Rise of David Levinsky*. In addition, Meyer Wolfsheim, the novel's worst speaker, creates a degraded copy of English through his transformation of "Oxford" into "Oggsford" and "connection" into "gonnegtion" (76, 75). Fitzgerald appears to endorse a kind of vocal nativism, in which the decline of English mimics Tom's anxieties about the decline of "Nordic" superiority.

However, where Daisy's "thrilling voice" (13) ostensibly evokes her aristocratic class and racial position, Jordan senses in it the conflict between repression and desire, noting that "perhaps Daisy never went in for amour at all—and yet there's something in that voice of hers" (82). Fitzgerald's manuscripts reveal the conflict between class, gender, and sexuality that Daisy's voice harbors: when Gatsby comments on Daisy's voice, Nick first responds, "She loves you. Her voice is full of it" (*Trimalchio* 96). Nick's sentimentalization of Daisy, notably absent from the novel's final version, reads her voice as the vessel for her suppressed emotions; Gatsby, who has forcibly assimilated the trappings of the leisure class, assesses it more coldly, interpreting the richness of her voice as a signifier of the class position she works to sustain.

Similarly, Wolfsheim's immigrant diction, which Fitzgerald takes such care to differentiate from the Anglo-American norm, reiterates one of *Gatsby*'s signal themes. In a novel whose plot turns on causal uncertainty— notably, Nick reads the fixing of the World Series as something "that merely *happened*, the end of some inevitable chain" (78; emphasis added)—references to "connection," or the lack thereof, suggest the repression of causal links necessary to the maintenance of both the Buchanan and Gatsby worlds. The word "connection," reshaped by Wolfsheim's immigrant accent, becomes literally unspeakable, underscoring the economic and homosocial imperatives underlying the novel's ambiguous causal linkages. Wolfsheim's business "gonnegtions" link men for profit, exposing the conflation of economic and gendered power that is partially responsible for Myrtle's death. Wolfsheim's interest in forging "gonnegtions" registers his mastery of American mores of class and gender rather than his failed imitation of them.

Reading *Gatsby* in tandem with narratives of racial passing and ethnic Americanization complicates Fitzgerald's class politics, transforming Gatsby's persona into one in which the ostensibly biological imperatives of "race" and the supposedly more fluid boundaries of class are complexly and ambiguously intermingled. Inauthenticity, the trope of identity in passing and Americanization fiction, emerges as close to the norm for almost all of *Gatsby*'s characters, even those whose class and ethnic status are usually considered unshakeable. Where this section has located *Gatsby* in respect to

African-American and Jewish-American ethnic literary texts of the 1910s, the next section situates it in relation to the racial and ethnic performance culture of the era, which lends Gatsby's West Egg parties their "spectroscopic gayety" (49).

MASS ENTERTAINMENT AT WEST EGG

Gatsby's parties, which glamorize mixing, mass entertainment, and imitation, the qualities most taboo in the Buchanans' East Egg milieu, serve as the setting for the reproducibility and travesty of white leisure-class identities. In one paradigmatic moment, a "gyps[y] in trembling opal ... moving her hands like Frisco dances out alone on the canvas platform ... the erroneous news goes around that she is Gilda Gray's understudy from the 'Follies.' The party has begun" (45). The allusion to Gilda Gray, one of Florenz Ziegfeld's most famous showgirls, complicates critical understandings of both the cultural politics of *The Great Gatsby* and the Americanization of immigrants in the 1920s culture industry. As Michael Rogin has extensively documented, some Jewish performers in early Hollywood facilitated their transition into Americanness through the donning and exploitation of blackface. However, Rogin's exclusive focus on male actors, Jewish immigrants, and the persistence of minstrelsy precludes the extent to which other white ethnics were engaged in similar processes of appropriative and performative Americanization. For example, Fitzgerald's "gypsy" popularizes African-American cultural forms for a white audience by emulating Joe Frisco, a black male performer who inaccurately touted himself as "The First Jazz Dancer" (Stearns and Stearns 190). In her history of the Ziegfeld showgirl, Linda Mizejewski has shown that impresario Ziegfeld racialized the image of the American Girl by insisting not only that the women he hired were American-born but also that their "parents and grandparents and remoter ancestors were also natives of this country" (qtd. in Mizejewski 109). Ziegfeld's preference for "Nordics" encouraged white ethnic dancers to engage in *Gatsby*-like name changes, and Gilda Gray was in fact the Polish-born Marianne Michalski (Mizejewski 120).

The racial connotations of the putative understudy's performance do not end there. In the *Follies* of 1922, which premiered in the summer of Gatsby's extravaganzas, Gray's signature number commented on the success of *Shuffle Along*, claiming that

It's getting very dark on old Broadway,
You see the change in ev'ry cabaret;

Just like an eclipse on the moon
Ev'ry café now has its dancing coon ...
Real dark-town entertainers hold the stage,
You must black up to be the latest rage. (qtd. in Woll 76)[10]

The song travesties notions of racial authenticity, with blackness infinitely reproducible through the vehicle of burnt cork. However, it also refers to the popularity of Broadway musicals featuring black actors, for as Susan Gubar has argued, "New York's theater district was undergoing a racechange" in the 1920s (114).[11] When Gray announces, "You must black up to be the latest rage" in the face of "[R]ealdark-town entertainers," she suggests the potential obsolescence of white performers like herself in the vogue of African-American performance. Mizejewski notes that the staging of this piece in the 1922 *Follies* made explicit "the acknowledgments and anxieties of cross-racial desire," using lighting and brown make-up to make the white showgirls resemble the "dusky belles" on stage in *Shuffle Along* (129). Drawing upon a constellation of rumor, the uncertainty of origins, and the collapse of authenticity into imitation, the dancer miniaturizes Gatsby's self-transformation.

Fitzgerald's renderings of Gatsby's mansion, car, and entertainments place him at the crossroads of middle-class Broadway realism (Owl Eyes calls Gatsby "a regular Belasco" in ironic praise of his ability to turn his house into a stage set [50]) and such popular spectacles as the circus (128), "amusement parks" (45), and the "world's fair" (86). Vladimir Tostoff's "Jazz History of the World"—described extensively in the manuscripts of *The Great Gatsby* but elided from the published version of the novel—emblematizes the tensions between bourgeois and popular culture that the parties expose. In the final published form of the manuscript, Gatsby's parties endeavor to rein in the carnivalesque energies of popular culture, but as Mitchell Breitwieser suggests, the "scars" of the revision haunt the final product (*"The Great Gatsby"* 66).[12] Shadowed by the excision of racial and ethnic performance, Gatsby's parties simultaneously celebrate the power of popular entertainment and manifest the efforts of bourgeois culture to contain it.

Just as Fitzgerald's revision of the party scenes mutes the presence of African-American and ethnic performance, it parallels similar efforts within 1920s popular culture itself. As Jeffrey Melnick has demonstrated, the composers and lyricists of Tin Pan Alley—many of whom were immigrant or second-generation Jewish Americans—crafted nostalgic representations of southern life that had little to do with the reality of urban Northern African Americans.[13] Gatsby's participation in the expressive culture of the 1920s marks a comparable effort to gain access to an idealized national past. In the manuscripts, for example, Gatsby has written songs reminiscent of Tin Pan Alley, a "vague compendium of all the stuff of fifteen years ago," "which dealt at length with the 'twinkle of the gay guitars' and 'the shining southern moon'" (*The Great Gatsby: A Facsimile* 177). Figuring Gatsby in the role of parvenu composer, writing songs reminiscent of a white southern past he did not experience, makes the mansion at West Egg more a distant outpost of Broadway than a possible competitor with the East Egg milieu.

The manuscript versions of the party scenes underscore Gatsby's exclusion from the narrative of American racial, class, and ethnic history in which Nick and the Buchanans are so comfortably situated. For example, Gatsby's second party was originally a costume party, allowing Fitzgerald to explore race and class tensions more openly than in the published version. In the design of the party, Gatsby attempts to screen contemporary urban race and class relations through the lens of an idealized agricultural past: "It was a harvest dance with the conventional decorations—sheaves of wheat, crossed rakes, corncobs, arranged in geometrical designs and numerous sunflowers on the walls. Straw was knee deep on the floor and a negro dressed as a field hand served cider which nobody wanted at a straw covered bar" (*The Great Gatsby: A Facsimile* 146). The "negro dressed as a field hand" suggests that Gatsby's tastes have not become too sophisticated to eschew the tropes of minstrelsy, while the harvest setting recalls the socially prescribed festive periods of an agricultural order, the changing seasons that comfort Jordan and Nick. Gatsby's nostalgia for African-American field hands, like that of Tin Pan Alley songs that glorified the sunny Southland, suggests his desire for a past not his own. That past resurfaces later in the excised version of the party, in which Gatsby asks Daisy to leave Tom. Daisy refuses, and when asked what she and Gatsby are discussing, remarks, "We're having a row ... about the future—the future of the black race. My theory is, we've got to beat them down" (152), a reprise of Daisy's first sarcastic allusion to Tom's theories of Nordic supremacy. After Daisy confesses the failure of her marriage—and thus Tom's infidelities—to Nick, she tells Tom that she and Nick "talked about the Nordic race" (*Gatsby* 24). In both cases, the rhetoric of white supremacy defends against cross-class adultery, casting sexual relations in race and class terms.

The most significant elision from the party scenes is that of the "Jazz History of the World," which links the popularization of an ostensibly "authentic" genre—jazz—with the ambiguous status of blacks and Jews in the popular cultural world of the 1920s. As Gerald Early argues, the "Jazz History" most probably refers to Paul Whiteman's "symphonic jazz" concert at Aeolian Hall, the moment at which jazz attained popular and critical acceptance. Whiteman's piece aimed to "make a lady out of jazz" (qtd. in Early 131) by creating a musical historical narrative of its evolution, beginning with the first recorded jazz piece, "Livery Stable Blues" (recorded in 1917 by the Original Dixieland Jazz Band) and ending with George Gershwin's *Rhapsody in Blue*. According to Early, the allusion to Whiteman "indicates that Gatsby is not only wealthy enough to hire" a large dance-band "to come to his house but pretentious and status-conscious enough not to have a 'hot' Dixieland-style jazz band play for guests" (131). As Melnick argues, by the 1920s, such Jewish immigrant artists as Gershwin and Berlin were instrumental in recasting jazz as an "American" art form by loosening it from its African-American moorings. Mitchell Breitwieser has commented with great depth and subtlety about the novel's whitening of jazz and the excision of the "Jazz History of the World" from the novel's final version; however, in Fitzgerald's original version, jazz wears not only a white face, but an ethnic and distinctly declassed one. In the published version of *The Great Gatsby*, the composer is the vaguely aristocratic Vladimir Tostoff, whose name, as Michael Holquist notes, suggests Gatsby's improvisatory approach to history and identity (466); in the original, the plebeian-sounding Leo Epstein is the composer. The composer's name change, like Jimmy Gatz's, sublimates ethnicity and class, making difference only faintly palpable.

As depicted in the manuscript, the best-received element of the "Jazz History" absorbs and popularizes racial and ethnic difference. Fitzgerald concludes his depiction of the "Jazz History" with "recognizable straws of famous jazz" (*The Great Gatsby: A Facsimile* 54), "Alexander's Ragtime Band," "The Darktown Strutters' Ball," and "The Beale Street Blues." Each piece Fitzgerald references marks the appropriation and domestication of black popular culture, whether through its composition or its performance. "Alexander's Ragtime Band" (1911), which launched the careers of both lyricist Irving Berlin and performer Al Jolson, mocks the pretensions of a black bandleader. The piece alludes to an idealized southern past through echoes of Stephen Foster's "Old Folks at Home," a minstrel piece voicing ex-slaves' ostensible nostalgia for the plantation.[14] African-American songwriter Shelton Brooks wrote "Darktown Strutters Ball," as well as "Some of These Days," for the Jewish-American singer Sophie Tucker, who rose to fame as a "coon shouter." Handy's number leads the listener on a tour through Memphis's gritty "Beale Street" (Breitwieser, "*The Great Gatsby*" 67), reproducing ostensibly authentic black working-class culture for white middle-class consumption.[15] Like Gatsby's techniques of class assimilation, the "Jazz History" substitutes imitation for authenticity: when the "Jazz

History" actually uses jazz, it uses only the pieces most familiar and unthreatening to a white middle-class audience. The ultimate excision of the "Jazz History" masks parallels between Gatsby's self-transformation, racial passing, and ethnic Americanization, driving a deeper wedge between notions of race, ethnic, and working-class difference.

To tell global history through jazz would turn a linear narrative of progress on its head, replacing it with what Michael Holquist notes is an "improvisatory" and contingent mode of change (470). However, such a mode of change would legitimate the Gatsbys of the world, elevating theatrical modes of identity formation over essences. The absent presence of the "Jazz History" parallels the absence of *Gatsby*'s narrative of self-transformation from the novel; the omission of the "Jazz History" provides a vivid example of how Fitzgerald's revisions obscure both the novel's and the hero's roots. My readings here have suggested affinities between Gatsby's performance of leisure-class masculinity and the black and ethnic popular culture of the era; the final section of this essay recuperates Gatsby's feminized, declassed, and consumerist mode of identity formation through an analysis of the semiotics and politics of color.

WHAT DID WE DO TO BE SO RED, WHITE, AND BLUE?: OR, FITZGERALD COLORIZED

Fitzgerald's rhetoric of color samples both the burgeoning consumer culture of the 1920s and the nativist paranoia of the era, metaphorizing class in racial terms. As William Leach reports, early-twentieth-century innovations in glass, lighting, and the dye process had introduced over a thousand new shades and hues into the color spectrum, engendering a new color vocabulary designed to increase consumption. In just one example of the new color rhetoric, Estelle DeYoung Barr asked participants for a survey in her Columbia University doctoral thesis in social psychology, "What simple names would you give these colors?" The colors in question were "beige, rose-rust, Chianti, new leaf, Clair de lune, egg-shell, sun dust, biscuit, Spanish flame, rust, mauve, Algerie, ambertone, blanc farina, parokeet, dahlia, taupe, blackberry, aquamarine, Chartreuse, and capucine" (19). If in the case of consumer culture, a new realm of signification threatened to unsettle a stable nineteenth-century notion of color, the results of *Plessy v. Ferguson* (1896) had altered the meaning of color in a radically different way. If white skin no longer guaranteed a legally white person, the tripartite function of whiteness as skin color, hue, and symbol, risked destabilization (Dyer 45).

Fitzgerald's rhetoric of color responds to the culturally and racially charged implications of color by subsuming the anxiety over the visual perception of color—and thus its stability as symbol—into the practice of viewing colorful objects of desire. Thus, Daisy Buchanan is neither a "Nordic Ganymede" like Gloria Gilbert (Fitzgerald, *The Beautiful* 106) nor a "white-Saxon-blonde" like Nicole Diver (*Tender* 67), but wears white dresses and pearls and owns a "little white roadster" (*Gatsby* 79), instantiating her whiteness and class position through her objects. As Alison Lurie notes, because white clothing is so easily soiled, it "has always been popular with those who wish to demonstrate wealth and status through the conspicuous consumption of laundry soap or conspicuous freedom from manual labor" (185). Daisy's commodity aesthetic filters race and class through the conventionally gendered lens of consumerism. Like Daisy, Gatsby and the novel's female consumers transform color into a volatile tool of social mobility, using colorful costumes and objects as tools of theatrical apparatus of self-fashioning.

As historian Matthew Jacobson has demonstrated, 1920s racial theorists argued fiercely for the relation of whiteness to American citizenship (68); similarly, Fitzgerald's rhetoric of color pinpoints the connections between racial and national identity. The title Fitzgerald pressed for at the last minute, *Under the Red, White, and Blue* (*The Great Gatsby: A Facsimile* xiv), attests to the power of the colors of the flag as national symbol. Both the proposed title and the novel itself hint at the flag's surveillant authority, suggested by the "red, white and blue banners" that "*tut-tut-tut-tut* in a disapproving way" as Jordan Baker walks by in wartime Louisville (*Gatsby* 79). Jordan's New Womanhood, signified in her skirt that rises with the wind, seems to offend the conservative ideology the flag represents; it appears to be no accident that Daisy's house has the biggest banner, suggesting the iconicity of her status as a white leisure-class southern woman. However, color marks both the idealized racial nation—white America in wartime—and its paranoid twin, the white nation fearing decline in the face of the rise of the "colored races." Walter Benn Michaels has identified Tom Buchanan's inaccurate citation of Lothrop Stoddard's *The Rising Tide of Color Against White-World Supremacy* (1922), the tract whose "stale ideas" fuel Tom's racial anxieties (25); Tom, whom Michaels characterizes as a "nonironic spokesman" of the "Klan's style of racism" (23), asserts that "The Rise of the Coloured Empires," as he terms it, is "a fine book and everybody ought to read it. The idea is if we don't look out the white race will be—will be utterly submerged" (17). However, one might argue for a more complex interplay between Stoddard and Fitzgerald than the simply allusive, for while Stoddard figures races as colors, Fitzgerald articulates color with racialized class positions. The centerfold map of *The Rising Tide* is filled in with red (ironically standing in for white), yellow, brown, black, and orange (for "Amerindians"), attesting to the difficulty of literalizing racial identity through color. Forecasting a battle between white Europeans and Americans and the world's "colored races" for global control, *The Rising Tide of Color* provides a competing model of history to the occluded "Jazz History of the World." In *Gatsby*, color alternately secures and confounds racial, ethnic, class, and national identities. The rising pile of Gatsby's shirts, for example, feminizes Stoddard's "rising tide of color," relocating Gatsby's ambiguously ethnic whiteness within the rising culture of consumption. The shades in the "soft rich heap" growing before Nick and Daisy's eyes are "coral" and "apple green" and "lavender" (98, 99), reflect the new color vocabulary of the 1920s but violate normative masculine dress codes of the period.[16] Significantly absent are the hues that decorate Daisy's southern home—red, white, and blue—marking Gatsby's exclusion from the color field of white American leisure-class masculinity.

Fitzgerald's semantic play with the word "white" suggests its pliancy as a signifier for racial purity, female virginity, and class superiority. The importance of whiteness as a symbol of sexual, national, and racial purity subjects Daisy to particularly intense scrutiny from her husband, who identifies Daisy as white only after a moment of "infinitesimal hesitation" (18). While Tom seems determined to prove that women in white are not necessarily white women, Daisy alerts the reader to the cultural sanctioning of her whiteness, and perhaps her own ironizing of it, through the incantational phrase "our beautiful white girlhood" (24), whose repetition Tom cuts off. In the Plaza scene, after Tom compares Daisy's affair with Gatsby to "intermarriage between black and white," Jordan murmurs, "We're all white here" (137). In the manuscript version, she tartly adds, "Except possibly Tom" (*Trimalchio* 103). Tom's "hesitation" before identifying Daisy as white recalls what Michaels calls the "feminine threat to racial purity" characteristic of nativist modernism (18, 41); however, Jordan's exclusion of Tom from whiteness primarily calls attention to his bad taste. Because the word "white" adheres to a variety of realms of identity, without fully belonging to any of them, it is particularly vital that Daisy have a child who resembles her—rather than Tom—and who dresses like her in white. The child forms the one unassailable link in Daisy's series of racialized objects: Nick notes that Gatsby had never "really believed in *its* existence before," underscoring Pammy's role as synecdoche for Daisy (123; emphasis added).

While Daisy's daughter vouches for her whiteness, the novel's working-class women are not so lucky. Although, as Klipspringer sings during Daisy's tour of Gatsby's mansion, "[T]he rich get richer and the poor get—children" (101), the novel betrays the song's assertion. Myrtle and George have been married for twelve years without reproducing, and Michaelis's question to George goes repeated and unanswered: "Ever had any children? ... Did you ever have any children?" (165). With the white working-class largely nonreproductive, the upwardly mobile women of the novel manipulate commodity culture to approximate white leisure-class femininity. As several scholars of late-nineteenth- and early-twentieth-century culture have noted, soap and cosmetic advertising propagated racialized ideals of beauty, linking clean, flawless skin to whiteness.[17] Powder emerges as the feminized version of the "foul dust" (*Gatsby* 6) that contaminates both Gatsby's dreams and the valley of ashes; while for leisure-class women, makeup serves as an effort to mask and enhance, it transforms independent, working-class women into degraded copies of their ostensible betters. Daisy's powder appears noticeable to no one but herself and Nick, as it floats into the air with her laughter (122), suggesting that Daisy powders herself only to protect her own beauty, rather than to enhance it. Powder subtly masks the brown hue on Jordan's fingers (122), referencing both the 1920s suntan craze (Piess 151) and Jordan's slightly masculine outdoor athleticism. In contrast, Catherine, the novel's fleeting portrayal of a bohemian flapper, seems in need of a makeover. With her "complexion powdered milky white," lending a "blurred air" to her countenance (34), Catherine's cosmetic self-fashioning transforms her white face into a white mask.

Although Myrtle Wilson attempts neither to mask nor to enhance her "smoldering" "vitality" through a layer of cosmetics (30), she endeavors to prove herself a woman of Daisy's status through a melange of color, fashion, and commodities. Fitzgerald signals Myrtle's thwarted desires for self-improvement, her sexual imprisonment, and her ultimate demise through the "list of things" that Myrtle has to "get," which include "a massage and a wave and a collar for the dog and one of those cute little ash trays where you touch a spring and a wreath with a black silk bow for mother's grave that'll last all summer" (41). Anyone who changes her clothes three times in one day has a point to make: on the day of the Harlem party, Myrtle begins in a "spotted dress of dark blue crepe-de-chine" (30), whose color suggests working-class respectability, while its fabric—a bit dressy for work in a gas station—implies Myrtle's yearning for mobility. After changing for her trip to town, Myrtle uses color in an attempt to approximate the Buchanans' class position. Selecting a "lavender-colored" taxi with "grey upholstery," Myrtle's style, as Ronald Berman writes, "suggests an ideal of moneyed tastefulness; while a gray interior goes with her communication of 'impressive hauteur,' signifying that she should indeed become Mrs. Buchanan" (53). The gray interior is more ambiguous than Berman suggests: even as the upholstery signifies her effort to master a new canon of taste, it simultaneously recalls the gray zone of the valley of ashes. Finally clad in "an elaborate afternoon dress of cream colored chiffon" (35), Myrtle attempts to signify access to the Buchanan class through color, costume, and gesture. Wilson's wife differs from Daisy in crucial ways, however: in the face of Daisy's singularity, Myrtle produces only copies, most obviously in her repetition of Daisy's name, which causes Tom to break her nose in a "short deft movement" (41). In contrast to the elaborateness of Myrtle's gown, Fitzgerald notes only the whiteness of Daisy's dresses, underscoring the simple elegance Myrtle lacks. The distinction between "cream" and "white" marks a colorized class boundary, as the two shades differentiate themselves along the lines of excess versus simplicity, maternal sexuality versus nonreproductive asceticism. As Myrtle attempts to craft a commodity aesthetic that aligns her with women of Daisy's class, racial, and sexual purity, the specificity of Fitzgerald's language suggests her inability to approximate it.

Gatsby's efforts at sartorial and commodity self-fashioning situate him within a distinctly feminized and middle- to working-class mode of identity construction. When Nick and Gatsby make their first trip into New York, he is clad in a "caramel-colored" suit, a color that matches his own "tanned skin" (69, 54). In a candy-colored suit, Gatsby presents himself as a desirable object of consumption for Nick; by harmonizing his brown suit with his tanned skin, which evokes his past as a manual laborer, he removes himself from the canon of whiteness established by Daisy's commodity aesthetic. Gatsby garbs himself in brown for his lunch with Wolfsheim, who is openly excluded from the possibilities of whiteness. Gatsby similarly manipulates color codes later at the rendezvous with Daisy, wearing a "white flannel suit, silver shirt and gold colored tie" (89). Ironically, the splendor of Gatsby's costume is at odds with his physical appearance, for he appears "pale as death," with "dark signs of sleeplessness beneath his eyes" (91, 89). Where working women might use powder to mask their exhaustion, men cannot; pallor links Gatsby to the other pale white men of the novel, Mr. Wilson and Mr. McKee, both workers on the edge of the middle class dependent on the leisure class for their subsistence.

While Gatsby appears able to approximate Daisy's racialized commodity aesthetic, it is his disruption of the masculine and class dictates of his culture that helps bring his masquerade to a close. While Gatsby's first two suits display his efforts to harmonize with his surroundings, providing him a means of camouflage, Gatsby arrives at the Buchanan mansion garbed in the feminized color pink. Significantly, Fitzgerald does not mention Gatsby's costume when he enters the Buchanan mansion, but notes that he "stood in the center of the crimson carpet and gazed around with fascinated eyes. Daisy watched him and laughed her sweet exciting laugh" (122). Gatsby's aesthetic choices mark his transgression of normative categories of class and masculinity in the eyes of Tom Buchanan, for whom wearing a "pink suit" marks the impossibility of being an "Oxford man" (129). Later, however, Nick notes, "I must have felt pretty weird by that time because I could think of nothing except the luminosity of his pink suit under the moon" (150). Significantly, Nick perceives the ability of the suit to transgress the codes of lineage: the "gorgeous pink rag of a suit ma[kes] a bright spot of color against the white steps" of what Nick ironically calls Gatsby's "ancestral home" (162). However, Nick also identifies the suit as a "rag," underscoring its hint of class violation but linking it to the syncopation common to the music of the elided "Jazz History of the World." If, as Ira Gershwin put it in 1918, "The Real American Folksong is a Rag," Gatsby's suit epitomizes the disruptive appropriation of African-American and ethnic codes underpinning his performance of white American masculinity.

Gatsby's death links him to Myrtle and Wilson, the novel's other working-class victims, and the final section of the novel blurs the boundaries between the wealthy communities at the tip of Long Island and the adjoining working-class towns. In the valley of ashes, the consumerist, class, racial, and ethnic implications of color meet and merge. The sheer preponderance of color imagery in this section marks the novel's efforts to categorize the white working class. The color imagery with which Fitzgerald marks Wilson suggests his class ambiguity: his skin "mingl[es] immediately with the cement color of the walls. A white ashen dust veiled his dark suit and his pale hair as it veiled everything in the vicinity" (30). In a suggestive repetition of W. E. B. Du Bois's metaphor for America's racial divide, Fitzgerald uses the image of the veil to demarcate the boundary between the working and leisure classes. Unlike passing protagonists, however, who typically manipulate their juxtapositions of black and white, Wilson appears a victim of his own intermixture. Elided from the ostensibly pure elite at the novel's center, he lacks the bloodline and the color (we learn that he is "anaemic" and "pale" [29, 30]) to secure the whiteness of the Carraway and Buchanan "clans." In the valley of ashes, grayness characterizes not only white working-class masculinity, but also marks the ambiguous status of the European immigrant: a "grey, scrawny Italian child" setting off firecrackers by the railroad tracks—

in an ironic allusion to national independence—matches the color of his surroundings, as does Wilson (30). Later laughing "in a colorless way" (144), Wilson—like the immigrant child and other inhabitants of the valley of ashes—lacks a firm place in the novel's race/color system.

In the aftermath of Myrtle Wilson's death, Fitzgerald's color imagery reprises the juxtaposition of African-American and immigrant modes of mobility Nick first glimpses on the Queensboro Bridge. Color serves as a key to culpability and agency here, as the police link the color of the car to its putative driver. The Greek immigrant Michaelis identifies the car as green, in a suggestive link to the immigrant's "greenhorn" state, the green light on Daisy's dock, and the "fresh, green breast of the new world" at the novel's conclusion (189). Then, however, a "pale, well-dressed Negro step[s] near" to assert that "[I]t was a yellow car ... Big yellow car. New" (147). Despite the momentary presence of the middle-class African-American man (although it is tempting to speculate that he is the unnamed second motorist who runs to Myrtle's body in the road), he is occluded from the official narrative of Myrtle's death. The Greek immigrant, exemplifying what Matthew Jacobson calls the "probationary whiteness" of southern and eastern European immigrants (177), serves as the "principal witness" at the inquest (143), mediating between the African-American eyewitness and the Anglo-American milieu of the courtroom.[18]

The silenced eyewitness provides Ralph Ellison with a synecdoche for the invisibility of African Americans in the European-American literary tradition. In "The Little Man at the Chehaw Station," Ellison creates a model for a resistant African-Americanist critic who sees the condition of blackness as part of the "American experience ... [as] a whole" and "wants the interconnections revealed" (499). He argues that the "little man," "[R]esponding out of a knowledge of the manner in which the mystique of wealth is intertwined with the American mysteries of class and color ... would aid the author [Fitzgerald] in achieving the more complex vision of American experience that was implicit in his material" (498). However, Ellison goes on to argue that Fitzgerald's treatment of the eyewitness demonstrates his failure to achieve such complexity: "How ironic it was in the world of *The Great Gatsby* the witness who could have identified the driver of the death car that led to Gatsby's murder was a black man whose ability to communicate (and communication implies moral judgment) was of no more consequence to the action than that of an ox that might have observed Icarus's sad plunge into the sea" (499). Ellison correctly notes, but overstates, Fitzgerald's flattening of the eyewitness.

The text suggests that the eyewitness saw the car, rather than the driver; Fitzgerald's eyewitness glimpses the (literal) vehicle of class privilege rather than its agent. The symbol of class privilege simultaneously figures class mobility: the identification of a parvenu by his car recalls the car of the "modish Negroes" on the Queensboro Bridge—the "limousine" that bears them out of town. Here the author reverses Nick's earlier examination of the black middle-class, allowing a representative of this group to return the gaze of the white elite, providing its definitive—albeit unrecorded—interpretation. Ellison's "little man," reading this incident from an African-Americanist revisionist perspective, might ask the following: What would it mean to consider *The Great Gatsby*'s analysis of white working- and leisure-class relations as framed, or even mediated, by the black middle-class gaze?

Situating *The Great Gatsby* against African-American and ethnic literary and popular culture of the 1920s demonstrates Fitzgerald's engagement—albeit tentative and ambivalent—with a culture shaped by racial and ethnic difference. Far from ignoring or repressing this aspect of his day, Fitzgerald sublimated difference to the level of style, engaging with the racially and ethnically diverse popular culture of his day through textual allusions and stylistic innovations. Ellison's sense that a "more complex vision of American experience" resided in Fitzgerald's material was thus correct (498); however, the novel's earlier, more palpable engagement with the interweaving of the "mystique of wealth" with "class and color" lay too deeply buried in manuscript material and dense cultural allusions for the "little man's" excavation (498).

The conclusion of *The Great Gatsby* registers the evacuation of the white Anglo-American elite from the shores of Long Island. Tom and Daisy "retreat back into their money or their vast carelessness or whatever it was that kept them together" (187–88), Jordan settles for marriage, and Nick withdraws into his fantasy of the "fresh, green breast of the new world" prior to the degradation of colonial expansion (189). The deaths of Myrtle, Gatsby, and Wilson—the novel's representatives of the white laboring class—foreclose on the possibilities of cross-class union or upward mobility. Despite the white flight that marks the novel's conclusion, however, traces of ethnic and racial difference haunt both the narrative's and the nation's outer limits. Perhaps the black middle-class eyewitness glimpses those traces, but he—like the excised passages, altered titles, fleeting images, minor characters, and oblique cultural references that haunt the novel—has too easily fallen to the side in *Gatsby*'s critical history. Illuminating the racial and ethnic subtexts of *The Great Gatsby* reveals the interdependence of white working-class identity formation with African-American and ethnic models, exposing an alternative genealogy for the man who remains, in Maxwell Perkins's words, "more or less a mystery" (Letter, 20 Nov. 1924. 83).

NOTES

I would like to thank Carmen Gillespie, Marie McAllister, Mason Stokes, and the editors of *Modern Fiction Studies* for their helpful comments with repeated drafts of this essay.

1. See Michael Rogin 73–120. Through a reading of Al Jolson's performance in *The Jazz Singer*, Rogin argues for the role of blackface performance and the appropriation of African-American popular culture as the medium for the transition from immigrant to American identity on screen. Rogin labels *The Jazz Singer* "the collective autobiography of the men who made Hollywood" (84), suggesting its importance in his argument as a paradigm for Jewish-American masculine identity formation.

2. In referring to the dialectic of imitation and authenticity, I allude to Miles Orvell's *The Real Thing: Imitation and Authenticity in American Culture, 1880–1940*. Although Orvell usefully charts the transition from a Victorian fascination with mimesis to a modernist search for the real, his location of this shift solely within Anglo-American culture detracts from the work's relevance for a multiethnic approach to modernism.

3. In *Our America: Nativism, Modernism, and Pluralism*, Walter Benn Michaels links Gatsby's liminality to the racial and ethnic others of the 1920s. However, the rhetoric of qualification and analogy pervade Michaels's argument, allowing him to claim in one section of *Our America* that "Gatsby isn't quite white, and Tom's identification of him as in some sense black suggests the power of the expanded notion of the alien" (25), while he asserts in the notes that "Gatsby needs to change his name to begin to count as a Jew" (150). Michaels deserves credit for identifying precisely the ambiguity around racial and ethnic identity in *Gatsby* and in modernist fiction generally that the slipperiness of his own prose implies. However, the paradigm shift he proposes in his reading of the novel—reading it as a site of solely racial and ethnic rather than class conflict—obscures rather than illuminates the novel's complexity.

4. Thomas Ferraro notes that the *Rise of David Levinsky* and *Autobiography of an Ex-Coloured Man* "insinuate, between ethnic and class mobility, a homosocial 'passing' into heterosexuality" (201). Siobhan Somerville argues for the homoerotics of *Autobiography of an Ex-Coloured Man* (111–25). On the ambiguous masculinity of both Nick and Gatsby, see Fraser and Kerr.

5. Thomas Pauly argues that both Gatsby and Wolfsheim echo representations of the Jewish gangster Arnold Rothstein and possibly one of Rothstein's fronts, Dapper Dan Collins (Robert Tourbillon), known for his fine clothes and grooming.

6. See, for example, "The Off-Shore Pirate" (1920), "A Diamond as Big as the Ritz" (1922), and "Dice, Brassknuckles and Guitar" (1923). While each places African Americans in highly conventional situations—as musicians, slaves, and servants, respectively—in each story, Fitzgerald demonstrates how white elite characters depend on African Americans for their wealth and comfort and how they appropriate speech and behavioral styles from African Americans.

7. Fitzgerald worried over his own ostensible "parvenu" status. As he wrote to John O'Hara in 1933:

> I am half black Irish and half old American stock with the usual exaggerated pretensions. The black Irish half of the family had the money and looked down upon the Maryland side of the family who had, and really had, that certain set of reticences and obligations that go under the poor old shattered word "breeding" (modern form "inhibitions")…. So were I elected King of Scotland tomorrow after graduating from Eton, Magdalene to Guards, with an embryonic history which tied me to the Plantagonets, I would still be a parvenu. (503)

On Fitzgerald's depiction of himself as a cross-regional and cross-class hybrid, see Irwin 4–6.

8. Gatsby's passion for costume recalls that of the two 1920s celebrities, the Prince of Wales, whose sartorial exploits were well-known in the early 1920s, and the racially and sexually ambiguous Rudolph Valentino. On Gatsby's affinities with Valentino, see Clymer.

9. Fitzgerald links almost all the novel's social climbers to the mass circulation of images, particularly photography. The question of mass circulation informs the ambiguity around Jordan Baker, who allows her image to be captured in the "rotogravure pictures of the sporting life" and lets her name be circulated through rumor (23). Her farewell scene with Nick underscores her reproducibility: as Nick tells his story, the narrator notes that "she looked like a good illustration" (185).

10. The enormous popularity of *Shuffle Along* and *The Follies* would have been difficult for Fitzgerald to ignore in 1922. The Fitzgeralds were such avid theatergoers in the early 1920s that, as Zelda Fitzgerald once wrote to her husband, "you took it off the income tax" (qtd. in Bruccoli 300). Ruth Prigozy shows that Fitzgerald knew and used lyrics of the Gershwins, Irving Berlin, Cole Porter, Jerome Kern, and a host of others.

11. Gray, who was believed to have invented the shimmy, explicitly denied the role of black performance in her success: "There weren't any Negroes in Milwaukee," she said, where she claimed to have invented the dance while "shaking her chemise" (qtd. in Stearns and Stearns 105). As Mizejewski notes, the staging and lyrics of "It's Getting Dark on Old Broadway" also "enact the wider appropriation of African-American musical traditions— Ziegfeld's purchase of acts from the *Darktown Follies* and his usage of African American choreographers to instruct white dancers" (129).

12. As Mitchell Breitwieser notes ("*The Great Gatsby*" 63), the most obvious moment of textual "scarring" in the final version of the novel comes immediately after the excision of the Jazz History. Nick remarks, "The nature of the piece eluded me" (54), which as Breitwieser suggests, intimates that he did not fully comprehend the piece, rather than not liking it or not listening ("*The Great Gatsby*" 64). Max Perkins echoed both Nick and Fitzgerald's ambivalence toward the piece: "it pleased me as a tour de force, but one not completely successful" (Letter, 20 Jan. 1925. 92).

13. In *A Right to Sing the Blues*, Jeffrey Melnick asserts that Jewish-American composers like George Gershwin and Irving Berlin claimed identities as makers of cultural fusion through the appropriation of African-American popular cultural forms and the denial of the contribution of black artists. Melnick documents how Jewish-American Tin Pan Alley composers often used their "seeming closeness to African American people and

expressive forms" in exploitative ways (13), and demonstrates how Jewish-American efforts to appropriate whiteness often involved a distancing from any ostensible affinities with African Americans (see especially chapters 1–3). However, a note of hostility toward his Jewish subjects—and even those African-American writers like James Weldon Johnson who were more sanguine than others about the possibilities of African American-Jewish American collaboration (147)—pervades Melnick's account, qualifying its richness as a source for students of early twentieth-century inter-ethnic relations.

14. See Melnick 40–44 for a detailed analysis of Berlin's "minstrel travesty" (43) in "Alexander's Ragtime Band."

15. W. C. Handy's autobiography, *Father of the Blues*, provides the reader with a good introduction to Handy's ambivalence on questions of race, music, and his own past.

16. That Gatsby's monograms, rather than the shirts themselves, are sewn in "Indian blue" only supports my argument (98). Signifiers of both his real and fake identities, the monograms (in a color associated with the flag, yet distanced through the label of "Indian") capture Gatsby's simultaneous Americanness and foreignness.

17. See, for example, McClintock 209–30 for a discussion of how Victorian soap advertisements associated domesticity with both whiteness and the denial of female labor. Piess demonstrates how early-twentieth-century cosmetics advertisements exploited "the aesthetic dimensions of racism—gradations of skin color, textures of hair" (42), linking lightened skin and straightened hair to greater marital and professional opportunities for African American women in particular. Dyer notes the linking of cleanliness, whiteness, and beauty in mid-twentieth-century cosmetics advertising (77–78).

18. In reading this episode and Ralph Ellison's response to it, Breitwieser makes a similar point: "the episode is brutally prohibitive ... but the act of exclusion *shows*" ("*The Great Gatsby*" 47). Breitwieser and I differ in our conclusions, however, regarding Ellison's critique of Fitzgerald and role of the immigrant in mediating the black eyewitness's account.

WORKS CITED

Agnew, Jean-Christophe. "A House of Fiction: Domestic Interiors and the Commodity Aesthetic." *Consuming Visions: Accumulation and Display of Goods in America, 1880–1920*. Ed. Simon Bronner. New York: Norton, 1982. 133–55.

Barr, Estelle DeYoung. *A Psychological Analysis of Fashion Motivation*. New York: Archives of Psychology, 1934.

Bergevin, Gerald. "Theorizing Through an Ethnic Lens." *Modern Language Studies* 26.4 (1996): 14–26.

Berman, Ronald. *The Great Gatsby and Fitzgerald's World of Ideas*. Tuscaloosa: U of Alabama P, 1997.

Breitwieser, Mitchell. "*The Great Gatsby*: Grief, Jazz and the Eye-Witness." *Arizona Quarterly* 47.3 (1991): 17–70.

———. "Jazz Fractures: F. Scott Fitzgerald and Epochal Representation." *American Literary History* 12 (2000): 359–81.

Bruccoli, Matthew J. *Some Sort of Epic Grandeur: The Life of F. Scott Fitzgerald*. New York: Harcourt, 1981.

Cahan, Abraham. *The Rise of David Levinsky*. 1917. New York: Harper, 1993.

Clymer, Jeffory. "'Mr. Nobody From Nowhere': Rudolph Valentino, Jay Gatsby, and the End of the American Race." *Genre* 29 (1996): 161–91.

Donaldson, Scott, ed. *Critical Essays on F. Scott Fitzgerald*. Boston: Hall, 1984.

Dyer, Richard. *White*. New York: Routledge, 1997.

Early, Gerald. "The Lives of Jazz." *American Literary History* 5 (1993): 129–46.

Ellison, Ralph. "The Little Man at Chehaw Station: The American Artist and His Audience." *The Complete Essays of Ralph Ellison*. Ed. John F. Callahan. New York: Modern, 1995. 489–519.

Ferraro, Thomas. *Ethnic Passages: Literary Immigrants in Twentieth-Century America*. Chicago: U of Chicago P, 1993.

Fitzgerald, F. Scott. *The Beautiful and Damned*. New York: Scribners, 1922.

———. "A Diamond as Big as the Ritz." Fitzgerald, *Short Stories* 182–216.

———. "Dice, Brassknuckles and Guitar." Fitzgerald, *Short Stories* 237–58.

———. *The Great Gatsby*. 1925. New York: Scribners, 1991.

———. *The Great Gatsby: A Facsimile of the Manuscript*. Ed. Matthew J. Bruccoli. Washington, DC: Microcard, 1973.

———. *The Great Gatsby: Revised and Rewritten Galleys*. Ed. Matthew J. Bruccoli. New York: Garland, 1990.

———. Letter to Carl Van Vechten. Summer 1926. Fitzgerald, *Letters* 490.

———. Letter to John O'Hara. 18 July 1933. Fitzgerald, *Letters* 503.

———. *The Letters of F. Scott Fitzgerald*. Ed. Andrew Turnbull. New York: Scribners, 1963.

———. "The Off-Shore Pirate." Fitzgerald, *Short Stories* 70–96.

———. *The Short Stories of F. Scott Fitzgerald*. Ed. Matthew J. Bruccoli. New York: Scribners, 1989.

———. *Tender Is the Night*. New York: Scribners, 1934.

———. *Trimalchio: An Early Version of The Great Gatsby*. Ed. James L. West III. Cambridge: Cambridge UP, 2000.

Fraser, Keath. "Another Reading of *The Great Gatsby*." Donaldson 140–52.

Gallagher, Catherine. "George Eliot and *Daniel Deronda*: The Prostitute and the Jewish Question." *Sex, Politics, and Science in the Nineteenth-Century Novel: Selected Papers from the English Institute*. Ed. Ruth Bernard Yeazell. Baltimore: Johns Hopkins UP, 1986. 39–63.

Gilman, Sander. *The Jew's Body*. New York: Routledge, 1991.

Gubar, Susan. *Racechange: White Skin, Black Face in American Culture*. New York: Oxford UP, 1997.

Handy, W. C. *Father of the Blues*. New York: Da Capo, 1941.

Holquist, Michael. "Stereotyping in Autobiography and Historiography: Colonialism in *The Great Gatsby*." *Poetics Today* 9 (1988): 453–72.

Irwin, John T. "Is Fitzgerald a Southern Writer?" *Raritan* 16.3 (1997): 1–23.

Itzkovitz, Daniel. "Secret Temples." *Jews and Other Differences: The New Jewish Cultural Studies*. Ed. Daniel Boyarin and Jonathan Boyarin. Minneapolis: U of Minnesota P, 1998. 176–202.

Jacobson, Matthew Frye. *Whiteness of a Different Color: European Immigrants and the Alchemy of Race*. Cambridge: Harvard UP, 1998.

Johnson, James Weldon. *The Autobiography of an Ex-Coloured Man*. 1912. New York: Knopf, 1989.

Kerr, Frances. "Feeling 'Half-Feminine': Modernism and the Politics of Emotion in *The Great Gatsby.*" *American Literature* 68 (1996): 405–31.

Kuehl, John, and Jackson Bryer. *Dear Scott/Dear Max: The Fitzgerald/Perkins Correspondence.* New York: Scribners, 1971.

Leach, William. *Land of Desire: Merchants, Power, and the Rise of a New American Culture.* New York: Pantheon, 1993.

Lurie, Alison. *The Language of Clothes.* New York: Holt, 1981.

McClintock, Anne. *Imperial Leather: Race, Gender, and Sexuality in the Colonial Contest.* New York: Routledge, 1995.

Melnick, Jeffrey: *A Right to Sing the Blues: African Americans, Jews, and American Popular Song.* Cambridge: Harvard UP, 1999.

Michaels, Walter Benn. *Our America: Nativism, Modernism, and Pluralism.* Durham: Duke UP, 1995.

Mizejewski, Linda. *Ziegfeld Girl: Image and Icon in Culture and Cinema.* Durham: Duke UP, 1999.

Orvell, Miles. *The Real Thing: Imitation and Authenticity in American Culture, 1880–1940.* Chapel Hill: U of North Carolina P, 1989.

Pauly, Thomas. "Gatsby as Gangster." *Studies in American Fiction* 21 (1993): 225–36.

Perkins, Max. Letter to F. Scott Fitzgerald. 20 Nov. 1924. Kuehl and Bryer 83.

———. Letter to F. Scott Fitzgerald. 20 Jan. 1925. Kuehl and Bryer 92.

Piess, Kathy. *Hope in a Jar: The Making of America's Beauty Culture.* New York: Holt, 1998.

Prigozy, Ruth. "'Poor Butterfly': F. Scott Fitzgerald and Popular Music." *Prospects* 2 (1976): 41–67.

Rogin, Michael. *Blackface, White Noise: Jewish Immigrants in the Hollywood Melting Pot.* Berkeley: U of California P, 1996.

Somerville, Siobhan. *Queering the Color Line: Race and the Invention of Homosexuality in American Culture.* Durham: Duke UP, 1999.

Stearns, Marshall, and Jean Stearns. *Jazz Dance: The Story of American Vernacular Dance.* 1968. New York: Da Capo, 1994.

Woll, Allen. *Black Musical Theatre: From Coontown to Dreamgirls.* Baton Rouge: Louisiana State UP, 1989.

PEARL JAMES

History and Masculinity in
F. Scott Fitzgerald's This Side of Paradise

F. Scott Fitzgerald prefaces *This Side of Paradise* with two epigraphs that express a skeptical attitude toward the novel's primary theme, masculine coming-of-age:

> ... Well this side of Paradise! ...
> There's little comfort in the wise.
>
> —Rupert Brooke

> Experience is the name so many people give to their mistakes.
> —Oscar Wilde

Brooke's presence has particular significance: he stands for the young men of Fitzgerald's generation who wanted to be heroes, who volunteered to fight, and who lost their lives in the First World War.[1] Taking the novel's title from him and placing his name on the title page, Fitzgerald uses Brooke's poetry, and the death it recalls, to signify romantic masculine heroism.

Oscar Wilde's bon mot—"Experience is the name so many people give to their mistakes"—dispels that aura of heroism.[2] Wilde's irony mocks the principle of development based on error and reflection, the principle undergirding the bildungsroman. One merely renames "mistakes" as

From *Modern Fiction Studies* 51, 1 (Spring 2005) pp. 1–33. © 2003 for the Purdue Research Foundation by the Johns Hopkins University Press.

"experience." Wilde's wit implies that wisdom *does* arrive, in the form of ironic distance, offering some consolation. But however consoling, Wilde's ironic pose introduces dangers of its own: by aligning himself (and his protagonist) with Wilde, Fitzgerald risks identification with a feminized dandy, with no nation to die for and no traditional masculinity to uphold.

Fitzgerald's epigraphs indicate the difficulties that confronted him as the author of a male bildungsroman in 1920. Together, the quotes from Brooke and Wilde find "little comfort" in wisdom and deflate the notion of individual progress. These references do allow Fitzgerald to trace the failure of his coming-of-age narrative to other writers, but they also betray anxiety about masculinity. Brooke and Wilde—both effete writers with ambiguous sexual identities—exemplify the importance of being on the right side of history. Brooke's heroism and Wilde's ignominy offer contradictory models that the novel's effeminate protagonist must master. From this (fallen) side of paradise, becoming a man seems a difficult prospect. Whether it was a pose to be struck (as it was for Brooke), or a fiction to be narrated (as it is in Wilde's epigram), masculine maturity is *not* a natural possession. Wilde's name and the fate it recalls imply the potentially dire consequences of not achieving it.[3]

This essay reads *This Side of Paradise* as a paradigmatic expression of an unease about masculine coming-of-age that surfaces in early-twentieth-century American culture generally and in the bildungsroman in particular. The novel speaks directly to Henry Adams's autobiography, *The Education of Henry Adams*—"one of the earliest expressions of modern nervousness" (Wieseltier xi)—following its popular republication in 1918. Adams's insistence that older myths of male self-fashioning seemed inadequate to the new, modern world finds profound resonance in Fitzgerald's novel. Both *The Education of Henry Adams* and *This Side of Paradise* describe a crisis in male formation. Scholars have traditionally read *Paradise* as part of Fitzgerald's apprenticeship, or as a thinly veiled autobiographical account of college life. (It is usually remembered as "the Princeton book.") I suggest that we read the novel's flaws as a reflection of a larger cultural anxiety about the coherence of masculinity in the early twentieth century, an anxiety exacerbated by World War I.

Writings from the early part of the twentieth century frequently voice an anxiety that modern life was taking a toll on the character of the American people, particularly American men. People seemed "nervous." In response to an accelerating pace of change, the American character seemed to be losing its firmness. Worse, the new, more fluid identity engendered by modern conditions seemed effeminate. Otto Weininger articulated this cultural logic in his notorious 1903 treatise on character, in which he defines femininity as a "lack of deep-rooted and original ideas" that manifests itself as "extreme adaptability." For Weininger, femininity *is* mobility: "because [women] are nothing in themselves, they can become everything" (320). According to this logic, the masculine type had become vulnerable precisely for those qualities—firmness and innate character—that had once assured his power. In his place, a prototypically feminine self seemed poised to rise. A new set of environmental givens threatened to undermine the coherence of masculine coming-of-age.

Anxiety about modernity and the dangers it posed to masculinity galvanized a variety of cultural formations and responses, including Teddy Roosevelt's popular call for "Strenuous Life," middlebrow movements such as the Boy Scouts, and increasingly popular forms of organized sports and recreation[4]—along with, eventually, the vituperative masculinism (even misogyny) of highbrow male modernists. While Fitzgerald's novel offers only one expression of this anxiety about masculine self-becoming, it was an expression that met with popular appeal: it resonated with readers and almost became a bestseller. It is worth remembering that, up until the time of his death in 1940, *Paradise* was Fitzgerald's most popular novel (Bruccoli 158).

Fitzgerald's novel betrays a suspicion that character, in the sense that it held for nineteenth-century writers, no longer seems tenable. Instead, identity is performed and relatively unstable. In the novel's lexicon, this shift appears as a move from "character" to "personality."[5] Fitzgerald registers this modern way of being in the world as a formal problem: his protagonist, Amory Blaine, can never achieve a coherent character, and, consequently, the novel never reaches a convincing culmination. This shift to "personality" begets the novel's (in)famous generic incoherence.[6] Critics have frequently diagnosed the novel's vagaries as signs of Fitzgerald's indecision about Amory's class position. Amory, like protagonists of the later novels, is both "within and without" the leisure class into which he is born.[7] But Amory struggles to find his place not just economically or in terms of his class, but in terms of gender: he fails to achieve masculinity, rather than adulthood or material comfort. That a desire to banish femininity, rather than immaturity, drives Amory's narrative is clear from Fitzgerald's conclusion: on the last page, Amory declares himself "free from all hysteria" (247)—free from the labile, feminine nervousness that has dogged him throughout the novel. This language draws our attention, first and foremost, to gender trouble.

Amory's story traces the development, not of manly character, but of personality—a new, inferior, and effeminate kind of identity. As the novel describes this more performative, shifting, and so feminine, mode of being in the world, it uncovers more alarming threats to notions of masculinity, including homoerotic desire. The desire to become a man, Fitzgerald suggests, is often accompanied by a desire *for* a particular man, an ideal who becomes both an object to emulate and to love. Amory Blaine's overdetermined desire for his ideal, Dick Humbird, profoundly threatens his ability to come of age and Fitzgerald's ability to narrate a convincing coming-of-age story.

Having depicted its new, modern, and problematically feminine attributes, Fitzgerald recuperates masculinity by connecting it to history. This essay traces the signature aspect of Fitzgerald's fiction—what Malcolm Cowley called Fitzgerald's "sense of living in history" (30)[8]—to an attempt to recuperate the coherence, integrity, and narratability of masculine identity. This signature aspect is a posture that Fitzgerald himself embraced and that has defined much of the criticism of his work. In *Paradise*, Fitzgerald imagines a certain attitude toward history—particularly the history of World War I—as a way to justify an American version of modernism's "new womanly man" (Joyce 403). While many critics have emphasized Fitzgerald's historical sense, we have yet to fully appreciate its origins in the fragility and incoherence of American masculinity. The novel figures masculinity as an unachievable ideal, complicated from without by contradictory cultural imperatives and from within by homoerotic desires, experiences of loss, and feelings of inadequacy. Fitzgerald's turn to history as partial attempt at masculine recuperation, I argue, adumbrates a larger American coming-of-age story scripted in the context of World War I.

GROWING UP NERVOUS: "AMORY, SON OF BEATRICE"

Amory Blaine embodies "American nervousness"—a pandemic, if ethereal, malaise. As Frederick Pierce worried in a 1919 issue of *North American Review*, "Our whole continent has been growing nervous. Everywhere we have had a steady increase in all forces making for neuroticism" (81). According to Pierce, this "neuroticism" preyed especially on men of prominent, New England families; it attacked the traditional masculinity upon which American national preeminence had been founded. In his depiction of Amory Blaine, Fitzgerald echoes this worry, paradoxically tracing his protagonist's effeminacy to his father's elite social origins. Amory's effeminacy is "handed down" by his father, Stephen Blaine. Wealth enables leisure, but leisure breeds degeneracy: inherited money enables Stephen Blaine to pass his life "drowsing" over books in his drawing room, but leaves him dependent upon the demise of male relatives (5). Along with the hope of a fortune, then, Amory inherits passivity. Echoing the work of William Dean Howells, Henry James, Henry Adams, Edith Wharton, and prefiguring that of George Santayana, Fitzgerald suggests that the emergence of a leisure class occasioned a widespread loss of national virility. If Amory follows his father's example, all he can do is drowse over books and wait. (In fact, this problem provides the entire premise for Fitzgerald's second novel, *The Beautiful and Damned* [1922].) Having wealth enables leisure, which engenders femininity; men can earn money, but only at the risk of becoming déclassé. This paradox, prefigured in nineteenth-century works analyzed by Ann Douglas in *The Feminization of American Culture* (1998)and by Eve Sedgwick in *Between Men: English Literature and Male Homosocial Desire* (1985), complicates Amory's accession to masculine independence. Reflecting on its own difficulty in providing a literary model for masculine self-becoming, *Paradise* suggests that reading provides an effeminate pastime—an escape from the world rather a lesson in how to conquer it.

His father's impotence leaves Amory in the hands of his mother, Beatrice, who provides him with an unorthodox, and potentially dangerous, education. She enforces habits of leisure: "Dear, don't *think* of getting out of bed yet. I've always suspected that early rising in early life makes one nervous. Clothilde is having your breakfast brought up. [... T]ake a red-hot bath [...] and just relax your nerves. You can read in the tub if you wish" (6–7).[9] It is as if Beatrice raises Amory as a girl, breeding within him a case of hysteria, or "nerves," which his mother repeatedly complains about. Amory's small rebellions fail to bring him independence. When he gets drunk and makes himself sick, Beatrice boasts, "'This son of mine [...] is entirely sophisticated and quite charming—but delicate—we're all delicate; *here*, you know.' Her hand was radiantly outlined against her beautiful bosom" (7). Beatrice appropriates her son's act of disobedience as evidence of their similarity, rather than their difference: "we're all delicate; *here*." Surrounded by references to Freud, Beatrice's dramatic gesture "*here*" assimilates Amory's exploit into a discourse of female hysteria: her hand on her body suggests the wandering womb that gives this "female trouble" its name. In contrast to the natural categories and physiological constants the word "hysteria" implies, Beatrice transmits it to Amory—despite his male body. After "too many meals in bed," Amory's nervousness reaches a crisis and his appendix bursts (9).

This rupturing of Amory's imaginary womb triggers the intervention of relatives, who separate him from his mother. Fitzgerald's plot traces a version of an actual masculine coming-of-age ritual: during the late nineteenth century, boys and girls were dressed alike in feminine clothing and kept together at home until (approximately) the age of seven, when they were divided into separate spheres. This universal girlhood came to an end for boys when they were dressed in pants and given more independence, being sent to school and allowed to play with other boys outside the home.[10] In *Paradise*'s version of this ritual, Amory is entrusted to an aunt and uncle and then to a boys' preparatory school, which promises to instill masculinity by "drill[ing] Beatrice out of him" (31). But despite its martial language and the rigor such language implies, the school fails to change the "fundamental Amory" (31). Rather than shaping Amory, the school puts a patina on his feminine qualities: "his moodiness, his tendency to pose, his laziness, and his love of playing the fool, were now taken as a matter of course, recognized eccentricities of a star quarterback, a clever actor, and the editor of the [school newspaper]"; after two years at St. Regis's, "small boys [imitated] the very vanities that not long ago had been contemptible weaknesses" (31). Ostensibly masculine activities (notably athleticism) fail to instill masculinity.

Despite the threat Beatrice poses to his masculinity, and despite the necessity of his move to a masculine sphere, Amory Blaine owes his ultimate attainment of masculinity (such as it is) to her. Beatrice is paradigmatically modern; her identity finds its perfect expression in the trends of her time: alcohol; conspicuous consumption; fashionable travel by car, steamer, and train; and the glib exaggerations in which the moderns announced their arrival in the public sphere. It is from his mother that Amory learns to navigate the modern world. She teaches him to manipulate social expectations and their idioms. Just as he will eventually parrot a discourse that relates masculine failure to the experience of World War I, so Beatrice manipulates a late-nineteenth-century discourse about feminine "nerves." Beatrice co-opts this discourse—which was used to naturalize notions of feminine weakness—and theatrically declaims its symptoms as alibis for her transgressions. Exploiting the imprecision of diagnoses such as "nervous breakdown" and "epidemic consumption," Beatrice describes her addiction to alcohol as a series of feminine physiological vulnerabilities (6). Masking her use of alcohol as "nerves" makes it socially acceptable. But if her female trouble is a mask for Beatrice, it seems more fundamental to her son Amory. Her example teaches him to assimilate his effeminate "nerves" within a discourse of masculine military experience and postwar disillusionment.

"DON'T READ HISTORY—MAKE IT"

As Fitzgerald develops his account of Amory's effeminacy, he also begins to identify history as a solution. The novel's division into three parts hints at this structure: Book I: The Romantic Egotist; Interlude: May 1917–February 1919; and Book II: The Education of a Personage. This triptych structure suggests that the youthful "egotist" will be transformed into a "personage" via an intermediary historical "Interlude," the war.[11] Although this transformation ultimately fails to be convincing, Fitzgerald makes its structure explicit. Throughout the novel, he uses episodic divisions and titles to make this process apparent. In Book I (the Princeton section of the novel), for instance, Fitzgerald juxtaposes two episodes—"Historical" and "Ha-Ha Hortense!"—that show Amory playing at becoming a character in relation to history. In the "Historical" episode, the important, public event takes place: the war breaks out. Amory's disconnection from it makes his egotism evident. Instead of taking part in history, as Rupert Brooke famously did, Amory indulges in homoerotic theatrics reminiscent of Oscar Wilde. Although he does not yet realize it, Amory must connect himself to a larger history—namely the war—if he is to overcome his egotistical effeminacy.

Amory's reaction to the outbreak of war signals the limits of his self-conception. "Historical" ironically demonstrates his failure to imagine himself as an agent of, or a participant in, history. He perceives the war as a melodramatic spectacle:

HISTORICAL

The war began in the summer following his freshman year. Beyond a sporting interest in the German dash for Paris the whole affair failed either to thrill or interest him. With the attitude he might have held toward an amusing melodrama he hoped it would be long and bloody. If it had not continued he would have felt like an irate ticket holder at a prizefight where the principals refused to mix it up.

That was his total reaction. (51)

Amory's lack of engagement in the war echoes a common association between spectatorship and femininity, which intensified during the war as it was evoked in propaganda. In a US Food Administration publicity campaign, the American consumer was depicted as a lazy, decadent, and female reader. James Montgomery Flagg used gendered images of spectatorship to appeal to men in his recruiting posters. This image, one in a series of designs that invite an ostensibly male viewer to "be a man" by joining the Navy, attributes reading and war-spectatorship to an aristocratic and effeminate figure. The two male figures in the poster form a contrast: the reader shields himself with his newspaper and turns away from the "real" theater of war, which Flagg pictures behind him on the sea. His features are delineated with fine, almost feminine, care: his lips are slightly pursed, his arched eyebrows disappear into a white brow. His clothes are those of a dandy, his shoes impossibly pointed. Despite similarly fine features, the Navy sailor forms a subtle contrast. He has a more active stance: his body leans forward; he grips the reader's shoulder with one hand, while using the other to gesture, rather grandly, to the sky, the war, and "history." The sailor beckons the reader to join him in an adventure sanctified by the nation and posterity, both of which are symbolized by the eroticized, and dehistoricized, female figure. "History" promises the chance for men to act and so to assert their fundamental difference from and attractiveness to women, who symbolize the nation but cannot, ostensibly, act for it in their own right. Many posters and other media included in the American recruitment campaign work to translate national anxiety about masculinity into war enthusiasm.

In the section following "Historical," Fitzgerald makes the dangers of effeminacy more ominous. This episode, "Ha-Ha Hortense!", features Amory's performance as a chorus girl in a musical put on by the Princeton Triangle Club. It conveys, in contrast to the world stage of "Historical," the smallness of the stage on which Amory acts. It also reiterates the effeminacy of that stage; the Triangle Club promotes a queer, almost camp, theatrical atmosphere:

> "All right, po*nies*!" [...] "Hey, *ponies*!"
> The coach fumed helplessly, the Triangle Club president, glowering with anxiety, varied between furious bursts of authority and fits of temperamental lassitude. [...]
> The ponies took last drags at their cigarettes and slumped into place; the leading lady rushed into the foreground, setting his hands and feet in an atmospheric mince; and as the coach clapped and stamped and tumped and da-da'd, they hashed out a dance.
> (51)

The president's split between "bursts of authority" and "lassitude," along with the coach's "helplessness," repeat Amory's failures to wield authority. The frivolity of the Triangle episode, narrated directly after the news of war, locates Amory within a discourse of a shallow, apathetic, entertainment-hungry—and paradigmatically feminine—home front.

"Ha-Ha Hortense!" indicates the overdetermined origins of Amory's gender crisis. In the first place, Amory's educational institutions foster a theatrical and inauthentic—and so feminine—self. Social success at

Princeton, one of the nation's most elite institutions, comes by acting like a girl; the popular college drag show teaches young men to perform as women, rather than as men. At the same time, this episode broaches the more threatening possibility that Princeton fosters same-sex passion. Here, alongside the other "ponies," the potential homosexuality of Amory's effeminacy emerges in a series of hints: the "leading lady" has a male body and "mince[s]," the "ponies" take "drags" at their cigarettes. Exhibiting a mode of signification that D. A. Miller has described as typical of homosexual subcultures within a larger oppressive culture (16), Fitzgerald makes the queer atmosphere of the Triangle Club an "open secret," requiring the reader to know something (what "drag" means or that "mince" implies sexual availability to other men) in order to interpret the scene's homosexual potential. The presence of Wilde is strong in this section, with the comedic play, the clever humor, the droll effeminacy, and all the queerness his name conjures up. (Not coincidentally, in 1914, when the Princeton administration faulted the Triangle Club for its show, they invoked Wilde's name in order to specify *without daring to name* what they disliked: Triangle participants were "lectured ... on the evil philosophy of Oscar Wilde and others of that ilk" and advised to change their show [Marsden 84].)

Some evidence suggests that the homosexual atmosphere of boarding school and college life was itself a kind of open secret in this period. In a summary of homosexual case studies first published in 1908, Xavier Mayne characterized "most schools" as "forcing-house[s]" of homosexual relationships (91). Furthermore, although cross-dressing in amateur and college theatricals was common in the first two decades of the twentieth century, it was increasingly associated with homosexuality.[12] Mayne reported a case study in which an incident of cross-dressing led to same-sex passion:

"My first irresistible love-affair of a homosexual kind was the outgrowth of a friendship with a chum at the University. J—was wonderfully clever at different 'female roles' in our college farces.... I had not appreciated his 'bisexual' sort of beauty, till he was made a 'flower-girl' in a burlesque.... J—'s photographs were sold all over the town, everybody talked of him. Then I realized how like a lovely, if rather robust, girl he was; and the feeling of sexual desire began to mount." (180)

The candor of Mayne's account may seem far-fetched as a context for *This Side of Paradise*. Taking women's roles was typical among college men of the 1910s and 1920s, and although the Triangle episode in Fitzgerald's novel is limned with homoerotic potential, it is accompanied by heterosexual adventures: Amory uses his popularity and attractiveness as a Triangle to appeal to "P.D.s" ("Popular Daughters"). But Fitzgerald himself was aware of the homoerotic potential of such performances: he performed in drag and encountered the passions such performances could arouse. He flawlessly enacted in his Triangle Club costume the usually feminine role of the beautiful object upon which the audience, and the camera, gazes.[13] Fitzgerald collected newspaper clippings that featured this photograph, along with fan letters and propositions it evoked from men. Fitzgerald knew that his female impersonations (both as a Triangle performer and as an individual partygoer) created sexual and gender ambiguities that many found exciting, uncomfortable, and even potentially dangerous. As he documented in his scrapbook, presidents of several colleges and universities debated the need to ban female impersonation as an activity that put America's elite male youth at risk.[14] The anxiety the Triangle Club's potentially queer atmosphere provokes in the novel pervaded elite colleges, where "American nervousness" seemed to be on the rise.

Having suggested its homoerotic implications, I want to emphasize another important aspect of the Triangle episode. This aspect resurfaces continuously in Fitzgerald's fiction and bears directly on the difficulty of representing a coherent ideal of masculinity. Simply, women's roles seem more stylized, more inauthentic, and thus, paradoxically, easier to con than men's. His female characters are canny, and therefore successful, performers.[15] I do not suggest that being like a woman comes more "naturally" to Fitzgerald, but that in his fiction, women understand what is expected of them, and so can more convincingly *perform* in character. Masculinity, on the other hand, seems incoherently conceived and inadequately scripted: Amory's performance as a "man" never comes to seem natural. Being inauthentic can, ironically, make one seem more coherent. Prefiguring theoretical accounts of performance as a particularly feminine prerogative, Fitzgerald repeatedly conveys femininity as a script. For him, women and their repertoire are to be envied and imitated, desired not in themselves as objects, but in the mobility and modernity that their way of being seems to enable. In Fitzgerald's fiction, masculinity differs from femininity not in offering a more authentic kind of identity, but in offering a less coherent social script.

Fitzgerald's emphasis on Amory's ability to perform illustrates an aspect of what the shift from "character" to "personality" encompassed. Both Fitzgerald's character and his emergence through a disjointed narrative structure depict a shift to what James Livingston has identified as a "discursive self" (144). The notion of the discursive self does away with simple notions of authenticity. This kind of self comes into being through imitation and acquisition rather than through introspection or contemplation. The discursive self, prodded by desire, comes into being in a social world, through relationships, posturing, and exchange. This model of self-becoming is pervasively imagined as a feminine process: a process that produces girls, women, and effeminate men. Amory's problem, then, is dual: the world fails to provide him with coherent masculine roles to play, and, consequently, he passes through a succession of personae. Because of this, the notion of an authentic and enduring self becomes increasingly untenable. Amory's deepest problem, then, is his protean artificiality, which is, ironically, his "fundamental" characteristic (*This Side* 31). Fitzgerald characterizes this artificiality as an essentially feminine way of being in the world. The wider cultural anxiety about masculinity thus provides a crucial context for appreciating the novel's appeal and the urgency with which it turns to history.

"THE MAGNIFICENT, EXQUISITE HUMBIRD"

Fitzgerald's depiction of the problems besetting young men embeds the inauthenticity of modern identity within a homoerotic atmosphere of all-male schools and colleges. He subtly establishes this atmosphere through allusions to Oscar Wilde. At Princeton, a young man initiates a friendship with Amory like this:

> "Ever read any Oscar Wilde?"
> "No. Who wrote it?"
> "It's a man—don't you know? [...] I've just finished a book of his, 'The Picture of Dorian Gray,' and I certainly wish you'd read it." (47)[16]

Such allusions hint at the dangers posed by male bonds. The allusion to Wilde's text reminds the reader that coming of age, when supervised by the wrong mentors, can lead to degeneration; as in the case of Dorian Gray, Amory's position as an attractive ingenue makes him vulnerable to other men's lessons of acculturation.

Amory's most dangerous idealization begins innocently but ends in death. Upon arrival at Princeton, Dick Humbird strikes Amory as the perfect "aristocrat." While "some people couldn't be familiar with a chauffeur without having it returned," Dick "could have lunched at Sherry's with a colored man, yet people would have somehow known that it was all right," Amory muses. Dick is attractive, athletic, and manly; he has "infinite courage, an averagely good mind, and a sense of honor." Dick's sophistication and high social status offer a model Amory strives to imitate. But, in an anticipation of Gatsby, Dick is a fraud: "the shocking truth" is that "his father was a grocery clerk" (71). Exposed as inauthentic, Dick's sophistication takes on other connotations, finally provoking the harshest rules of narrative discipline, and he dies in a car crash.

In the wake of Dick's death, Amory's masculine failure reaches a crisis. Although this scene has received little critical commentary, it constitutes a pivotal event in the novel's plot. Dick's loss is weird; it prompts Amory to seek a series of failures that indirectly repeat his loss. Dick's death is central to the failure of narrating Amory's masculine coming-of-age story: because the meaning of Dick's death is both overdetermined and queer, it cannot be spoken about directly. Its meanings emerge in a series of displaced substitutes that readers of the novel have failed to appreciate.

Interpreting Dick's death requires connecting a series of disparate and interrupted moments. After going drinking in New York, Amory, Dick, and their companions return in two cars to Princeton. Amory, a passenger in the following car, mentally composes a prose poem: "*So the gray car crept nightward in the dark and there was no life stirred as it went by.* [...] *A moment by an inn of lamps and shades, a yellow inn under a yellow moon—then silence, where crescendo laughter fades ... the car swung out again* [...] *then crushed the yellow shadows into blue*" (78). Amory's poetic reverie evokes a "*crush*[ing]" embrace and boundary loss. His latent fantasy is quickly disciplined. As the car rounds the bend, the poetic vision becomes uncannily real: the lead car has "swung out" and overturned by an "inn" and "crushed" its inhabitants, leaving Humbird dead and two others, including a character named Sloane, injured. This disaster seems to have no consequences. Fitzgerald abruptly passes on to other scenes, as if Dick's death is quite forgotten. But it haunts Amory, and that haunting becomes more pronounced as the novel departs from an otherwise realistic mode of narration and takes on increasingly gothic proportions. (The gothic often signifies homosexual panic in literature, as Sedgwick and others have noted.) Some pages after Dick's death, Amory returns to New York City with Sloane, where they are entertained by two chorus girls. At this point, just on the verge of a sexual encounter, Amory finally seems affected by Dick's death: he has a vision of the devil (whom he identifies as Dick); he runs deliriously from the girls' apartment and is chased down the street by the sound of footsteps—footsteps that then seem to be ahead of him. This directional and temporal confusion repeats an aspect of the accident, in which Amory imagined disaster in advance of its occurrence. These temporal disruptions evoke a sense of the demonic, of destiny, and of traumatic repetition: Amory's feeling of terror "fit[s] like a glove everything that had ever preceded it in his life" (104).[17] The evening resembles the one of Dick's death, and this repetition—of place (New York City), of companion (Sloane), of mood (dissipation)—triggers Dick's reappearance. Disoriented and sexually frightened, Amory returns to Princeton, only to see Dick's ghostly face at his window. He tries to ward off the evil by reading H. G. Wells and Rupert Brooke and by narrating the frightful events to D'Invilliers (transforming into what he names as an "experience" [107]). He attempts to bring the feeling of demonic and traumatic destiny under his control, as if to retain the feeling of teleological arrival, without the terrifying loss of self that accompanied it.

In this episode, we encounter the paradigmatic overdetermination of the causes and manifestations of Amory's masculine failure. The day after Dick's death, instead of mourning his friend, Amory leaves to see his girlfriend Isabel, hoping to consummate their relationship. Just as their passion culminates (in a section called "Crescendo!", which both alludes to sexual climax and echoes the poem preceding the accident), the affair is over. Amory "hurt[s]" Isabel with his shirt stud; Isabel faults him for being "not very sympathetic," voicing a reproach that applies, more accurately, to his reaction to Dick's death (82).[18] Through these echoes, Fitzgerald represents elements of grieving, but in dislocated places and times. Instead of mourning for Dick, Amory encounters his loss through the displaced, heterosexual loss of Isabel. Other disasters follow: Amory nearly flunks out of school; his father dies, leaving drastically less money than expected; his friends start leaving for the war. These disappointments—in Isabel, his performance, the loss of his father, his financial circumstances—delay, mask, and justify his melancholic reaction to Dick's death. The impact of Dick's death is disguised as a disappointment in a heterosexual love plot and in other normative male coming-of-age story lines. Love for another man can only find disguised expression. Fitzgerald creates an overabundance of reasons for Amory's feelings of panic.

Amory's fascination with Dick takes on erotic charge after his death: the episode with Dick's ghost is pervaded by a certain *flânerie*, an atmosphere of urban cruising. He catches Amory's attention in a bar, "smile[s] faintly," then he follows him home: "Amory became aware that someone [...] was looking at him. He turned and glanced casually ... a middle-aged man dressed in a brown sack suit, it was, sitting a little apart at a table by himself and watching their party intently. At Amory's glance he smiled faintly" (100). And later, with Phoebe in the apartment,

> There was a minute while temptation crept over him [...] and he took the glass from Phoebe's hand. That was all; for at the second that his decision came, he looked up and saw [...] the man who had been in the café. [...] There the man half sat, half leaned against a pile of pillows [...] His face was cast in [...] yellow wax [...]—rather a sort of virile pallor [...] like a strong man who'd worked in a mine or done night shifts in a damp climate. Amory looked him over carefully and later he could have drawn him after a fashion, down to the merest details. His mouth was the kind that is called frank, and he had steady gray eyes that moved slowly from one to the other of their group, with just the shade of a questioning expression. Amory noticed his hands; they weren't fine at all, but they had versatility and a tenuous strength ... they were nervous hands that sat lightly along the cushions and moved constantly with little jerky openings and closings. Then, suddenly, Amory perceived the feet, and with a rush of blood to the head he realized he was afraid. The feet were all wrong ... with a sort of wrongness he felt rather than knew.... It was like a weakness in a good woman, or blood on satin; one of those terrible incongruities that shake little things in the back of the brain. (101–02)

Fitzgerald's words ("evil," "virile," "wrongness," the "mouth that is called frank") and ellipses are part of a homophobically coded description of homoerotic desire. Amory's gaze seems sensually, if not sexually, motivated: he pays close attention to the man's mouth, his hands, his eyes; his description asks us to imagine not just how the man looks now, but how he might look if he were hot and dirty and seen in low light (working in a mine), or what it might be like to touch and to be touched by him. This gaze gives way to a certain structure of feeling: panic, revulsion, terror. Amory's revulsion has traditionally been glossed as an instance of Fitzgerald's so-called Puritan strain: heterosexual temptation leads to a feeling of shame.[19] But the revulsion Amory experiences in this passage—though admittedly grounded in a possibility of sex with a woman (Phoebe)—is triggered by the presence of Dick's ghost. Dick's ghost is a figure of reproach, not just for sexual dissipation in a general sense, but also for disloyalty: Amory's desire for Phoebe seems to recall an unresolved desire for Dick to mind.

But if Dick's death brings Amory's identity confusion to its crisis, it also triggers his discovery of an idiom that will help him manage such contradictions. Dick's loss becomes the event around which Amory discovers a consoling discourse: one that uses "History"—and in particular tropes used to describe the war—to bestow meaning on otherwise obscene, unspeakable, or unbearable losses. The reasons such losses should be felt to be unspeakable are overdetermined, but the element of homoeroticism should not be overlooked. Homoeroticism pervades both Amory's "problem" and his "cure": the war rhetoric and poetry to which he turns is laced with homoerotic feelings for beloved comrades.[20]

This idiom of loss suits both Amory's admiration and inarticulable desire for Dick because it emerges in relation to heroic death, which freezes time and therefore stabilizes contradiction: Dick is "like those pictures in the Illustrated London News of the English officers who have been killed" (71). Although death threatens Dick's meaning, the discourse of heroic death circulating in relation to the war (in which Brooke was a central iconic figure) offers Amory a way of symbolizing his loss. In arguing that Amory's most intense crisis begins with Dick's death and ends with a talismanic faith in Brooke's power to ward off "evil," I suggest that the wartime rhetoric of manly, heroic sacrifice signifies a great deal more than its official referent. "Rupert Brooke" subsumes Amory's inarticulate feelings of stimulation, loss, and guilt, and the masculine failure that those feelings provoke. It triggers his turn to "history," and to the war, in hope of consolation.

Amory's confusion about what is expected of him as a man and how he can assert a recognizably masculine identity predate his complicated identification with and desire for Dick. But as Amory finds himself able to express his admiration for Dick in an idiom of heroic military masculinity, he becomes better able to symbolize his failures. History becomes a masculinizing trope, not because it eradicates Amory's failures, but because it makes them speakable. History becomes a trope that impersonalizes loss, and so impersonality becomes for Amory, as it had been for an earlier generation of writers, an "antidote for the egotistical, the subjective, the solipsistic" (Cameron 2–3).[21] Most important, a relationship with history seems to offer a cure for effeminacy. The desire for an "impersonal" way of writing about emotional loss was one Fitzgerald shared with other American modernists, particularly Eliot and Pound.[22] A myth of war experience—which reached an apotheosis as millions gave their lives in World War I—becomes the single most important trope of the novel in that it allows Amory to justify his masculine crisis, simultaneously allowing Fitzgerald to justify his protagonist.[23]

"Should we be a Turning Point in History?":
The Myth of War Experience

Death rarely comes when it is expected; it finds most of us inadequately prepared to perform for others. Perhaps for this reason, literature is filled with deathbed scenes; we use fiction to order the unpredictable. Dick's death does not work according to any such literary logic, and so he dies a double death in *This Side of Paradise*: after his death, his shape as a character unravels. In life, Dick's words and gestures always seem "intangibly appropriate," but death transforms him into "a heavy white mass" (79). The spectacle of Dick's inanimate body—a body that is no longer recognizable as Dick—challenges Amory to reconsider his ideal. After Dick's death, Amory's search for identity takes on a more desperate quality. Amory seems to need to attach himself to an external reality that will transcend the vicissitudes both of fate and of his own short attention span. The sophistication of class superiority has been exploded as a myth and a source of vulnerability. As it did for some of Amory's real-life counterparts, including Fitzgerald himself, the war in Europe, "the war to end wars," seemed to offer a solution.[24] As Amory renounces Dick as his model, Fitzgerald places increasing importance on a closely related figure, the soldier-poet, Rupert Brooke. Brooke seems strong exactly where Dick was weak: in his relationship to death. Brooke seemed to understand that death was the ultimate pose to strike.

To sketch the portrait of Brooke familiar to readers in 1920 is to notice that he shared a great deal with the fictional Amory Blaine: he had a literary ambition, he was athletic, and he attended the best schools. Brooke was a member of the ruling class and the social elite; here he may be, as Robert Roulston has pointed out, Amory's (and Fitzgerald's) ideal rather than his equal (129).[25] Brooke had a penchant for student theatricals. He even lost a beloved male companion, his older brother, named Dick.[26] He was also effeminate; a bare-shouldered and ethereal portrait of him made the rounds at Cambridge and earned him homophobic censure.[27] Edward Marsh's "Memoir,"published in 1918 as a preface to the first edition of Brooke's *Collected Poems*—one of Amory's college "discoveries" (96)—hints at Brooke's effeminacy.[28] Most important, however, is the coincidence of Brooke's effeminacy with the difficulty he had in finding his place, his métier—and that the war banished this difficulty once and for all. In January 1915, Brooke wrote an enthusiastic letter describing his military assignment:

> I'm filled with confidence and glorious hopes.... Do you think *perhaps* the fort on the Asiatic corner will want quelling, and we'll

land and come at it from behind, and they'll make a sortie and meet us on the plains of Troy? ... Should we be a Turning Point in History? Oh God!

I've never been quite so happy in all my life, I think. Not quite so pervasively happy; like a stream flowing entirely to one end. I suddenly realize that the ambition of my life has been—since I was two—to go on a military expedition to Constantinople. And when I *thought* I was hungry or sleepy or aching to write a poem—*that* was what I really, blindly, wanted.[29]

Brooke rejoices at the delightfully romantic goal provided by war; his life seems "suddenly" teleological rather than aimless, "like a stream flowing entirely to one end." As his life begins to trace a culturally shared narrative, Brooke can retrospectively attribute a new significance to his entire life story. Otherwise vague and unspoken longings become the prelude to nationally sanctioned masculinity.

Brooke expressed his enthusiasm for his role in the war in a series of widely printed war sonnets. In the most famous of these, "The Soldier," Brooke asserts the meaningfulness of the soldier's death:

> If I should die, think only this of me:
> That there's some corner of a foreign field
> That is forever England. There shall be
> In that rich earth a richer dust concealed;
> A dust whom England bore, shaped, made aware.
> Gave, once, her flowers to love, her ways to roam,
> A body of England's, breathing English air,
> Washed by the rivers, blest by suns of home.
> And think, this heart, all evil shed away,
> A pulse in the eternal mind, no less
> Gives somewhere back the thoughts by England given;
> Her sights and sounds; dreams happy as her day;
> And laughter, learnt of friends; and gentleness,
> In hearts at peace, under an English heaven. (316)

Here Brooke positions himself in relation to the death he knew he was risking, predicting that death will do away with "evil." When that death occurred, he seemed to have possessed an uncanny ability to see history unfolding and to have placed himself strategically within its narrative. This, at least, is how Winston Churchill remembered him to the nation in Brooke's obituary: Brooke "expected to die" and "was willing to die for the dear England whose beauty and majesty he knew" (qtd. in Marsh 170). The ironic fact that Brooke died of blood poisoning before reaching his military target did not matter. Brooke's example taught that history has a way of dignifying mistakes—historical narratives bestow meaning on otherwise arbitrary events. Brooke's death took on the aura of destiny; Dennis Browne (a friend of Brooke's) described passing Lesbos a few weeks after his burial: "We passed Rupert's island at sunset.... Every colour had come into the sea and sky to do him honour; and it seemed that the island must ever be shining with his glory that we buried there" (qtd. in Marsh 170). Brooke's example suggests that one man's weakness and lack of agency can become significant, poignant, and meaningful when dignified as history; a young man with largely unrealized potential can become a national hero in a manly, masculinist tradition.

Brooke's death offered Fitzgerald a model for how to masculinize and justify Amory's effeminacy. Fitzgerald uses the model explicitly by referring to Brooke and implicitly by developing history as a trope that structures manhood. As we've seen, an explicitly historical section, "INTERLUDE: May 1917—February, 1919," divides Amory's development into two phases (139). The dates, inscribed on the page as if on a monument, situate Amory in a public history: the young egotist goes off to war, as if to die and be reborn as a man.[30] Fitzgerald avoids the necessity of narrating a realistic war experience he did not have by structuring this "interlude" with documents and letters—the primary sources of historical narrative. (Indeed, these letters were authentic historical documents insofar as Fitzgerald received them from other people and simply inserted them into his manuscript.[31]) In one letter, Amory's spiritual guide, Monsignor Darcy—the effeminate and celibate priest, hardly the masculine ideal Amory ostensibly needs—suggests that the war will make Amory "hard": "for better or worse you will never again be quite the Amory Blaine that I knew [...] your generation is growing hard, much harder than mine ever grew" (139). He imagines Amory's death: "Amory—I feel, somehow, that this is all; one or both of us is not going to last out this war...." (141). Neither does die, but Fitzgerald uses the war to mark a change, a coming-of-age, a relinquishing of effeminacy. Amory, like his generation, will never be as young (or as *soft*) again.

Fitzgerald marks the difference the war makes by giving Amory a new epithet: prewar Amory is an "egotist," "Narcissus off duty"; postwar Amory is a "personage." "We're not *personalities*, but personages," Darcy tells him (94; emphasis added). Darcy explains what a personage is, helping Amory formulate it as an explicit goal: "he"—and the gender of the pronoun is not unimportant—is "never thought of apart from what he's done" (94). This emphasis on "what he's done" identifies a "personage" with events, actions, history: someone whose record speaks for itself: "He's a bar on which a thousand things have been hung—glittering things [...] but he uses those things with a cold mentality back of them. [... W]hen you feel that your garnered prestige and talents and all that are hung out, you need never bother about anybody; you can cope with them without difficulty" (94). Darcy's description evokes the decorated military hero, on whose breast "glittering things" are hung; the hero whose "cold mentality" enables him to take action without becoming hysterical. Darcy's definition captures Amory's imagination and becomes a key word for Fitzgerald, who uses it persistently to describe Amory's development. Nevertheless, becoming a personage is no simple matter. Darcy himself confuses Amory: one page after admonishing him to be a personage, Darcy "[gives] him more egotistic food for consumption" (95). This metaphor emphasizes the physical nature of egotism, which, like that fatuous but inferior quality, "personality," is a "physical matter almost entirely," and so—like Dick's body—is vulnerable.

The idea of being a "personage"—as opposed to having "personality"—offers Amory a way to order his gender confusion. "Egotism" and "personality" become condensed ways of referring to a whole series of problematic feminine qualities Amory inherits from Beatrice: self-indulgence, emotional excess and hysteria, self-absorption, a body with unseemly appetites and desires. Fitzgerald's formulation echoes T. S. Eliot's call for an "extinction of personality" ("Tradition" 40), a use of artistic form to control and discipline somatic feelings and their sentimental expression. By defining femininity through this series of associations, Amory's performance as a man stands to become more consistent and convincing. With these terms, Fitzgerald attempts to order his novel's narration of male self-becoming.

But Fitzgerald's distinctions are not as absolute as he might like to imply, and so becoming a man remains difficult, if not impossible. Darcy, who formulates the definition of a personage, is himself something of a failure as a man. His flamboyant purple costume, his gushing enthusiasm, his solicitous attention to younger men are all inappropriate when Amory imitates them. He is, like Amory, pretentious and inauthentic. Even his religion is "a thing of lights and shadows"—more an aesthetic than a spiritual experience (233). In other words, even religion fails to offer perfect immunity from personal failings. But all this ambiguity seems to be banished, as it had for Brooke, by death. Crucially, the Monsignor's performance culminates, rather than fails, in death: "Amory kept thinking how Monsignor would have enjoyed his own funeral" (232). Unlike Dick, Beatrice, Stephen Blaine, and the various friends Amory loses in the war, Darcy stays in character even after he dies. Rejecting the religious—and effeminate—source of the Monsignor's personagehood, Amory adapts his lesson and selects a more masculine truth on which to found himself: not religion, but history.[32] After all, this solution had worked for Brooke. Just as Darcy—or Darcy's image—survived death and did not wholly unravel (as Dick had), so did Brooke. Situating oneself in a history of men provides consolation not merely for mortality, but for inadequate manhood.

Fitzgerald attempts to compensate for the novel's disjunctions and his character's inconsistencies through its emphasis on history. In fact, Amory never attains an ideal manliness. Even after the war, he remains vulnerable and effeminate. Fitzgerald makes this particularly clear when Amory loses Rosalind, the most important female romantic character in the novel. When her parents insist that she refuse Amory and marry for money, he is powerless to convince her otherwise. Amory reveals himself as a still unmanly man:

> AMORY: Rosalind, we're on each other's nerves. It's just that we're both high-strung, and this week— [...] (*A little hysterically*) I can't give you up! I can't, that's all! I've got to have you!
>
> ROSALIND: (*A hard note in her voice*) You're being a baby now.
>
> AMORY: (*Wildly*) I don't care! You're spoiling our lives! (169–70)

Rosalind suffers with Amory, but, as Fitzgerald describes the scene, "*there is a difference somehow in the quality of their suffering*" (170). The difference appears in gendered terms that mark Rosalind as masculine (hard, firm, matter-of-fact) and Amory as feminine (hysterical, histrionic). The repressed language from the novel's beginning returns: Amory's "nerves" resurface here. He is "a baby" again and, as his mother had once intimated, he seems too much *like* a woman ("weak *here*") to win a woman.

What should we make of this relapse? Has "history," then, failed? It seems that going to war has failed to make Amory a man—he is not "hard," despite Darcy's prophecy. His compromised masculine agency resurfaces, again, as a repetitive failure with women—itself, in turn, the result of his failure in other masculine arenas, such as financial and professional accomplishment (or, perhaps, as a sign of a recurrent lack of heterosexual desire). In contrast, women continue to succeed where he fails; Rosalind is weirdly both inauthentic and true to her self-interest.

However, Fitzgerald does not wholly give up on history, or personagehood, as a solution for Amory and his plot. If Amory's hysteria resurfaces, it does so with a difference: he can now speak in an idiom of war experience, which transforms his weaknesses into a masculine ailment. This is Amory after leaving Rosalind:

> The Knickerbocker Bar, beamed on by Maxfield Parrish's jovial, colorful "Old King Cole," was well crowded. Amory stepped in the entrance and looked at his wrist-watch; he wanted particularly to know the time, for something in his mind that catalogued and classified liked to chip things off cleanly. Later it would satisfy him in a vague way to be able to think "that thing ended at exactly twenty minutes after eight on Thursday, June 10, 1919." This was allowing for the walk from her house—a walk concerning which he had afterward not the faintest recollection. (172)

Amory identifies himself with history. Focusing on historical details ("twenty minutes after eight") allows him to compensate for feelings of inadequacy. Rosalind's rejection becomes "that thing" that "ended." His interest in recording time and his plan to memorialize his wound emerge directly from the experience of the war, echoing the rituals in which the war was collectively remembered. (The incantatory quality of the public remembrance that the war had ended "exactly" at eleven o'clock on the eleventh day of the eleventh month of 1918 has an echo here.[33]) Amory's attention to the scenery, the time, and the historical layers of fashionable New York allow him to distract himself (and perhaps the reader) from his psychological unreliability ("he had not the faintest recollection" of whole parts of his evening). The sharpness of some details compensates for the omission of others. Thinking like a social historian, or a chronicler of his age, brings the power of selection. One renames "mistakes"—failures—as historical "experience."

This selection resembles the ways in which the war would be remembered. Just as this example is, accounts of the war are pervasively characterized by a fetishism of historical detail, while many of the war's hardest truths remain unexplored.[34] Paradoxically, the detail of such accounts seems designed to enable as much forgetting as remembering. Amory proceeds to get drunk and to "discourse volubly" about his war experience, calling it a "was'e" [waste]. He blames the war for his "los' idealism" and for the fact that it turned him into a "physcal anmal"; although he used to "be straight 'bout women in college," now he does not "givadam"—he has become "Prussian 'bout ev'thing" (173). Just as the alcohol slurs Amory's pronunciation, his talk of the war offers a spurious and blurred account of his wound: he is not a brutal, militaristic "Prussian" at all; he has just been acting "hysterical" and "weak" and been called a "baby." Amory *misremembers* the war as the origin for his depression. The war takes the place of a more direct statement that he has lost Rosalind because he's broke. The war serves as a cover story for a more personal blow to his masculinity that Amory disguises as war-weariness. Disillusionment as a result of the war is a mythic and fraudulent explanation offered for emasculation at the hands of a materialistic, "hard," New Woman. Talking about history becomes a way of both leaving the New Woman out *and* of implicating her in the traumas that modern history seemed to visit on men.

Amory's war experience becomes a cover story for other, more personal and more shaming, failures. Though fighting the war does not permanently resolve Amory's feminine weaknesses, it does offer an idiom for them and make them speakable in culturally acceptable terms. He gains an alibi: after the war, Amory attributes his lack of agency to the war, and explains his impotence as part of a disillusioned postwar zeitgeist that reckons "all Gods dead, all wars fought" (247). In this way, Fitzgerald depicts the "myth of war experience" as an answer to a need for a useable past. To borrow another relevant term from Eliot, the war serves as an objective correlative: a metaphor that successfully justifies (and could evoke in its reader) an overwhelming feeling of loss. Folded within this loss are all those that must remain unspoken or unmourned. In the last few pages of the novel (prefiguring a scene in *Tender is the Night*), Amory visits a cemetery where he looks at the gravestones of Civil War soldiers. As he imagines them lying in perpetual and heroic intimacy, the desire for closeness with other men is implicitly sanctified through the idiom of military sacrifice. This process—of impersonalization through reference to a romanticized military history—constitutes the novel's main method of cloaking inadmissible homoerotic desire, of working through trauma, and thus, of masculinizing its subject. It enables Amory to declare himself "free from all hysteria" (247).

Perhaps because the war ended before Fitzgerald was sent to Europe, his rhetorical uses of the war and its idioms have not received the attention they warrant, despite the appreciation of Fitzgerald's fascination with his contemporary milieu. Some readers of *Paradise* emphasize Amory's late espousal of socialism as the "solution" to his inconsistencies as a character. According to that reading, class-consciousness gives Amory (and Fitzgerald) what he has been lacking all along. But to other readers, Amory's snobbery, along with his political apathy, make the turn to socialism ironic, if not simply ridiculous. Perhaps both his socialist speech and his identification with reminders of the war can be read as part of the same desperate attempt for resolution. Becoming a socialist, like being a soldier in the war, implies taking a position, joining the fray that will later become known as history. This perspective was essential to popular discourse about the war. Joining the march of history and "be[ing] a man" were the dominant lures in recruitment campaigns, and those tropes remained central in how war experience was recalled and memorialized. Being part of history, like being a man, was compensation for enduring traumatic experience. After the war, it became a way of containing, and of glossing over, male wounds. At the end of *Paradise*, historical consciousness—variously expressed—offers Amory a rhetorical means of declaring himself "free from all hysteria."

Its ability to represent history is what Fitzgerald's writing is known for: what Cowley identified, and what subsequent critics have continued to celebrate, as a "sense of living in history"—his ability to transform his and his generation's "actual experiences" into narrative.[35] Recognizing the sexual and gender anxieties that precipitate this turn, we can newly understand both the appeal and the selectivity of Fitzgerald's "sense of living in history." Fitzgerald would continually rework the problem *This Side of Paradise* presents: how to narrate the losses and wounds at the center of a certain kind of male subjectivity (embodied alike by Nick Carraway, Dick Diver, and Monroe Stahr) within discourses that emblematized contemporary culture.

Though Fitzgerald is particularly known for his historical sense, his use of the war is far from idiosyncratic. What is idiosyncratic, I think, is the self-consciousness with which Fitzgerald's novel demonstrates the manipulation of history as a strategy to accommodate gender anxiety. In a variety of discourses and media, the postwar era saw a new myth of war experience, which was used to stereotype male suffering as disillusionment. As cultural historians have reconsidered the experience and impact of World War I, the importance of questions of gender has been increasingly apparent.[36] While it would be too simple to blame the war on a crisis in masculinity, texts from the period make it clear that anxiety about masculinity was central to the enthusiasm for the war, which led directly to its outbreak and to its continuance and to American participation. The war gave men a chance to be men in an honorific and absolute sense: it gave them the chance to do something that women could not do, which—in a world where women were increasingly independent socially, politically and economically—had very tangible appeal. For reasons *Paradise* explores, some Americans felt a need for a more coherent sense of manliness. The war is imagined in *Paradise*, as it was at large, as an opportunity for men to put an otherwise stymied desire for heroism into action and to free themselves from the contagious "hysteria" of an overcivilized and feminized world. Enlistment in an all-male army draws the male body within a special and sanctified sphere: although male bodies were counted cheap individually, they were held dear at the level of national symbolism. As Brooke's sonnet makes plain, male bodies were imagined to be the locus of national identity and coherence. All bodies die, but male bodies that die in the service of the nation have a special value, and so individual men's stories gain a central place in the nation's own, historical, coming-of-age narrative. The myth of war experience continued to be invoked after the war, particularly insofar as masculinity continued to be a locus of cultural anxiety.

This Side of Paradise also suggests that war experience was not, in and of itself, enough to overcome the perceived cultural crisis in masculinity. That crisis continued to be felt, and continued to inform and shape postwar society and how Americans went about commemorating and translating modern war experience into a new myth that would be handed down to subsequent generations. If *This Side of Paradise* offers a false account of the war's meaning, it reminds us to be suspicious about a history that was reinterpreted and reinvented over the course of the twenties and thirties, as the war itself receded into an ever-contested past.

NOTES

I would like to thank Mitchell Breitwiese, Michael Trask, Vera Kutzinski, Alan Trachtenberg, and Leon Sachs for their helpful comments on this essay. I am also grateful to Anna Lee Pauls of Princeton University Library for her help using the Fitzgerald Papers and to Chris Lee for his research assistance.

1. Fitzgerald quotes from Brooke's poem "Tiare Tahiti," which is essentially a carpe diem complaint, disdaining the wisdom that comes with age (Brooke 305–07). *This Side of Paradise* refers to Brooke's *Collected Poems*, which were published in 1918 and prefaced by William Marsh's almost hagiographic *Memoir*.

2. Fitzgerald takes the line from Wilde's *The Picture of Dorian Gray*; see *The Letters of F. Scott Fitzgerald* (323).

3. According to Alan Sinfield, the Wilde trials produced "a major shift in perceptions of the scope of same-sex passion. At that point, the entire, vaguely disconcerting nexus of effeminacy, leisure, idleness, immorality, luxury, insouciance, decadence and aestheticism, which Wilde was perceived, variously, as instantiating, was transformed into a brilliantly

precise image" of "the queer" (3). From then on, he argues, talking about Wilde was a way to refer indirectly to homosexuality (124–25).

4. John Higham describes the popularity of the Boy Scouts and a cult of sports as part of the masculine reaction against industrialization.

5. In chapter 14 of his *Culture as History*, Warren Sussman identifies these keywords as indicators of a shift in cultural notions of identity, but does not refer to gender.

6. In his introduction to the Cambridge edition of *Paradise*, James L. W. West provides an account of the novel's composition, which involved suturing together different material not originally written with the novel in mind. This process undoubtedly contributed to the novel's discontinuities. But the inconclusiveness of Amory's plot cannot be explained away as a simple product of the novel's composition. As West points out, Fitzgerald did substantial revision and intentionally left his portrayal of Amory full of both contradiction and open-endedness. West even restores Fitzgerald's original dash to the novel's ending. I am not the first to treat the novel as a bildungsroman: Jack Hendriksen places *This Side of Paradise* within the bildungsroman tradition and reviews its critical record for earlier (limited) treatment of the issue. I disagree with Hendrikson's conclusions: his claim that "the formal problems in *Paradise* all but dissolve when it is seen how well it fits into the *Bildungsroman* genre" ignores the novel's loose ends (4).

7. This quotation refers to Nick Carraway in *The Great Gatsby* (30).

8. Cowley asserted that Fitzgerald "never lost a quality that very few writers have been able to acquire: a sense of living in history" (30). This aspect of his writing has been a recurrent subject of critical commentary. On Fitzgerald's relationship to history, see also James R. Mellow.

9. Fitzgerald's novel uses ellipses for effect on several occasions. Ellipses that I am using to indicate omissions will appear in brackets throughout the essay.

10. Anthony Rotundo analyzes the importance of this ritual, in which boys were separated from their mothers and the domestic sphere and initiated into an outdoor world of "boy culture." See chapters 2 and 5 of *American Manhood*.

11. Frederick John Hoffman offers the insight that "[t]he division of *This Side of Paradise* into two books was designed to show a process of growth from the 'Egotist' to the 'personage'" [102]). In identifying the binary aspect of Fitzgerald's design, he and others overlook the significance of the short, but important, middle section—the war.

12. Writing about drag shows in the Navy in 1919, George Chauncey, Jr. reports that "female impersonation was an unexceptional part of navy culture during the World War I years.... The ubiquity of such drag shows and the fact that numerous 'straight'-identified men took part in them sometimes served to protect gay female impersonators from suspicion.... But if in some circles the men's stage roles served to legitimate their wearing drag, for most sailors such roles only confirmed the impersonators' identities as queer" (297–98).

13. "Ha Ha Hortense!" evokes the Triangle Show in which Fitzgerald played and for which he wrote the lyrics "Fie Fie Fi-Fi!" (see Bruccoli, chap. 6 and 7; and Marsden 90–94). As Chip Deffaa notes, "Fitzgerald was pleased ... that *The New York Times* and other papers ran a publicity photograph of him—as one of the members of the all-male show who appeared in drag—saying he was 'considered the most beautiful show girl' in the new Triangle Club production, *The Evil Eye*" (5).

14. In the collection of his papers at Princeton University, Fitzgerald's scrapbook contains newspaper clippings of his publicity photograph and the letters that he

received in response; one writer urged Fitzgerald to consider working as a female impersonator. In the same book, he also clipped and saved newspaper articles in which college presidents debated the danger that cross-dressing posed to their students. Yale enacted a rule that men could only perform as women once every two years, lest their sense of themselves as men be damaged. Perhaps disappointed over his suspension from the Triangle Club (and other extracurricular activities as a result of his grades), Fitzgerald took it upon himself to attend a University of Minnesota fraternity party in drag while home for Christmas vacation. This performance also hit the papers ("He's Belle of the Ball Until Astonished Co-eds Find Blond Wig on Chair") and appears in Fitzgerald's scrapbook.

15. Fitzgerald repeatedly imagines femininity in dramatic terms: in *Paradise*, he presents the debutante Rosalind in the form of a play; in "Bernice Bobs her Hair," Marjorie coaches Bernice how to be a socially successful girl by fulfilling male expectations; in *Tender is the Night* (1933), Rosemary Hoyt's role as "Daddy's Girl" prepares her for a "real life" romance with the paternalistic Dick Diver. Fitzgerald's letters and fiction both establish his sense that femininity was an act—he wrote letters to his sister advising her on what to wear, how to carry herself, and how to be a successful woman. He also incorporated such friendly advice to girls in his fiction, particularly his magazine fiction; in "Bernice Bobs Her Hair," one female character advises another:

> You have no ease of manner. Why? Because you're never sure about your personal appearance. When a girl feels she's perfectly groomed and dressed, she can forget that part of her. That's charm.... you never take care of your eyebrows.... you dance straight up instead of bending over a little.... you've got to learn to be nice to men who are sad birds. (367)

16. This encounter marks the beginning of Amory's friendship with Thomas Parke D'Invilliers (a figure based on John Peale Bishop), a poet whose literary passion and sophistication Amory admires. Although D'Invilliers ultimately exerts a positive influence on Amory, other friendships disrupt his development.

17. Fitzgerald's episode conforms to a temporal organization that Cathy Caruth, in chapter 1 of her *Unclaimed Experience* (10–24), identifies as a literary signifier of trauma. According to this description of traumatic temporality, awareness of Dick's death (the trauma) returns after a latency period during which it could not, or would not, be called to mind.

18. The post–car-accident romantic failure strangely recalls an earlier scene in the novel, in which the child Amory invents a fictional automobile accident in order to gain a girl's affections, only to feel revulsion at his success.

19. Bruccoli asserts that Fitzgerald "remained Puritanical about sex" in his life and that that attitude is maintained in his fiction (79). This opinion was also expressed by Leslie Fiedler and has remained general in Fitzgerald criticism. For instance, Sy Kahn asserts, "All of Fitzgerald's heroes, his 'brothers,' as he called them, from Amory Blaine to Dick Diver, were men concerned with fashioning a code or sustaining a belief and, most important, all feel the restraints of the American Puritan heritage.... 'Evil' is identified with sex" (174). I would counter that not all sex is equally evil for Fitzgerald, and using the stark binaries that the "Puritan" code suggests in discussions of Fitzgerald blunt and normalize more complicated attitudes in his fiction.

20. On homoeroticism as an aspect of war writing, see Sarah Cole's essay on "Modernism, Male Intimacy, and the Great War."

21. Sharon Cameron usefully summarizes Ralph Waldo Emerson's definition of "impersonality" in these terms. Cameron is not interested in the implications this term had in terms of gender.

22. In his essay "Tradition and the Individual Talent," Eliot insisted that a true "artist" strives for "a continual extinction of personality" (40). That Pound shared this opinion can be deduced from the cuts he made when he edited *The Waste Land*: he eliminated autobiographical references; see Eliot's *The Waste Land: A Facsimile and Transcript*. This insistence on "impersonality" seems related to their shared desire, as male modernists, to make their writing "new," "hard," and unsentimental, as opposed to literature they identified with women writers and readers. On their collaboration, see chapter 4 of Wayne Kostenbaum's *Double Talk*.

23. George Mosse analyzes the importance of the "myth of war experience" in mobilizing the volunteer armies that fought in the First World War: "All [men who volunteered for war] were affected by the aim of the war, to recapture 'law, morality, faith and conscience' as a means of personal and national regeneration. Manliness was understood as the embodiment of those ideals, and through fighting the good fight men attempted to translate them into action" (26). Although Mosse takes Germany as his primary example, this "myth of war experience" is generally shared by all the combatant nations including America—Amory learns to manipulate this "myth." In addition to Mosse's, I am drawing on the accounts of the following authors of how World War I was memorialized and mythologized: Paul Fussell, Lynne Hanley, John Limon, and Jay Winter.

24. In an earlier draft of the novel, Fitzgerald had used the war more bluntly to bring his novel into shape: when Charles Scribner's Sons rejected the manuscript in 1918 because "neither the hero's career nor his character [were] shown to be brought to any stage which [justified] an ending," Fitzgerald rewrote it with the war in mind: he "dispatched" his protagonist "to the war and callously slew him." More significantly, both Fitzgerald and his sponsor Stephen Leslie used the fact that Fitzgerald might die in combat to try to convince Scribner's to accept the novel. Fitzgerald did not get over to Europe before the war ended, which he would later remember as a major disappointment. See Bruccoli 88–89.

25. Roulston has given the most extensive analysis of Brooke's importance in *Paradise* to date. Many critics have commented on Fitzgerald's use of Brooke's line for his title and have mentioned in passing his enthusiasm for Brooke, including Arthur Mizener, Andrew Turnbull, Henry Dan Piper, and Robert Sklar.

26. Marsh devotes several pages to Brooke's roles in student and amateur theatricals: "Rupert was not a good actor, nor even a good speaker of verse. Yet I feel now that anyone who remembers *Comus*, and remembers it with ever so slight a sense of beauty, will think of Rupert as the central figure of it; and watching rehearsals daily, as I did, I felt that, however much his personal beauty might count for, it was his passionate devotion to the spirit of poetry that really gave [a performance of Milton's] *Comus* its peculiar and indescribable atmosphere" (47–48). This is only one of several grounds on which Fitzgerald would have been likely to identify with Brooke: Fitzgerald shared Brooke's love of Keats (Marsh 39) and, especially, Brooke's air of simultaneous involvement and detachment (Brooke wrote, "I am actor and spectator as well" [Marsh 30]), which

Fitzgerald attributed to himself and to many of his fictional protagonists (most obviously Nick Carraway). For more on Brooke's brother Dick's death, see Marsh 38.

27. A friend of Brooke's, Jacques Raverat, wrote in a letter to Geoffrey Keynes in April 1913, "It's positively obscene about Rupert. Let us write him a very insulting letter, suggesting that a photo of him completely in the nude would doubtless find a large sale" (qtd. in Cole, "'A Body of England's'" 1).

28. This "effeminacy" is never identified as such but only hinted at as "self-absorption," theatricality, and an overly enthusiastic response to "ninety-ish" literature, such as Pater, Wilde, and Dowson (Marsh 30–31, 51–57).

29. This letter from Rupert Brooke, addressed to Miss Asquith and dated January 29, 1915, is included in Marsh's "Memoir" on page 150.

30. That the army took boys (effeminate and otherwise) and made them men was a common trope in film, posters, and fiction during the war; two examples that were popular with American audiences occur in Charlie Chaplin's film *Shoulder Arms* (1918) and in Edith Wharton's novella *The Marne* (1918). In the postwar era, the assertion that male coming-of-age was a direct result of military service was for some a truism and for others a clichéd lie—what the war meant in the lives of the young men who fought in it was at the very center of a debate about how to remember the war.

31. See West's introduction to the Cambridge edition of *Paradise*.

32. The most important limitation that Darcy's example poses is it would require Amory to forsake women once and for all—a requirement that would not satisfy Fitzgerald, who simply insists too much on Amory's romantic inclinations. (Perhaps the loss of Dick would weigh too heavily on the narrative if Amory were to relinquish, in a final way, all heterosexual intrigues.) Following Darcy's example would imply, somehow, that Amory was still indirectly controlled, even castrated, by his mother: Darcy became a "celibate" priest after having been refused by Beatrice; when she said no to him, his sexual life ostensibly ended. To follow in his footsteps would be to fail too utterly.

33. For a detailed account of the remembrance of the Armistice in England, see Adrian Gregory. But in the 1920s and 1930s in all combatant nations, including America, references to the "11th hour of the 11th day of the 11th month" are myriad in films, novels, letters, newspapers, and so on.

34. Recent historians have made this observation about primary sources and the historiography of the war. For instance, Joanna Bourke writes, "The characteristic act of men at war is not dying, it is killing.... What is striking is the lengths some commentators will go to deny the centrality of killing in modern battle" (1–2).

35. The claim to represent "actual experiences" is Fitzgerald's own language from the cover of the first edition of *This Side of Paradise*; see Cowley 30.

36. For considerations of the war's impact on gender and the reciprocal consideration of gender's role in shaping the war, see especially Sandra M. Gilbert and Susan Gubar's *No Man's Land* and *Behind the Lines: Gender and the Two World Wars*, ed. Margaret Randolph Higonnet, et al.

WORKS CITED

Bourke, Joanna. *An Intimate History of Killing: Face-to-Face Killing in Twentieth Century Warfare*. London: Granta, 1999.

Brooke, Rupert. *Rupert Brooke, the Collected Poems, with a Memoir by Edward Marsh*. 1918. 4th ed. London: Sidgwick, 1987.

Bruccoli, Matthew. *Some Sort of Epic Grandeur: The Life of F. Scott Fitzgerald*. New York: Harcourt, 1981.

Cameron, Sharon. "The Way of Life by Abandonment." *Critical Inquiry* 25 (1998): 1–31.

Caruth, Cathy. *Unclaimed Experience: Trauma, Narrative and History*. Baltimore: Johns Hopkins UP, 1996.

Chauncey, George, Jr. "Christian Brotherhood or Sexual Perversion? Homosexual Identities and the Construction of Sexual Boundaries in the World War I Era." *Hidden from History: Reclaiming the Gay and Lesbian Past*. Ed. Martin Bauml Duberman, Martha Vicinus, and George Chauncey, Jr. New York: Pantheon, 1989. 294–316.

Cole, Sarah. "'A Body of England's': Rupert Brooke, Gender, and Purification." MA Thesis. Columbia University, 1998.

———. "Modernism, Male Intimacy, and the Great War." *ELH* 68 (2001): 469–500.

Cowley, Malcolm. *A Second Flowering: Works and Days of the Lost Generation*. New York: Viking, 1973.

Deffaa, Chip. *F. Scott Fitzgerald: The Princeton Years, Selected Writings, 1914–1920*. Fort Bragg, CA: Cypress House, 1966.

Eliot, T. S. "Tradition and the Individual Talent." 1919. *Selected Prose of T. S. Eliot*. Ed. Frank Kermode. New York: Harcourt, 1975. 37–44.

———. *The Waste Land: A Facsimile and Transcript of the Original Drafts including the Annotations of Ezra Pound*. Ed. Valerie Eliot. New York: Harcourt, 1971.

Fitzgerald F. Scott. "Bernice Bobs Her Hair." 1920. *Novels and Stories 1920–1922*. Ed. Jackson R. Bryer. New York: Library of America, 2000. 356–82.

———. *The Great Gatsby*. Ed. Matthew J. Bruccoli. Cambridge: Cambridge UP, 1991.

———. *The Letters of F. Scott Fitzgerald*. Ed. Andrew Turnbull. New York: Scribner's, 1963.

———. Scrapbook: A Scrapbook Record CO 187 I. Writings Oversize, microfilm. F. Scott Fitzgerald Papers. Department of Rare Books and Special Collections, Princeton U Lib.

———. *This Side of Paradise*. 1920. *Novels and Stories 1920–1922*. Ed. Jackson R. Bryer. New York: Library of America, 2000. 1–252.

Fussell, Paul. *The Great War and Modern Memory*. New York: Oxford UP, 1975.

Gilbert, Sandra M., and Susan Gubar. *No Man's Land: The Place of the Woman Writer in the Twentieth Century*. New Haven: Yale UP, 1988.

Gregory, Adrian. *The Silence of Memory: Armistice Day 1919–1946*. Oxford: Berg, 1994.

Hanley, Lynne. *Writing War: Fiction, Gender, and Memory*. Amherst: U of Massachusetts P, 1991.

Hendriksen, Jack. *This Side of Paradise as a Bildungsroman*. New York: Lang, 1993.

Higham, John. "The Reorientation of American Culture in the 1890s." *The Origins of Modern Consciousness*. Ed. John Weiss. Detroit: Wayne State UP, 1965. 25–48.

Higonnet, Margaret Randolph, et al., eds. *Behind the Lines: Gender and the Two World Wars*. New Haven: Yale UP, 1987.

Hoffman, Frederick John. *The Twenties: American Writing in the Postwar Decade.* New York: Viking, 1955.

Joyce, James. *Ulysses.* Ed. Hans Gabler. New York: Vintage, 1986.

Kahn, Sy. "*This Side of Paradise*: The Pageantry of Disillusion." 1966. *F. Scott Fitzgerald: Critical Assessments.* Ed. Henry Claridge. Vol. 2. Mountfield, Eng.: Helm Information, 1991.

Kostenbaum, Wayne. *Double Talk: The Erotics of Male Literary Collaboration.* New York: Routledge, 1989.

Limon, John. *Writing After War: American War Fiction from Realism to Postmodernism.* New York: Oxford UP, 1994.

Livingston, James. *Pragmatism and the Political Economy of Cultural Revolution, 1850–1940.* Chapel Hill: U of North Carolina P, 1994.

Marsden, David. *The Long Kick-Line: A History of the Princeton Triangle Club.* Princeton: Princeton UP, 1968.

Marsh, Edward. "Memoir." Brooke 25–170.

Mayne, Xavier. *The Intersexes: A History of Similisexualism as a Problem in Social Life.* 1908. New York: Arno, 1975.

Mellow, James R. *Invented Lives: F. Scott and Zelda Fitzgerald.* Boston: Houghton 1984.

Miller, D. A. *Bringing Out Roland Barthes.* Berkeley: U of California P, 1992.

Mizener, Arthur. *The Far Side of Paradise: A Biography of F. Scott Fitzgerald.* Boston: Houghton, 1951.

Mosse, George L. *Fallen Soldiers: Reshaping the Memory of the World Wars.* New York: Oxford UP, 1990.

Pierce, Frederick E. "Nervous New England." *North American Review* June 1919: 81–85.

Piper, Henry Dan. *F. Scott Fitzgerald: A Critical Portrait.* New York: Holt, 1965.

Rotundo, Anthony. *American Manhood: Transformations in Masculinity from the Revolution to the Modern Era.* New York: Basic, 1993.

Roulston, Robert. "*This Side of Paradise*: The Ghost of Rupert Brooke." *Fitzgerald/Hemingway Annual* (1975): 117–30.

Sinfield, Alan. *The Wilde Century: Effeminacy, Oscar Wilde, and the Queer Moment.* London: Cassell 1994.

Sklar, Robert. *F. Scott Fitzgerald: The Last Laocoön.* New York: Oxford UP, 1967.

Sussman, Warren. *Culture as History: The Transformation of American Society in the Twentieth Century.* New York: Pantheon, 1973.

Turnbull, Andrew. *Scott Fitzgerald.* New York: Scribner's, 1962.

Weininger, Otto. *Sex and Character.* 1903. New York: Putnam's, 1908.

West, James L. W. Introduction. *This Side of Paradise.* By F. Scott Fitzgerald. Cambridge: Cambridge UP, 1995. xiii–liii.

Wieseltier, Leon. Introduction. *The Education of Henry Adams.* New York: Library of America, 1990. xi–xxii.

Winter, Jay. *Sites of Memory, Sites of Mourning.* Cambridge: Cambridge UP, 1995.

HAROLD BLOOM

Afterthought

It is reasonable to assert that Jay Gatsby was *the* major literary character of the United States in the twentieth century. No single figure created by Faulkner or Hemingway, or by our principal dramatists, was as central a presence in our national mythology as Gatsby. There are few living Americans, of whatever gender, race, ethnic origin, or social class, who do not have at least a little touch of Gatsby in them. Whatever the American Dream has become, its truest contemporary representative remains Jay Gatsby, at once a gangster and a Romantic idealist, and above all a victim of his own High Romantic, Keatsian dream of love. Like his creator, Scott Fitzgerald, Gatsby is the American hero of romance, a vulnerable quester whose fate has the aesthetic dignity of the romance mode at its strongest. Gatsby is neither pathetic nor tragic, because as a quester he meets his appropriate fate, which is to die still lacking in the knowledge that would destroy the spell of his enchantment. His death preserves his greatness, and justifies the title of his story, a title that is anything but ironic.

Gatsby, doom-eager yet desiring a perfect love, or perhaps doom-eager out of that desire, is a wholly American personality, as tender as he is tough. Indeed, Gatsby's Americanism is so central to him that any other national origin would be impossible for him. Fitzgerald memorably remarked of his protagonist that "Jay Gatsby ... sprang from his Platonic conception of himself," and for "Platonic" we could substitute "Emersonian," the proper name for any American Platonism. As a son of God, Gatsby pragmatically seems to have fathered himself. And that may be why Fitzgerald had to portray his hero in the Conradian mode, with Carraway mediating Gatsby for us as Marlow mediates Jim in *Lord Jim*. Gatsby does not reveal himself to us, but to Carraway, who plays Horatio to Gatsby's Hamlet. Perhaps a character who lives in a consuming and destructive hope always has to be mediated for us, lest we be confronted directly by the madness of a Wordsworthian solitary or a Blakean emanation. It is Gatsby's glory that he is not a "realistic" character. How could he be, since his essence is his aspiration, which again is at once sordid and transcendental?

Since Gatsby is a character in a romance, and not a realistic fiction, we cannot apply the criteria of moral realism to his love for the absurdly vacuous Daisy. She is to Gatsby as his enchanted Dulcinea is to Don Quixote: a vision of the ideal. Just as Daisy's love for her brutal husband can be sublimely dismissed by Gatsby as "merely personal," so her defects of character and taste cannot affect Gatsby's attitude towards her, as Carraway teaches us:

> There must have been moments even that afternoon when Daisy tumbled short of his dreams—not through her own fault, but because of the colossal vitality of his illusion. It had gone beyond her, beyond everything. He had thrown himself into it with a creative passion, adding to it all the time, decking it out with every bright feather that drifted his way. No amount of fire or freshness can challenge what a man can store up in his ghostly heart.

It must seem odd to argue for Gatsby's religious significance, since his mindless idealism has no relevance to Christian terms. But it takes on a peculiarly intense meaning if the context is the American religion, which is oddly both Protestant and post-Christian. Gatsby's mythic projection is one of a more-than-Adamic innocence, in which his perpetual optimism, amoral goodness, and visionary hope all are centered in an escape from history, in a sense of being self-begotten. Daisy Buchanan, according to the late Malcolm Cowley, is named for Henry James's Daisy Miller, and *The Great Gatsby*, for all its debt to Conrad, partakes more in the Americanism of Henry James, though the Jamesian dream of innocence is marked by a more pervasive irony. But then Gatsby's Daisy is a snow-queen, ice-cold, while Daisy Miller has more of Gatsby's own warmth. A heroine of American romance, she shares Gatsby's deprecation of time and history, and his exaltation of the questing self.

Is Gatsby, as Marius Bewley once wrote, a criticism of America? I hardly think so, since his effect upon Nick Carraway, and so upon the reader, is so wonderful, and so affectionate. Nick, like Fitzgerald, declines to culminate in the irony of irony; Gatsby saves Nick from that abyss of nihilism, as well as from the pomposities of mere moralizing. More subtly, he seems to give Nick an image of the male side of heterosexual love that can be placed against the sadistic masculinity of Tom Buchanan. We do not know what life Carraway will return to when he goes West, but evidently it will be a life somewhat illuminated by Gatsby's dream of an ideal, heterosexual Romantic love, though the illumination may not prove to be pragmatic.

What would it mean if we interpreted Gatsby the dreamer as an ignorant and failed American lyric poet, whose value somehow survives both ignorance and failure? Gatsby cannot tell his dreams; every attempt he makes to describe his love for Daisy collapses into banality, and yet we no more doubt the reality of Gatsby's passion for Daisy than we doubt the terrible authenticity of the dying Keats's intense desire for Fanny Brawne. It seems absurd to compare the vulgar grandiosity of poor Gatsby's diction to the supreme eloquence of John Keats, but Gatsby is profoundly Keatsian, a direct descendant of the poet-quester in *The Fall of Hyperion*. I take it that a repressed echo of Keats is behind Carraway's sense of a lost, High Romantic music even as he listens to Gatsby's turgid discourses:

> Through all he said, even through his appalling sentimentality,
> I was reminded of something—an elusive rhythm, a fragment of
> lost words that I had heard somewhere a long time ago. For a
> moment a phrase tried to take shape in my mouth and my lips
> parted like a dumb man's, as though there was more struggling
> upon them than a wisp of startled air. But they made no sound,
> and what I had almost remembered was incommunicable forever.

What Carraway (and Fitzgerald) almost remembered may be a crucial passage in *The Fall of Hyperion*, where the poet-quester is nearly destroyed by his silence and his inability to move:

> I heard, I looked: two senses both at once,
> So fine, so subtle, felt the tyranny
> Of that fierce threat and the hard task proposed.
> Prodigious seemed the toil; the leaves were yet
> Burning—when suddenly a palsied chill
> Struck from the paved level up my limbs,

And was ascending quick to put cold grasp
Upon those streams that pulse beside the throat:
I shrieked, and the sharp anguish of my shriek
Stung my own ears—I strove hard to escape
The numbness; strove to gain the lowest step.
Slow, heavy, deadly was my pace: the cold
Grew stifling, suffocating, at the heart;
And when I clasped my hands I felt them not.
One minute before death, my iced foot touched
The lowest stair; and as it touched, life seemed
To pour in at the toes ...

Carraway remains mute; the anguish of Keats's shriek reawakens the
poet to life, and to poetry. Part of Carraway's function surely is to contrast
his own recalcitrances with Gatsby's continual vitality and sense of wonder,
But Carraway anticipates his own narrative of Gatsby's destruction. Gatsby's
foot never touches the lowest stair; there is for him no purgatorial
redemption. But how could there have been "something commensurate to
his capacity for wonder"? The greatness of Gatsby is that there was no
authentic object for his desire, as Daisy's inadequacies render so clear. Like
every true quester in Romantic tradition, Gatsby is both subject and object
of his own quest, though he never could hope to have learned this
bewildering contingency.

Many readers sense that there is a "drowned god" aspect to Gatsby's
fate, doubtless suggested to Fitzgerald by Eliot's *The Waste Land*. Yet it is
difficult to fit such a figure into American myth, as we can see by contrasting
the powerful but enigmatic figure of Whitman's drowned swimmer in "The
Sleepers" to the more evocative and contextualized image of President
Lincoln in "When Lilacs Last in the Dooryard Bloom'd." The American
visionary can die as a father, or as a son, but not as a ritual sacrifice to
rekindle the dead land, because even now our land is far from dead. Gatsby,
a son of God, dies with a curiously religious significance, but one that is
beyond Carraway's understanding. What is best and oldest in Gatsby cannot
die, but returns to the living fullness of the American Dream, itself undying
despite all of its cancellations and farewells, which prove never to have been
final.

What Carraway does come to understand is that Gatsby's freedom was
invested in solitude, and not even in the possibility of Daisy, since marriage
to the actual Daisy could not have sufficed for very long. If your belief is in
"the orgiastic future that year by year recedes," then your belief is in what

Freud called repression, a process that implies that everything significant is already in your past. Gatsby's deepest need was to reverse time, to see his lateness as an ever-early origin. To fulfill that need, you have to be Emerson or Whitman, or if you are a fictive self, then Huck Finn will serve as example. Loving a dream of freedom will work only if you can detach that dream from other individuals, and Gatsby was too open and generous to exercise such detachment.

It does seem, after all, that Fitzgerald placed much of the best of himself in Gatsby. His relation to Gatsby is quite parallel to Flaubert's rueful identification with Emma Bovary. Even Flaubert could not protect himself by his own formidable irony; he suffered with Emma, and so do we. Fitzgerald did not protect himself at all, and he contaminated us with his vulnerability. Perhaps Gatsby does not suffer, being so lost in his dream. We suffer for Gatsby, as Carraway does, but what mitigates that suffering is the extent to which we too, as Americans, are lost in the same dream of love and wealth.

Chronology

1896	Born Francis Scott Key Fitzgerald on September 24, 1896 in St. Paul, Minnesota to Edward Fitzgerald and Mary McQuillan Fitzgerald.
1911	Attends the Newman School, a Catholic boarding school in Hackensack, New Jersey.
1913	Matriculates at Princeton. Works on productions for the university's amateur theatrical company, the Triangle Club.
1917	Leaves Princeton without receiving a degree. Joins the US Army as a Second Lieutenant and goes for training at Fort Leavenworth, Kansas.
1918	Completes his first novel, *The Romantic Egotist*. Meets Zelda Sayre when transferred to Camp Sheridan, Montgomery, Alabama. In October *The Romantic Egotist* is rejected by Scribner's.
1919	After being discharged from the Army, moves to New York, works as a copywriter for an advertising agency. In July, returns to the familial home in St. Paul. Begins revising *The Romantic Egotist*. Under its new title, *This Side of Paradise*, the book is accepted by Scribner's in September.
1920	*This Side of Paradise* published in March. Marries Zelda Sayre on April 3. In September Scribner's publishes *Flappers and Philosophers*, a collection of stories.
1921	Daughter Frances Scott Fitzgerald born on October 26.

1922	*The Beautiful and Damned* published by Scribner's in March. The short story "The Diamond as Big as the Ritz" appears in the *Smart Set* in June. *Tales of the Jazz Age*, a second story collection, published by Scribner's in September.
1925	*The Great Gatsby* published by Scribner's.
1926	A third collection of stories, *All the Sad Young Men*, published by Scribner's.
1927	Spends two months in Hollywood writing scripts for United Artists.
1930	Zelda has a serious nervous breakdown while traveling in Europe.
1931	"Babylon Revisited" published in *The Saturday Evening Post*.
1932	Zelda suffers from a second breakdown, after which she is committed to a psychiatric clinic in Baltimore. She is discharged in June and her novel, *Save Me the Waltz*, is published the same year.
1934	Writes short stories in a desperate attempt to repay his debts after *Tender is the Night* appears to disappointing sales. Suffers a nervous breakdown in June.
1935	Declining physical health attributed to heavy drinking. Recuperates in Asheville, North Carolina.
1936	"The Crack-Up" essays appear in *Esquire* magazine. Zelda sent to a sanitarium in Asheville, where she remains until her death.
1937	Moves to Hollywood to work as a scriptwriter for MGM. Begins a relationship with Sheilah Graham.
1940	"Pat Hobby" stories published in *Esquire*. Dies from a heart attack on December 21.
1941	*The Last Tycoon*, an unfinished novel, published by Scribner's.
1945	*The Crack-Up*, edited by Edmund Wilson, published by New Directions.
1948	Zelda Fitzgerald dies in a fire at the sanitarium in Asheville.

Contributors

HAROLD BLOOM is Sterling Professor of the Humanities at Yale University. He is the author of 30 books, including *Shelley's Mythmaking* (1959), *The Visionary Company* (1961), *Blake's Apocalypse* (1963), *Yeats* (1970), *A Map of Misreading* (1975), *Kabbalah and Criticism* (1975), *Agon: Toward a Theory of Revisionism* (1982), *The American Religion* (1992), *The Western Canon* (1994), and *Omens of Millennium: The Gnosis of Angels, Dreams, and Resurrection* (1996). *The Anxiety of Influence* (1973) sets forth Professor Bloom's provocative theory of the literary relationships between the great writers and their predecessors. His most recent books include *Shakespeare: The Invention of the Human* (1998), a 1998 National Book Award finalist, *How to Read and Why* (2000), *Genius: A Mosaic of One Hundred Exemplary Creative Minds* (2002), *Hamlet: Poem Unlimited* (2003), *Where Shall Wisdom be Found* (2004), and *Jesus and Yahweh: The Names Divine* (2005). In 1999, Professor Bloom received the prestigious American Academy of Arts and Letters Gold Medal for Criticism. He has also received the International Prize of Catalonia, the Alfonso Reyes Prize of Mexico, and the Hans Christian Andersen Bicentennial Prize of Denmark.

PAUL ROSENFELD was a prolific essayist and critic. Though known primarily for his music criticism, he also wrote on art and literature for *Vanity Fair* and the *New Republic*. A close friend of Sherwood Anderson and Alfred Stieglitz, he edited posthumous volumes on both. *Port of New York*, a collection of essays, and *Discoveries of a Music Critic* are among his more well-known works. He died in 1946.

GLENWAY WESCOTT was part of the American expatriate community of Paris in the 1920s. Throughout his life he wrote reviews and essays, in addition to short stories and poetry, for the *New Republic* and magazines like it. His many books include the critically-acclaimed novels *The Grandmothers* and *The Pilgrim Hawk*.

WILLIAM TROY taught English at New York University, the New School, and Bennington College. A one-time film critic for *The Nation*, he was a frequent contributor to *The Kenyon Review* and *The Partisan Review*. His *Selected Essays* were published posthumously in 1967.

W.J. HARVEY was a beloved professor at both the University of Keele in Great Britain and Queen's University in Belfast, Ireland. With F.W. Bateson he edited the journal *Essays in Criticism*. At the time of his death in 1967 he had written two important book-length works of criticism: *Character and the Novel* and *The Art of George Eliot*.

JOHN W. ALDRIDGE is Professor of English, Emeritus, at the University of Michigan, where he taught for twenty-eight years. His works of criticism include *After the Lost Generation*; *Talents and Technicians: Literary Chic and the New Assembly-line Fiction*, and *Classics & Contemporaries*. In 1994 he was named one of the "Top Ten Fiction Critics" of the twentieth century in *The Dictionary of Literary Biography*.

SEYMOUR L. GROSS taught at the University of Notre Dame. In the early 1960s he spent a year as Visiting Professor of American Literature at the University of Skopje in Yugoslavia (now Macedonia). He edited, with John Edward Hardy, *Images of the Negro in American Literature* and, with Milton R. Stern, the *Viking Portable American Literature Survey*.

LEONARD A. PODIS is director of the Rhetoric and Composition Program in the English Department at Oberlin College, where he has taught since 1975. In addition to editing (with Yakubu Saaka) *Challenging Hierarchies: Issues and Themes in Colonial and Postcolonial African Literature*, he has written several books on writing and teaching.

SCOTT DONALDSON is the Louise G.T. Cooley Professor of English, Emeritus, at the College of William and Mary, where he taught for twenty-six years. Best known as a writer of literary biography, his books include *By Force of Will: The Life and Art of Ernest Hemingway*; *Fool for Love: F. Scott*

Fitzgerald; John Cheever: A Biography and, most recently, *Hemingway vs. Fitzgerald: The Rise and Fall of a Literary Friendship.*

JUDITH FETTERLEY, widely recognized for her pioneering scholarship on American women writers, recently retired after a long career from SUNY Albany, where she was Distinguished Teaching Professor of English. Her early work focused on the recovery and reevaluation of texts by American women. To this end, she edited (along with Joanne Dobson and Elaine Showalter) the *American Women Writers* series for Rutgers University Press. Her own books include *The Resisting Reader: A Feminist Approach to American Fiction* and, with Marjorie Pryse, *Writing Out of Place: Regionalism, Women, and American Literary Culture.*

ROBERT GIDDINGS teaches in the Bournemouth Media School at Bournemouth University in Great Britain. He has edited critical studies of Mark Twain, Charles Dickens, J.R.R. Tolkien, and Matthew Arnold, among others. He serves as a consultant to the BBC on matters of film and television adaptation. His most recent books include *The Classic Novel From Page to Screen*, with Erica Sheen, and *The Classic Serial on Television and Radio*, with Keith Selby.

JOHN F. CALLAHAN, Morgan S. Odell Professor of Humanities at Lewis & Clark College, is the author of *Illusions of a Nation: Myth and History in the Novels of F. Scott Fitzgerald* and *In the African-American Grain: The Pursuit of Voice in Twentieth-Century Black Fiction.* As literary executor of Ralph Ellison's estate, he edited the Modern Library Edition of *The Collected Essays of Ralph Ellison*, as well as a book of Ellison's uncollected short fiction, *Flying Home and Other Stories*, and the unfinished novel *Juneteenth.*

NANCY P. VAN ARSDALE is currently the Chair of the English Department at East Stroudsburg University in Pennsylvania. Her research projects have focused on both modern literature and aspects of business communication: professional writing, public relations, and advertising. She was a Fulbright Scholar in Belgium and Luxembourg in 1995.

MEREDITH GOLDSMITH was educated at Columbia University and held a Fulbright Teaching Fellowship in American Literature in Zagreb, Croatia. With Lisa Botshon she edited *Middlebrow Moderns: Popular American Women Writers of the 1920s.* She teaches at Whitman College in Walla Walla, Washington.

PEARL JAMES received her Ph.D. in English from Yale University. She is currently Visiting Assistant Professor of English at Davidson College.

Bibliography

Allen, Joan M. *Candles and Carnival Lights: The Catholic Sensibility of F. Scott Fitzgerald.* New York: New York University Press, 1978.

Berman, Ronald. *The Great Gatsby and Modern Times.* Urbana: University of Illinois Press, 1994.

———. *"The Great Gatsby" and Fitzgerald's World of Ideas.* Tuscaloosa: University of Alabama Press, 1997.

Bloom, Harold, ed. *Gatsby.* Major Literary Characters. New York: Chelsea House, 1991.

———, ed. *F. Scott Fitzgerald.* Bloom's Major Novelists. New York: Chelsea House, 2000.

———, ed. *The Great Gatsby.* Bloom's Modern Critical Interpretations. Philadelphia: Chelsea House, 2003.

Bruccoli, Matthew J. *Some Sort of Epic Grandeur: The Life of F. Scott Fitzgerald.* New York: Harcourt Brace Jovanovich, 1979.

———. *F. Scott Fitzgerald: A Descriptive Bibliography.* Revised edition. Pittsburgh: Pittsburgh University Press, 1988.

———, ed. *New Essays on "The Great Gatsby."* Cambridge: Cambridge University Press, 1985.

Bruccoli, Matthew J., and Jackson R. Bryer, eds. *Fitzgerald in His Own Time: A Miscellany.* Kent, OH: Kent State University Press, 1971.

Bryer, Jackson R. *The Critical Reputation of F. Scott Fizgerald.* New Haven, CT: Archon, 1967.

————. *F. Scott Fitzgerald: The Critical Reception.* New York: Burt Franklin, 1978.

————. "Four Decades of Fitzgerald Studies: The Best and the Brightest." *Twentieth Century Literature* 26 (Summer 1980): 247–67.

————, ed. *The Short Stories of F. Scott Fitzgerald: New Approaches in Criticism.* Madison: University of Wisconsin Press, 1982.

Bryer, Jackson R., Alan Margolies and Ruth Prigozy, eds. *F. Scott Fitzgerald: New Perspectives.* Athens: University of Georgia Press, 2000.

Callahan, John F. *The Illusions of a Nation: Myth and History in the Novels of F. Scott Fitzgerald.* Urbana: University of Illinois Press, 1972.

Chambers, John B. *The Novels of F. Scott Fitzgerald.* London: Macmillan, 1990.

Claridge, Henry, ed. *F.Scott Fitzgerald: Critical Assessments.* 4 vols. Near Robertsbridge, UK: Helm Information, 1991.

Cowley, Malcolm, and Robert Cowley, eds. *Fitzgerald and the Jazz Age.* New York: Charles Scribner's Sons, 1966.

Crosland, Andrew T. *A Concordance to F. Scott Fitzgerald's "The Great Gatsby."* Detroit: Gale Research, 1975.

Curnutt, Kirk, ed. *A Historical Guide to F. Scott Fitzgerald.* Oxford: Oxford University Press, 2004.

Dixon, Wheeler Winston. *The Cinematic Vision of F. Scott Fitzgerald.* Ann Arbor: UMI Research Press, 1986.

Donaldson, Scott, ed. *Critical Essays on F. Scott Fitzgerald's "The Great Gatsby."* New York: G.K. Hall, 1984.

Fahey, William A. *F. Scott Fitzgerald and the American Dream.* New York: Crowell, 1973.

Fitzgerald, F. Scott. *The Crack-Up.* ed. Edmund Wilson. New York: New Directions, 1945.

————. *Trimalchio: An Early Version of "The Great Gatsby."* ed. James. L. W. West III. Cambridge: Cambridge University Press, 2000.

Hindus, Milton. *F. Scott Fitzgerald: An Introduction and Interpretation.* New York: Holt, Rinehart, and Winston, 1968.

Kazin, Alfred, ed. *F. Scott Fitzgerald: The Man and His Work.* Cleveland: World, 1951.

Kuehl, John. *F. Scott Fitzgerald: A Study of the Short Fiction.* Boston: Twayne, 1991.

Latham, Aaron. *Crazy Sundays: F. Scott Fitzgerald in Hollywood.* New York: Viking Press, 1970.

Lee, A. Robert, ed. *Scott Fitzgerald: The Promises of Life*. Estover, UK: Vision
    Press, 1989.

Lehan, Richard D. *F. Scott Fitzgerald and the Craft of Fiction*. Carbondale:
    Southern Illinois University Press, 1966.

Lockridge, Ernest H., ed. *Twentieth Century Interpretations of "The Great
    Gatsby."* Lewisburg, PA: Bucknell University Press, 1979.

Mangum, Bryant. *A Fortune Yet: Money in the Art of F. Scott Fitzgerald's Short
    Stories*. New York: Garland, 1991.

Mellow, James R. *Invented Lives: F. Scott & Zelda Fitzgerald*. New York:
    Ballantine Books, 1984.

Milford, Nancy. *Zelda*. New York: Avon, 1970.

Miller, James E., Jr. *F. Scott Fitzgerald: His Art and Technique*. New York: New
    York University Press, 1964.

Mizener, Arthur. *The Far Side of Paradise: A Biography of F. Scott Fitzgerald*.
    Boston: Houghton Mifflin, 1951.

————, ed. *F. Scott Fitzgerald: A Collection of Critical Essays*. Englewood Cliffs,
    NJ: Prentice-Hall, 1963.

Pelzer, Linda C. *Student Companion to F. Scott Fitzgerald*. Westport, Conn:
    Greenwood Press, 2000.

Perosa, Sergio. *The Art of F. Scott Fitzgerald*, trans. Charles Metz and Sergio
    Perosa. Ann Arbor: University of Michigan Press, 1965.

Prigozy, Ruth, ed. *The Cambridge Companion to F. Scott Fitzgerald*.
    Cambridge: Cambridge University Press, 2002.

Roulston, Robert, and Helen H. Roulston. *The Winding Road to West Egg:
    The Artistic Development of F. Scott Fitzgerald*. Lewisburg, PA: Bucknell
    University Press, 1995.

Schlacks, Deborah Davis. *American Dream Visions: Chaucer's Surprising
    Influence on F. Scott Fitzgerald*. New York: Peter Lang, 1994.

Sklar, Robert. *F. Scott Fitzgerald: The Last Laocoön*. New York: Oxford
    University Press, 1967.

Stern, Milton R. *The Golden Moment: The Novels of F. Scott Fitzgerald*. Urbana:
    University of Illinois Press, 1970.

Turnbull, Andrew, ed. *The Letters of F. Scott Fitzgerald*. New York: Charles
    Scribner's Sons, 1965.

Trilling, Lionel. *The Liberal Imagination*. New York: Viking, 1950.

Way, Brian. *F. Scott Fitzgerald and the Art of Social Fiction*. London: Edward
    Arnold, 1980.

Wilson, Edmund. *The Shores of Light: A Literary Chronicle of the Twenties and Thirties.* New York: Farrar, Straus & Giroux, 1958.

Acknowledgments

"F. Scott Fitzgerald" by Paul Rosenfeld From *Men Seen: Twenty-Four Modern Authors*, pp. 215–224. © 1925 Lincoln Macveagh, The Dial Press. Reprinted by permission of Random House.

"The Moral of F. Scott Fitzgerald" by Glenway Wescott. From *The* New Republic (February 17, 1941). © 1941 by The New Republic, LLC. Reprinted by permission.

"F. Scott Fitzgerald: The Authority of Failure" by William Troy. From *Selected Essays of William Troy*, pp. 140–146. Originally published in *Accent* 6, no. 1. © 1967 Rutgers University Press. Reprinted with permission from the estate of William Troy.

"Theme and texture in The Great Gatsby" by W.J. Harvey. From *English Studies*, Vol. 38, No. 1. pp. 12–20. (c) 1957 Taylor & Francis Ltd., http://www.tandf.co.uk/journals. Reprinted by permission of Taylor & Francis Ltd.

"The Life of Gatsby" by John W. Aldridge. From *Twelve Original Essays on Great American Novels*, Charles Shapiro, ed. Pp. 210-237. © 1977 by Charles Shapiro. Reprinted by permission.

"Fitzgerald's 'Babylon Revisited'" by Seymour L. Gross. From *College English* 25 (November 1963), 128–135. © 1963 by the National Council of Teachers of English. Reprinted with permission.

"The Beautiful and Damned: Fitzgerald's Test of Youth" by Leonard A. Podis. From *Fitzgerald/Hemingway Annual* 1973, pp. 141–147. Reprinted by permission.

"The Crisis of Fitzgerald's Crack-Up" by Scott Donaldson. From *Twentieth Century Literature* Vol. 26 (Summer 1980), pp. 171–188. Reprinted by permission.

"Who Killed Dick Diver? The Sexual Politics of *Tender is the Night*" by Judith Fetterley. This article originally appeared in *Mosaic*, a journal for the interdisciplinary study of literature, Vol. 17, Issue 1 (Winter 1984), pp. 111–128. © 1984 *Mosaic*. Reprinted by permission.

"*The Last Tycoon*: Fitzgerald as Projectionist" by Robert Giddings. From *Scott Fitzgerald: The Promises of Life*, A. Robert Lee, ed. pp. 74–93. © 1989 Vision Press. Reprinted by permission.

"F. Scott Fitzgerald's Evolving American Dream" by John F. Callahan. From *Twentieth Century Literature* Vol 42, No. 3 (Autumn, 1996), pp. 374–395. Reprinted by permission.

"Princeton as Modernist's Hermeneutics" by Nancy P. Van Arsdale. From *F. Scott Fitzgerald: New Perspectives*, Jackson R. Bryer, Alan Margolies, and Ruth Prigozy, ed. pp. 39–50. © The University of Georgia Press. Reprinted by permission.

"White Skin, White Mask: Passing, Posing, and Performing in *The Great Gatsby*" by Meredith Goldsmith. From *Modern Fiction Studies* 49, 3 (Fall 2003) pp. 443–468. © 2003 for the Purdue Research Foundation by the Johns Hopkins University Press. Reprinted by permission.

"History and Masculinity in F. Scott Fitzgerald's *This Side of Paradise*" by Pearl James. From *Modern Fiction Studies* 51, 1 (Spring 2005) pp. 1–33. © 2005 for the Purdue Research Foundation by the Johns Hopkins University Press. Reprinted by permission.

Every effort has been made to contact the owners of copyrighted material and secure copyright permission. Articles appearing in this volume generally appear much as they did in their original publication with few or no editorial changes. Those interested in locating the original source will find bibliographic information in the bibliography and acknowledgments sections of this volume.

Index

Characters in literary works are indexed by first name (if any), followed by the name of the work in parentheses